A SPELL IN SCARLET

BY SONIA LEONG

To Noah
with love ♥

sweatdrop studios
INDEPENDENT ART & COMICS COLLABORATIVE

Story, art and design by Sonia Leong, cover design by En Gingerboom
Editing by Matthew Bentham and Morag Lewis
A Spell Of Scarlet

Published by Sweatdrop Studios
www.sweatdrop.com
ISBN 978-1-905038-63-3
First printed in 2022 in the United Kingdom

CONTENTS

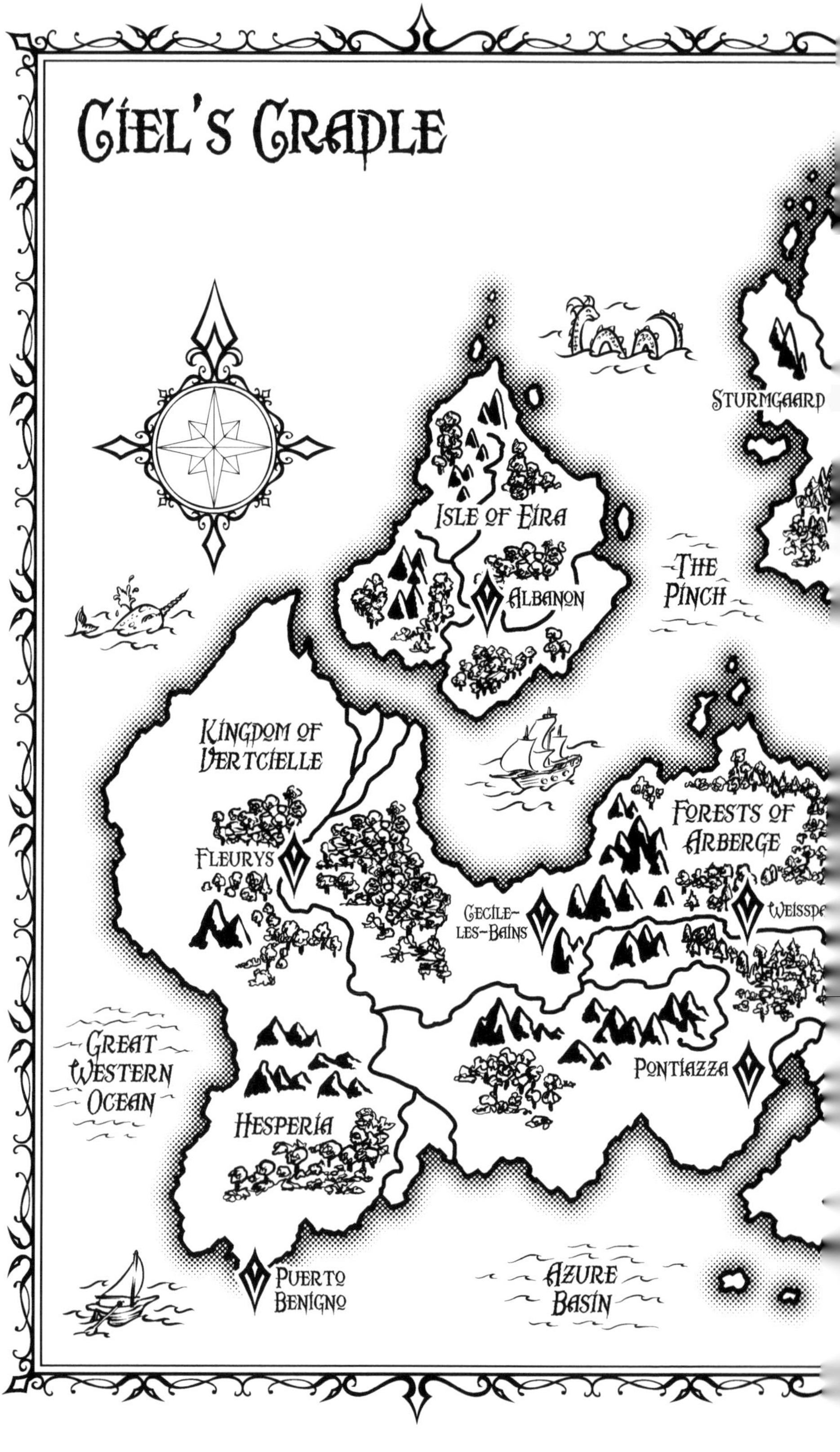
Ciel's Cradle
Sturmgaard
Isle of Eira
The Pinch
Albanon
Kingdom of Vertcielle
Forests of Arberge
Fleurys
Cecile-les-Bains
Great Western Ocean
Pontiazza
Hesperia
Puerto Benigno
Azure Basin

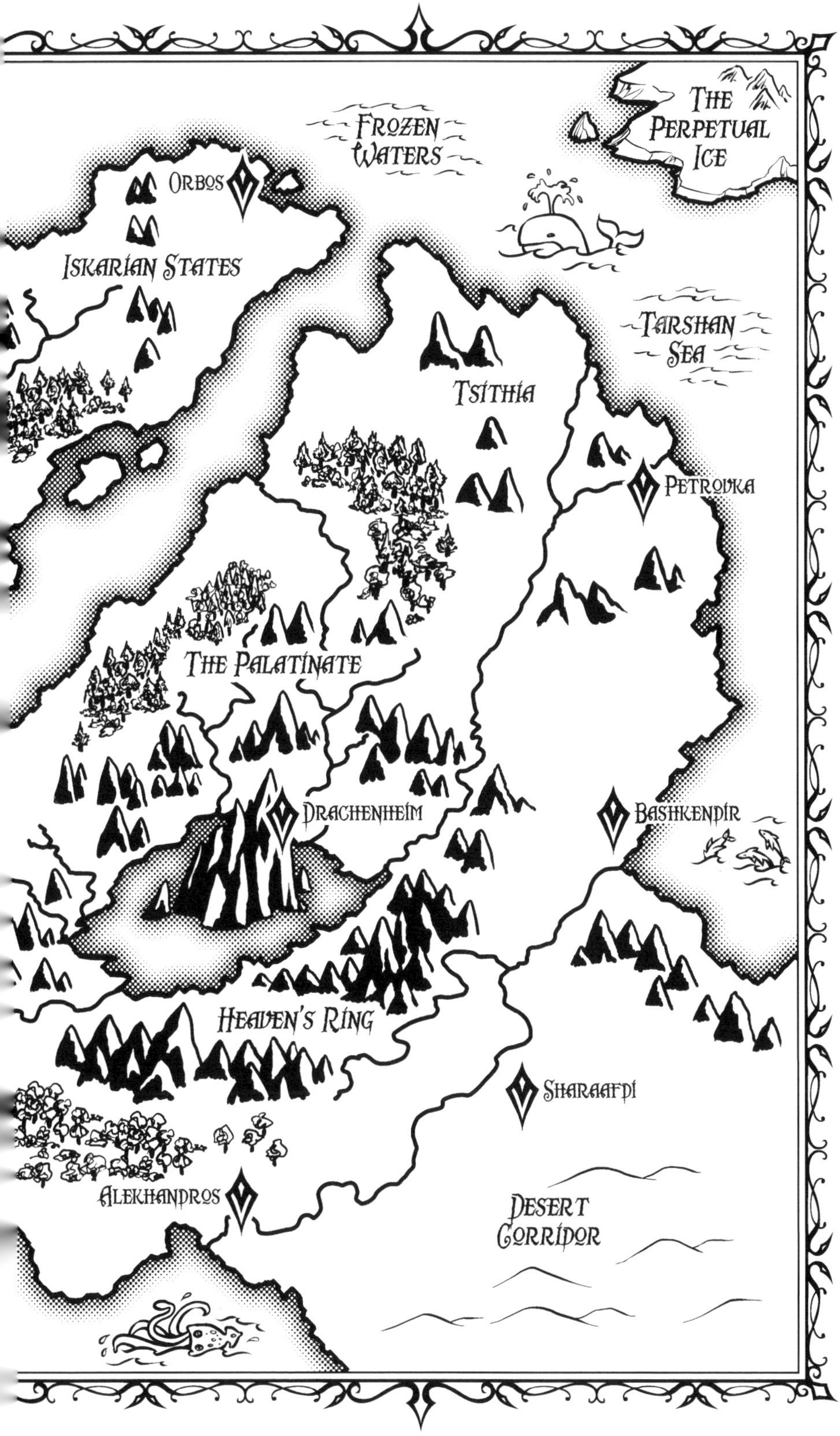
The Perpetual Ice
Frozen Waters
Orbos
Iskarian States
Tarshan Sea
Tsithia
Petrovka
The Palatinate
Drachenheim
Bashkendir
Heaven's Ring
Sharaafdi
Alekhandros
Desert Corridor

STORY & CHARACTERS

Ciel, the Goddess of Light, blessed her strongest warrior with divine powers of regeneration, tasking her with protecting the innocent and dispensing justice throughout the world. After centuries on her own, the warrior was given a partner by the Goddess; a pure-hearted mage with divine elemental sight. Amidst threats of terrorism and assassination, how will the pair overcome the fears and anxieties they had been accumulating over the years from being so different to everyone else?

Ruaidhri'ogan (Rua). A Vulpine warrior chosen as the Dagger of Ciel, the deadliest fighter who has ever lived... and died. Again and again.

Silas L'Heritier. A PhD student and battle mage. Known as the Weaver, this young Elf can use all five elements of magic at once.

Reynard Débonnaire. The newly elected Vulpine Councillor of Vertcielle. A suave playboy... and Rua's ex-boyfriend.

Gildas L'Heritier. Silas's brother. A Chevalier in Albanon leading the Eiran-Vertciellen military exchange programme. Bold and loyal.

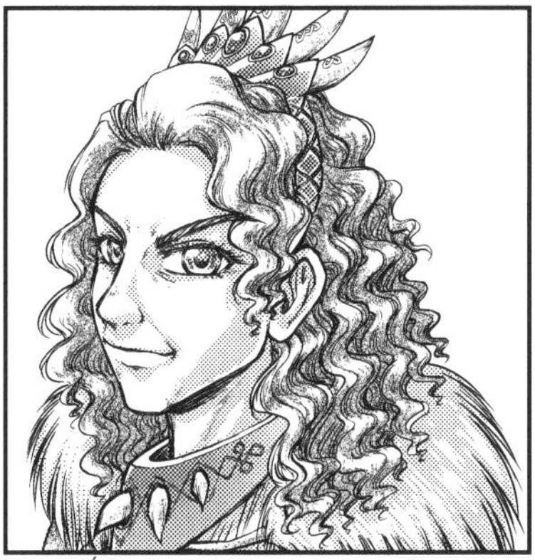

Queen Éilís the Enlightened. Aside from Silas, the wise warrior queen of Eira is the only other mortal Rua answers to.

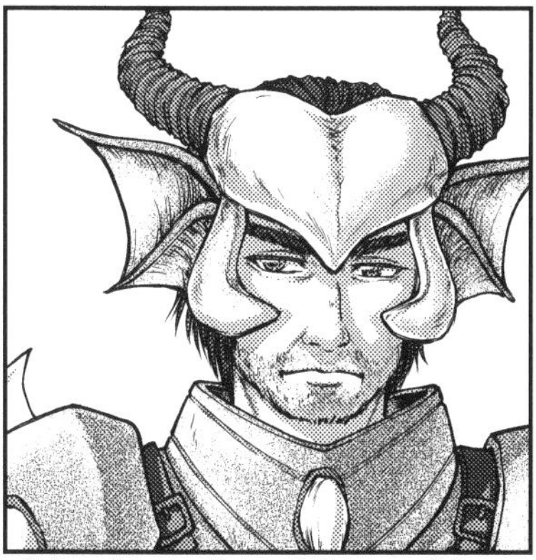

Prince Consort Owyn. A fearsome fighter, devoted husband to Queen Éilís and father of her two children. Stoic and mostly silent.

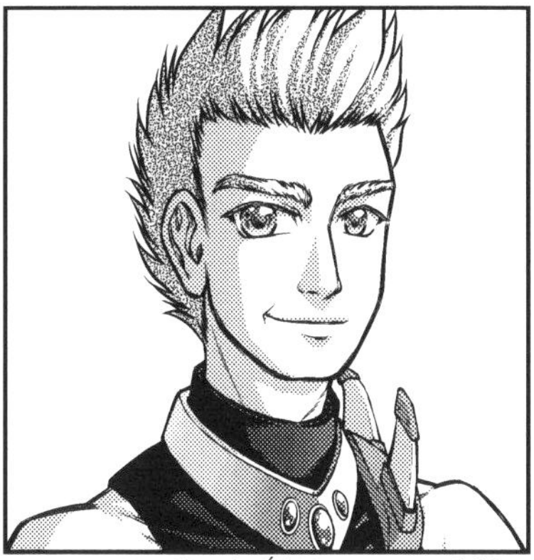

Teagan Fiag'Arach. Éilís's youngest child. Keen to prove himself in the royal duty of dragonslaying, like the rest of his family.

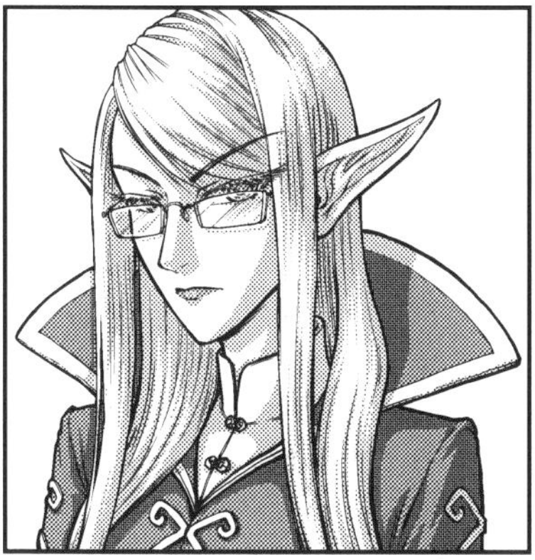

Véronique Tempête. Chancellor of the Lyceum Arcanus and Silas's mentor. Trusted advisor to King Xavier IV.

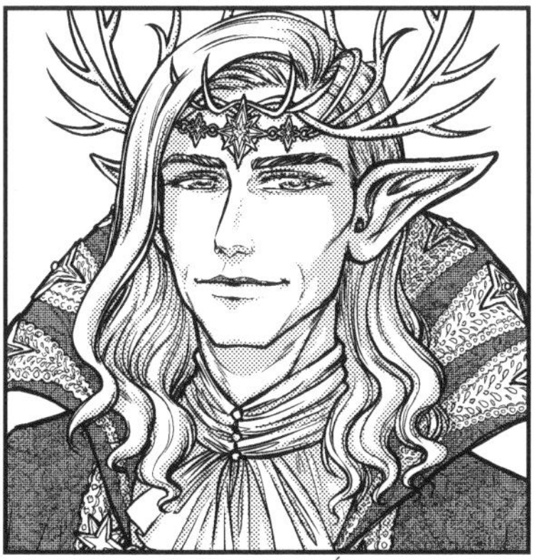

King Xavier IV. *L'Elfe Roi-Étoiles:* the Elven Star King. Beautiful and blasé, he has mastered the game of Houses.

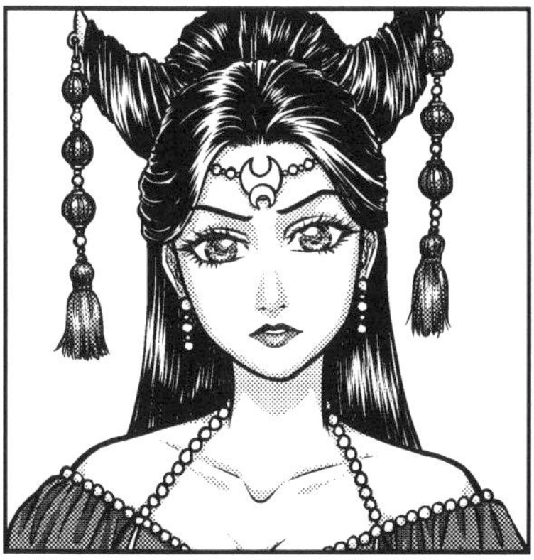

Arafel Crescentia Eltares von und zu Aristarchus. Soon-to-be Empress of the Palatinate. Nervous, but determined.

~Prelude~
Coping Mechanism

***

'…And that, *mes amis*, was how I managed to slip out of her bathroom before her father could catch me!'

His friends roared with laughter as Reynard took a bow, his tail swishing back and forth with self-satisfaction. He was always pleased to be the centre of attention, even when he was off-duty.

'*Mais, oui*, only you Vulpines could get away with something like that!' Henri said. 'There is no way the rest of us would risk a two-storey drop!'

'Ah, but you're an Elf; her father would not have objected in the first place!'

'Then what about me and Victor?' asked Pascal.

'Completely screwed.'

Pascal grinned down at Victor and toasted his glass.

'*Tant pis!* To Dwarves and Humans! Always getting the raw deal!'

Reynard looked at his empty glass. He brandished it at the others.

'Hey, I think my tale was worth a drink, *non*? Buy me another and I'll sing–'

The door crashed open and the inn grew quiet as everyone looked at the small figure standing in the doorway.

Reynard's nostrils flared; his keen sense of smell was assaulted by the metallic tang wafting in. Drenched in blood, he could barely see her face; only her yellow irises. Her black-tipped ears stuck out above her cropped hair, but her heavily stained cloak obscured everything else.

She looked over the room. When her calculating gaze lingered on him, he felt a chill in his bones. He was no stranger to fierce glares from other Vulpines – irate vixens and cuckolded dogs, usually – but her eyes were different. He felt as if he was her prey and she had gracefully allowed him to live.

She prowled past them in silence, drips of blood falling in her wake.

The fluidity in her motion was mesmerising.

'*M-madame*,' the innkeeper ventured. 'D-do you need... anything...?'

She stopped halfway up the stairs.

'A bath. I'll pay extra.'

His troubadour's mind went into overdrive. Hard vowels, rolled 'r's. South Eiran. A high timbre, but dark notes. A soprano, lyrical. Not a girl. A woman's voice.

The innkeeper motioned to a scullery maid who was standing there, open-mouthed, like everyone else.

'Nanette! Boil some water, *allez, tout de suite.*'

Reynard watched the vixen disappear upstairs. Feeling lightheaded, he realised that he hadn't been breathing.

Like a shroud had been lifted, the inn gradually eased back into life. But there was only one topic on everyone's lips.

'That,' Pascal exclaimed. '...Was one helluva scary bitch.'

Reynard was fascinated.

'*Dites-moi*, what do you know about her? I've not been in Pas-Droit recently.'

'She's not from around here, I'll tell you that much,' Victor whispered. 'I've only seen her these past two weeks. I think she's rented a room from Rémy.'

'I hear she's a mercenary,' Pascal pitched in. 'I'd not heard her speak until now, but I suspected she'd be Eiran; it's what most of them do abroad.'

'She must work alone. Never seen her with anyone.'

Henri shuddered.

'All that blood. And those eyes... the way she looks at you. *Non, non, elle est folle.* Can we talk about something else now?

Reynard reluctantly let it drop and picked up his lute to lighten the mood.

'Well, I know plenty of songs about crazy women!' he said.

His bawdy poem about a lady who challenged a knight to fulfil her specific tastes in bed went down a storm with his friends. By the time he got to the verse where she insisted he do the same for her other lover, the rest of the inn had started listening. He finished to much laughter and applause along with offers of free drinks just as more minstrels arrived for their set; the Brothers Fournier. He gave them a nod as they had shared gigs before. Once they began playing, it didn't take long for people to start singing and dancing after his complimentary warm up act. As his friends started clapping along to the songs, he placed his empty glass on the table and looked towards the bar, considering a refill.

Then he noticed her coming down the stairs.

Bit by bit, she came into view. Her lean, muscled legs were bare from her toes to her thighs and free of the blood stains, her tawny brown skin was flawless. Her sword belt hung low on her hips; the hilt of her dagger glinting in the lamplight.

Yes, she was a warrior, alright. But she was all woman, too.

She was wearing black shorts and a cropped vest that revealed a toned midriff and sculpted arms. The knitted fabric was form fitting, her long, bushy tail pulled through a slit in her shorts. When she turned around to sit at a bar stool in the corner, he drew in his breath sharply.

She was younger than he had initially thought. Her breasts were small and high in her tight vest. And her face: the full cheeks, snub nose and pointed chin already made a disarmingly cute combination, but with those wide, golden eyes, he was totally doomed.

Reynard was walking towards her before he could stop himself. She had already downed a shot of brandy and was handing the glass back to the innkeeper when he sat down next to her. He nodded to the innkeeper.

'Rémy, two more brandies, *s'il vous plaît*. One for me and one for... *la femme*.'

She twisted away from him in her seat.

'I'm not in the mood,' she spat.

'Well, it is just a drink,' he said, shrugging. 'And it is going free, if you want it.'

After a few moments, she flicked him a sideways glance.

'Thanks... don't think that entitles you to anything.'

'Of course not, *cherie*,' he assured.

But that wasn't going to stop him trying.

The glasses plonked onto the counter. He handed one to her and raised his.

'*Bon. Santé,*' he toasted.

'Cheers,' she replied, brusquely.

They both drank, him studying her as she knocked it back with abandon.

Her dark red hair wasn't particularly unique, but the blonde streaks that framed her face: that was something he had never seen before. And yet, it felt familiar somehow.

Like he had read about it as a child.

'Tough day?' he began. 'You look tired... though your beauty still shines through.'

She glared at him.

'You have no idea.'

Those fierce eyes made him shiver. It was exciting.

'Maybe you will feel better if you let it out? I will listen.'

In a flash, she pulled her knife from its sheath and rammed its point into the counter. The blade was lodged perfectly in the gap between his thumb and forefinger.

'You were here when I came back. Did you fail to notice the amount of blood on me? None of it was mine.'

He swallowed and withdrew his hand slowly. He wasn't going to give up.

'And all I could think about was how you really looked like, underneath the blood. I am not disappointed.'

She clicked her tongue and shook her head. Then she narrowed her eyes at him.

'Tell me boy... do you really want to play with fire?'

'I am but a moth to your flame,' he said, with a crooked grin.

He saw the exact moment she made her choice; it was almost unnerving when her eyes transformed from suspicious slits into languorous and inviting pools.

She leant into him, placing her hand on his thigh, tracing lines with her claws.

'Then make me burn,' she growled.

He obliged, grabbing her roughly and kissing her.

She ran her fingers through his hair and gripped the back of his head, pulling herself onto his lap, still glued to his lips.

He could taste the brandy on her tongue. And the way she ground her hips...

She pulled back, her predatory eyes glazed over in lust.

'Shall we skip everything and just head up to my room?' she breathed.

'Oh, yes, *cherie.*'

She sheathed her dagger then slid off his lap, her tail trailing between his legs.

By Ciel, he loved it when a vixen did that.

He followed her upstairs to the surprise and astonishment of his friends below, some of whom gave him congratulatory gestures whilst the others shook their heads.

As soon as he closed her door, she grabbed him and pushed him onto the bed. She tugged off her vest and started pulling at his shirt; a button came off before he took over undressing himself and directing her hands elsewhere. What she was doing to him with her mouth was very distracting though, and he lost another button before she straddled him, riding him to within an inch of his life.

***

13

Reynard awoke, feeling the cold, night air against his skin. His mouth was dry and his throat felt hoarse; all that drinking and strenuous activity must have done it. He shifted around in the bed, his nose picking up the heady smells of her sweat and musk. But he couldn't feel her beside him. He sat up, looked around the room and found her.

Lit by the full moon and a clear sky, full of stars, she was sitting on the window sill, still naked, save for a sheet she had wrapped around herself.

She was crying.

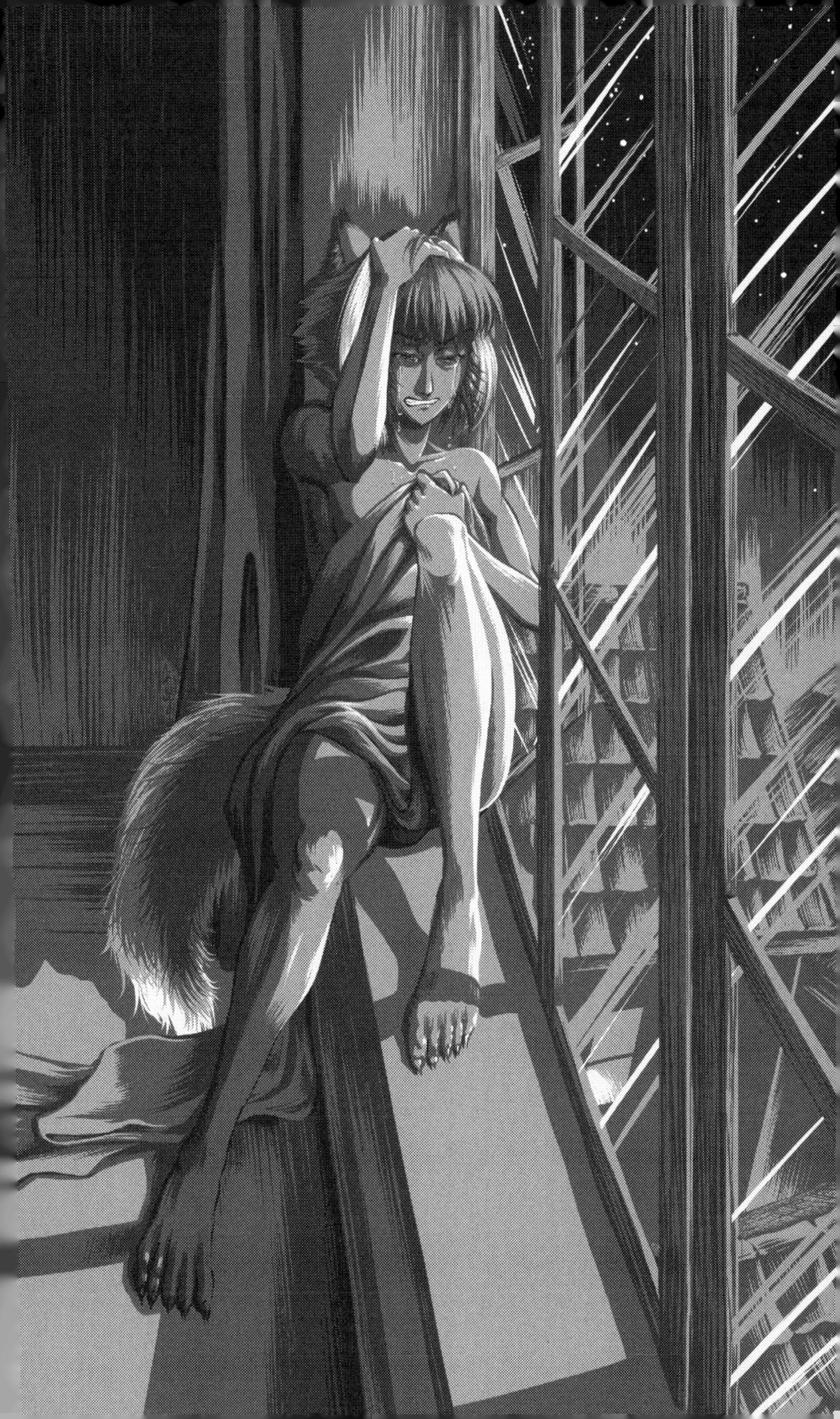

~PART ONE~

OUTFOXED

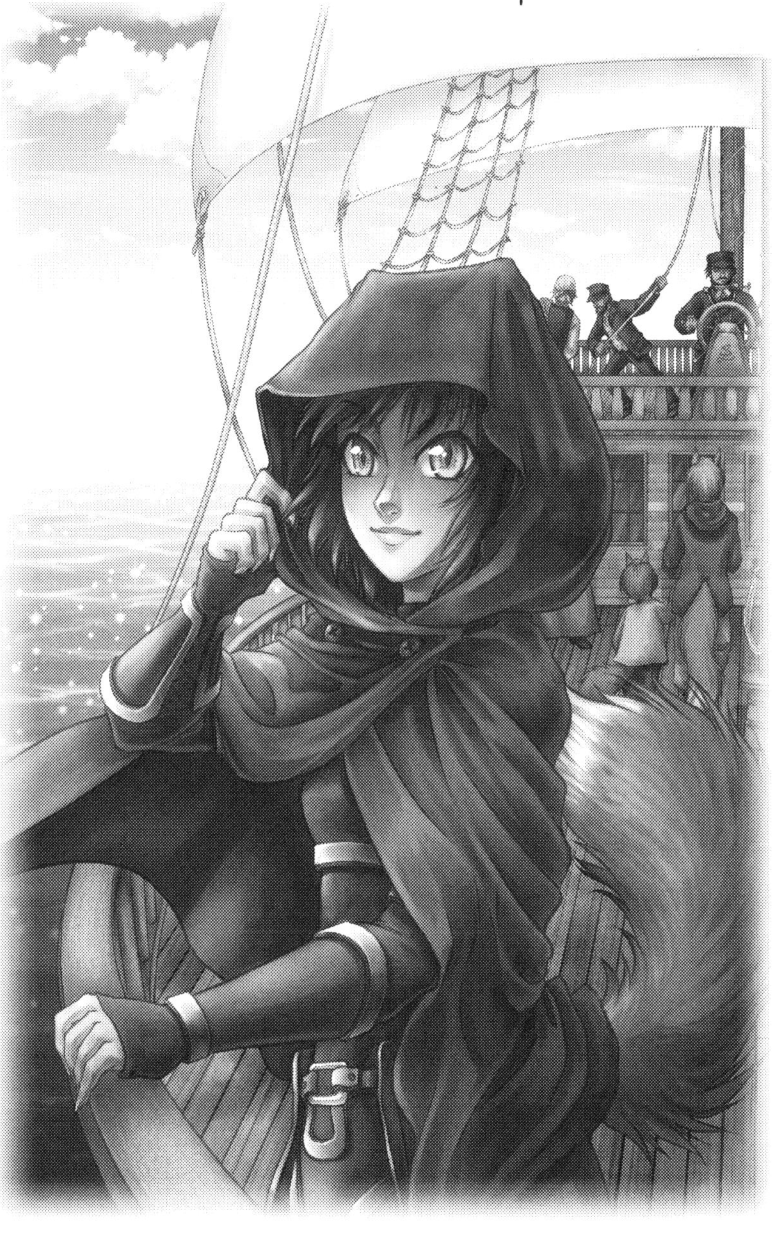

I

The ferry dipped, riding down the crest of a wave, then lurched as it hit the bottom of the swell. The resulting sea spray caught a few of the passengers off guard; some tutted, others squealed. They were obviously from Vertcielle; Eirans knew to stay well in the middle, or simply didn't care about getting wet.

Rua laughed from the bow of the boat. A little saltwater wasn't going to dampen her mood; the sun was out, the breeze was brisk, so that meant good sailing.

Carefully keeping her gold-streaked hair under the hood of her cloak, she shook the water out of her tail. She hopped up onto the side rail and shaded her eyes against the sunshine. A sliver of land on the horizon. Her heart thumped louder in anticipation.

Eira. Of course, Rua loved her fierce, proud homeland. A warrior with a big voice and a bigger heart, she was Eiran to the core. The problem was that the rest of the country knew it too; it was considerably harder for her to travel incognito when she was the nation's greatest legend. And she hated the attention.

She checked her hood again. It wasn't the most graceful of solutions, but the autumnal wind had enough of a chill to warrant its use. She'd previously caused a ruckus amongst Eirans who recognised her, so she knew better than to go without. But this was the first time on the ferry for him.

She looked back at the tall figure she had grown to love.

He stood near the stern, gripping the starboard rail with his gloved hands as he looked out to sea. His shoulder length hair ruffled about his pointed ears, the strawberry-blond strands barely restrained in his half ponytail. The wind whipped at his blue and gold cloak, fastened tightly around his slender waist. Its skirt flapped around his legs, wind-proofed by tall leather boots. His gold-trimmed grimoire swung in the breeze, suspended from a long strap slung across his shoulder.

Silas L'Heritier. When she had rescued the young mage from bandits early in the spring, she had had no idea just how much he would change her life.

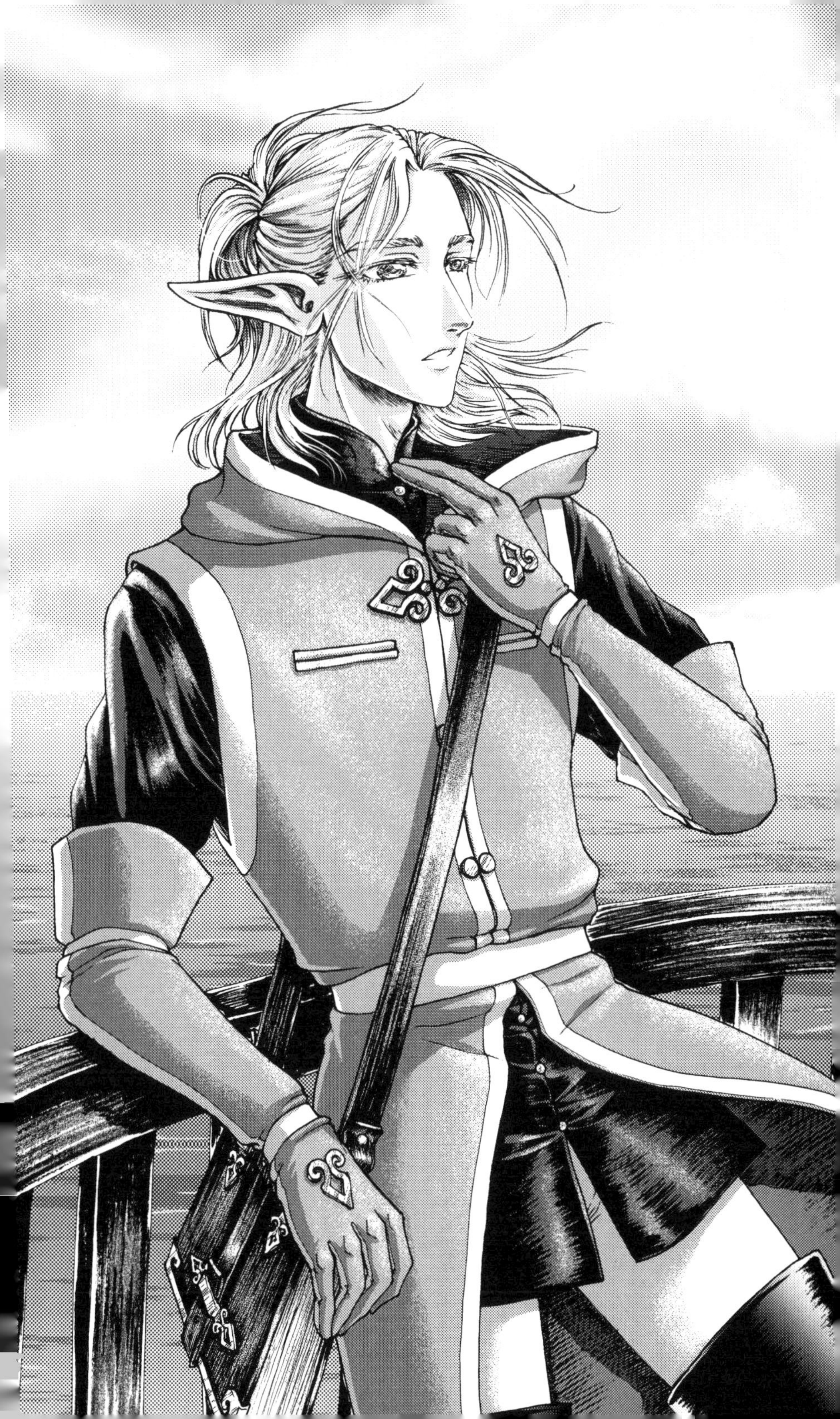

For six hundred years she wandered the world, giving her strength to the forces of good and dispensing her brutal form of justice as the Dagger of Ciel. Honed over the centuries, her deadly skills and her divine ability to regenerate made her the ultimate warrior and assassin; even if she had to die to do it, she always got her mark. But six hundred years was a long time to be doing this on her own. When loneliness and isolation drove her to the edge of madness, Ciel, the Goddess of Light, the Creator and Mother to all, brought her back with words of love, encouragement... and a promise.

This man was the embodiment of that promise. An Elf blessed with divine sight, he had the ability to weave all five elements of magic at once, giving him immense powers of protection and destruction. The Weaver was her partner, her equal, her beacon of light in the darkness. And more recently, her lover.

Perhaps it was too soon to call him that. They were taking things slow. It had only been a few weeks since they admitted their feelings to each other. They barely even held hands in public; both of them were so used to putting up barriers, it was hard to break the habit. And behind closed doors when they did indulge in a few kisses, she was almost afraid of taking it further. She was steeped in the blood of thousands. She had used men in a haze of lust: to forget her feelings, to punish herself with loveless unions and to remind herself of the animal she was.

Silas released the ship's rail to turn around and lean back on it. Closing his eyes, he took a deep breath. As he reached up to loosen the high necked collar of his black tunic, his silver eyes fluttered open and he noticed Rua's scrutiny.

With his pale skin, high cheekbones and sweeping eyelashes, he was more beautiful to her than any Elf maiden.

He's so young, so pure. No woman in the world is worthy of him.

But he looked even paler than usual. Actually, he looked a little grey.

Rua rushed to him as he doubled over, his hands on his knees, his breathing shaky.

'No, love, you need to face the other way,' she advised.

She turned him around and bent him over the rail. Holding his hair back, she patted his back gently as he retched overboard. She winced in sympathy.

'Better out than in. It's not much farther. Come now – d'you think you're done?'

He nodded and straightened up, swaying slightly. His ears dipped in dismay.

'I avoided a heavy lunch, stayed at the back of the boat, kept my eyes in the distance and yet... please forgive me for being such a nuisance.'

A hand holding a small, damp rag appeared between the two of them. It was offered by a vixen with a baby strapped to her back. Another little one huddled behind her tail, staring up at them with big eyes.

'You look like you could use this, lad,' the lady said with a kind smile. 'It's clean – I always have some washcloths and a water canteen on me. Keep it, I've plenty spare.'

'How awfully kind of you! Thank you so much.'

Silas accepted the rag, bowing to her as she walked away. He dabbed at his mouth delicately and tucked it into his pocket.

Despite his seasickness, he was no stranger to travelling. Prior to meeting Rua, he had already established a reputation at the Lyceum Arcanus as an adventurer. Tasked with researching rare scrolls and rediscovering ancient magic, it was the perfect PhD for someone with his unique skill set. But she suspected his wanderlust was down to similar reasons as her own; the need to get away from others who knew what he was.

The past few weeks had been a welcome break for them; after months on the road, they spent the summer at his family's villa in Fleurys. When Rua told him about her role at the next Vulpine Council in Albanon, he was eager to accompany her. There were no incidents travelling by land, but as soon as the ferry left Port Profond and headed into the salt water of The Pinch, she could see that he wasn't one for sailing.

'Ha! I make that the third one to empty his belly this journey!'

Rua glared at the crewman, who hastily held up his hands to placate her.

'Oh, missy, your eyes cut me to the core! T'was in jest.'

He grinned and walked past her to the control line to adjust its tension.

'I'm no stranger to your kind, miss, but I've noticed a lot of Vulpines takin' this here ferry recently. There a shindig goin' on?'

Her disapproval vanished as she nodded, happy to satisfy his curiosity.

'Sure is! And there'll be plenty more, from all over the world in the next couple of days. It's the Vulpine Council meeting next week; a summit that only happens once every twelve years, so there'll be loads of parties. This year, it's being held in Albanon, timed to match with celebrations for the Queen's Silver Jubilee.'

His eyes widened and he whistled through his teeth in wonder.

'So that's why some've been wearing funny clothes 'n all. I've not seen their get up in Ciel's Cradle before.'

'Eira doesn't have Spirit Gates, so travellers from further afield use Fleurys–'

She was cut off by a high-pitched squeal and a woman screaming.

'Barrie! No! Someone, please help him!'

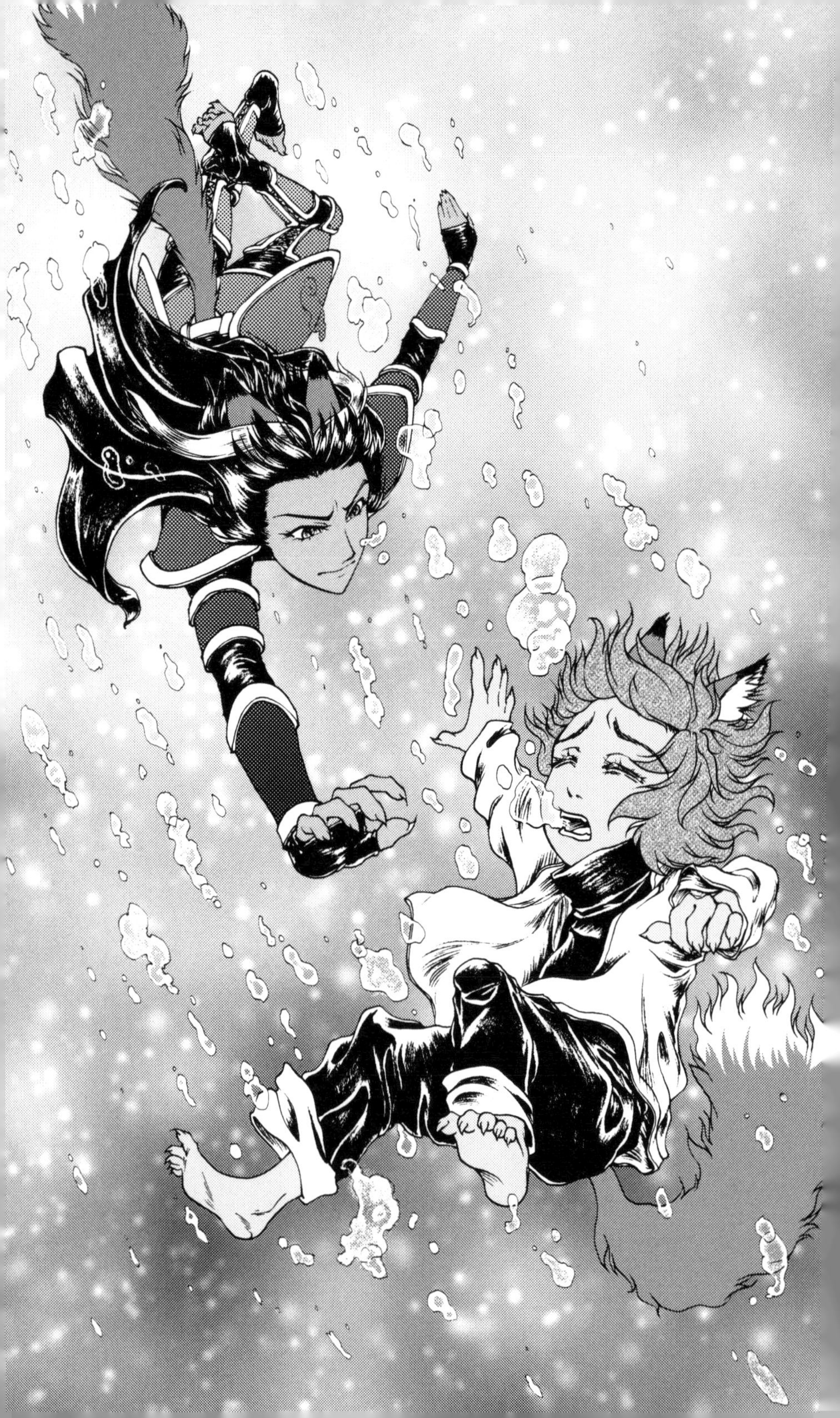

It was the vixen from before. Her baby was crying, but the little boy was gone.

Another Vulpine came running over, his ears flattened in fear.

'Nuala, where's Barrie?!' he cried.

The vixen sobbed and pointed overboard.

Rua spotted a flash of brown fur in the sea.

She took a massive leap from the side of the ship, arcing into a dive. Plunging in deep, the chilly waters would have knocked the breath out of all but the most experienced swimmers. The boy was getting drawn into the depths by a strong undertow. She kicked hard to push through the current and soon reached him.

The poor thing was flailing helplessly, his eyes scrunched up tight.

She grabbed him around the waist and started swimming back up.

They broke the surface with loud gulps of air. To preserve her strength, Rua leant back and steadied the boy on her stomach.

'It's alright, I've gotcha,' she soothed. 'Stay still, Barrie, it's easier to float.'

He was coughing, but did as he was told.

Only then did she notice the water was strangely calm.

'Rua! Are you alright?!' Silas called.

She looked up at him standing at the stern; even from this distance, she could see that his eyes had a soft, blue glow. Of course – he'd woven a Water spell.

'We're both fine!' she replied.

'Thank the Goddess! Please, relax, I will guide the currents for you.'

True to his word, all she had to do was float; the waters carried them straight back to the ferry. As they got close, the crewman threw her a line. She let herself be pulled up the hull and pushed the child through the gap in the side rails.

He clambered to his feet and ran to his anxious parents. She swung herself over the rail with the ease of an acrobat and lobbed the line back at the ship's hand with a wink.

Before she could protest, Silas was giving her a hug.

'But I'm all wet!' she squeaked.

'I do not care.'

She harrumphed, but allowed it.

After a long squeeze, he leant back with a relieved smile, still holding onto her. His eyes were back to their usual silver now.

A pity she missed it; she liked seeing his eyes flash and change colour.

'Thank Ciel we had you two on board!'

She broke out of his arms as the ship's captain approached them and frantically made a show of wringing out her sodden cloak.

'What were the chances of having a Water Master with us as a passenger? My thanks to you, Magus, for your magic, and to you, mi'lady, for your bravery.'

Silas, despite the wet patches she'd left on his clothes, still managed to look elegant as he performed his well-practised bow with a flourish.

'It was a pleasure to assist, Captain,' he said.

'Yeah, it wasn't a problem at all!' added Rua cheerfully, untying her cloak and draping it over the side rail to dry off.

There was a collective gasp from the Vulpine passengers on the ship.

Rua froze and swallowed nervously.

Oh, damn it.

'By Ciel, that hair... could it be her?'

'It's really her! It's *the* Dagger!'

'The Queen's Champion?!'

Slowly, she turned around to a sea of awestruck and curious faces. As soon as the golden streaks in her hair caught the sun, several passengers dropped to their knees. Others followed, bowing their heads. The whispers continued.

'The Divine Dagger...'

'The Chair of the Council!'

An old man tried to kneel. She went straight to him and lifted him back up.

'Please,' she insisted. 'There's really no need for it.'

'But there is,' he responded. 'The young 'uns might not believe, but...' his voice dropped to a whisper. 'The old guard do and we will not forget. The warrior who has stood by our queens for centuries.'

He kissed her hand, then gave her his best salute, puffing up his chest.

'Queen's Guard. I served with you in Bashkendir in 2325. It was an honour.'

She stared at his face. No, she couldn't remember him. She could never remember them all. But she remembered that peacekeeping mission and the long, freezing nights in the desert, stalking and hunting down slave traders.

She shook her head and took his hand down from his forehead. She positioned it along her wrist, so they could clasp each others' forearms. She squeezed as forcefully as she dared without hurting him; to show mutual respect, soldier to soldier.

His eyes became bright with tears.

She faced the rest of them.

'I am but a soldier,' she pleaded. 'One who's served their queen, their country and their Goddess, like this man here. I don't want any special treatment – Ciel knows the amount of pomp and ceremony I'm already gonna have to deal with next week! So please can we just... keep calm and carry on? Pretty please?'

II

Taken by Rua's disarming manner, the crowd obliged, gradually dispersing across the deck – though some still bowed and curtsied before moving on.

She breathed a sigh of relief and turned to the captain.

'Really sorry about the delay,' she said, scratching the back of her neck. 'Silas, is there any way we can help them keep to time?'

Silas straightened up.

'O-of course! Captain, please return to the helm. I will work the currents for you.'

The captain nodded and directed his slack-jawed ship mate to the sheet.

Rua watched as Silas's eyes flickered from light grey to a luminous blue. With thin rivulets of water trailing his fingertips, he traced a sinuous pattern in the air, like overlapping ripples on a lily pond. Then he held out his hands underneath. The symbol splashed into his cupped hands. He threw the glowing water into the sea.

'Aqua, ducere nos.'

For just a second, she could see the glow ripple through the waves before it disappeared. Then, the ship lurched as the current took hold, pushing at the hull.

Silas went pale again, and grabbed at the rail.

Rua rubbed the small of his back, trying to ease his seasickness.

He stared into the distance for a minute, breathing deeply before he spoke.

'I did not realise how easily you would be recognised on this ship.'

He looked down at her, his eyes still glowing blue as he monitored the spell.

She sighed.

'It's not normally that bad, it's just that... what, with the timing and all, every Vulpine is on their way here and on the lookout for the mythical Chair of the Council, and as soon as anyone calls me the Queen's Champion, every Eiran will want a look.'

Silas stroked his chin, frowning.

'I hope you do not mind me asking but... why did the old soldier whisper to you?

26

How much do the public know about... what you really are?'

She shuffled closer to him and lowered her voice.

'All Vulpines abide by the laws of the lands we reside in. But we have elected Councillors in various regions to represent us in their respective governments. Eiran Vulpines used to select a Councillor too, and six hundred years ago, I was the main candidate. The Council took place in Eira that year. As part of the celebrations, the Councillors attended our local ritual and bore witness when it took an unexpected turn as Ciel herself showed up and made me into...'

She gestured at herself.

'...This. Since then, every fox cub has been told about it. It's like a bed time story; The Dagger with Golden Hair. They can choose to believe it or not. Eiran Vulpines overwhelmingly do. But only the Councillors know it as fact when I am introduced to them as the Chair. They don't need much convincing when I meet them twelve, twenty four, thirty six years later, looking exactly the same.'

Silas nodded, earnestly soaking up the information.

'As for the old man,' Rua continued. 'They may not know me on sight, but all Eirans, no matter what race, know of the Queen's Champion. It used to be that the best warrior in Eira was selected as head of her personal guard. I was already the Champion of Queen Liadán the Grey before *it* happened. And in the years following, no one could best me, obviously. Liadán and I agreed that it would be a military advantage to keep my powers secret, so only the royal family and the Queen's Guard know the truth. Everyone else thinks that I'm a descendant of... well, me. That my line has a tradition of giving a daughter to be trained up as the next Champion. You get the odd fool who challenges me for the title, but I soon beat that idea out of their head.'

She broke off when she noticed the ship's hand coming.

'Mi'lord Magus, mi'lady Champion,' he said, with considerably more deference than before. 'Cap'n told me to tell you we've caught up now, we'll be mooring soon.'

Silas smiled in response and made a sweeping gesture with his hands towards the water. He turned back to face the sailor as the blue glow faded from his eyes.

'Thank you. Please relay to the Captain that I have dismissed the currents, so the ship is fully under your control again.'

The man bowed nervously and headed back to the helm.

Rua took her cloak from the rail and grimaced; it was still quite wet.

Silas studied it and frowned.

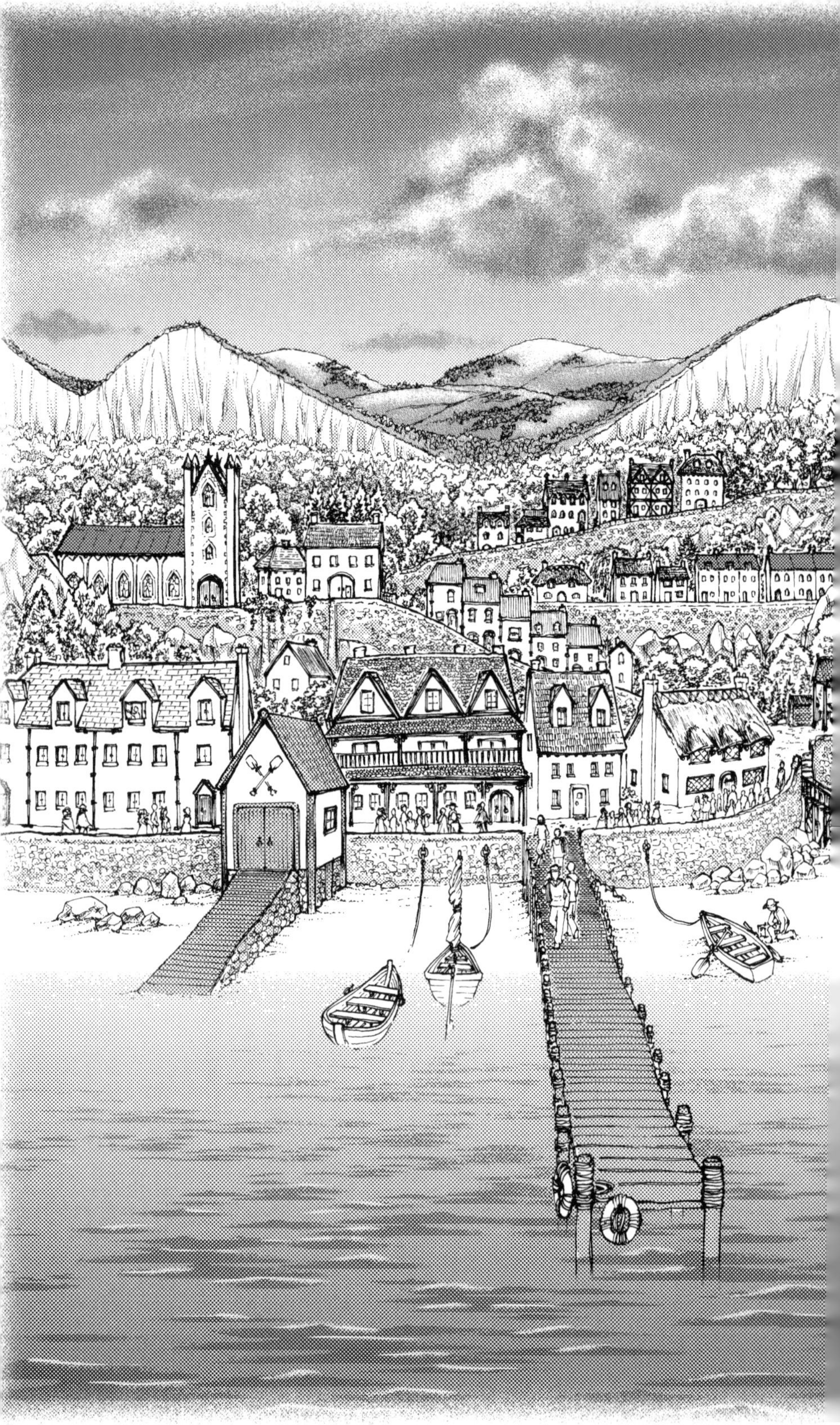

'I do apologise, I would help with an Air spell, but as I had already cast a Water spell, I have to maintain the appearance of being a Water Master. Although... I could have made the ship travel much faster had I been allowed to use both elements.'

'Hah! I don't think they could've handled the shock of you after me.'

***

The sun was on its way down when the ferry pulled into Seacht Sisters Harbour, painting the chalk cliffs orange all the way up each of their seven peaks, topped off with dark green grass. The surf crashed onto the pebble beach; the wet stones sparkling like diamonds as each wave receded.

As the ship moored, Rua felt a tug on her cloak.

It was Barrie, the little boy.

'I'm so sorry, mi'lady Dagger,' called his mother, rushing over.

Rua grinned at the boy and ruffled his hair.

'Aw, it's okay. You're just saying hello, ain'tcha?'

He sucked on his thumb and nodded.

The vixen bobbed her head.

'Um, would you like to travel with us tomorrow morning, if you're not already sorted?' she asked. 'We've booked a private coach to Sienna Vale, it should be less crowded than the other stagecoaches?'

Rua pricked her ears in surprise and beamed.

'Oh! Yeah, thanks, that'd be great!'

'It leaves at nine from the front of The Black Bull, you know of it? Just say Nuala sent you, if you get on before we do.'

'Perfect, we're hoping to stay at the Bull tonight. See you tomorrow!'

Rua crouched down and wiggled her claws at Barrie.

'Bye bye, little man.'

He waved back, then skipped to his father, who scooped him up as the family crossed the gangplank. Rua waited until all the other passengers disembarked before motioning for Silas to follow her.

The Black Bull was an inn that she knew well. It was behind the warehouses on the docks, so it wasn't as crowded or expensive as the fancy places on the seafront.

The innkeeper hailed them as they walked in.

'Ah, if it isn't Miss Rua! It's been a few years since I saw you last, but you keep getting better-looking as I get worse, haha!'

'Come now, Declan,' she said with a wink. 'You're a sight for sore eyes.'

'Damn right: you'd have to be blind! Now, what can I do for you? I take it this handsome chap's with you?' he said, nodding at Silas. 'D'you need a twin or...?'

There was a disparaging grunt from one of the drinkers at the bar.

'An Elf bedding a Vulpine?' he sneered. 'No way.'

In a flash of irritation, she looked at Silas, who set his jaw in defiance.

'Double!' they both declared at once, putting an arm around each other.

The customer choked on his beer.

The innkeeper laughed and threw her a key.

'And why not? Enjoy yourselves!'

It was only when she got to the top of the stairs that she lost her bravado. They'd always slept in separate beds. She didn't want to cross that line yet, but her damned temper had just forced it.

She found their room. It was tiny and the bed filled most of it; no space for one of them to go on the floor.

How was she going to fix this?

It took her a whole minute to notice Silas looked as nervous as she felt.

'We do not have to...' he said, haltingly. 'I mean... not that I would refuse but... that man was so rude, I just... I-I will keep to one side of the bed.'

She sighed with relief. Ever the gentleman.

'Thank you, Silas. We'll sleep, nothing more.'

Oof, that came out harsh. Try again, girl.

'I mean... I do want to, but... not just yet. Okay?'

'Okay.'

Rua's travelling cloak was still uncomfortably damp. She reluctantly hung it up to dry before heading back downstairs with Silas for dinner, hoping that any travelling Vulpines would leave her alone in this quieter inn. Her gamble paid off and she was left undisturbed as she caught up on the latest gossip with the innkeeper. He always had his finger on the pulse, often tipping her off on the latest opportunities for mercenaries.

The available jobs seemed pretty typical for the time of year; bounties on thieves who preyed on tourists or protection detail for travelling dignitaries. But they soon moved on to talk about the royal family and the queen's Silver Jubilee celebrations.

There would be a grand procession through the whole city. Her son, Prince Teagan, was finally old enough to join his sister, the Princess Royal, Niamh, at the head of the procession. As Lieutenants of the Household Cavalry, they would be the outriders before being followed by the Dragoons and the ceremonial carriage for Queen Eílís and her Prince Consort Owyn. The Queen's Champion was to ride solo closely behind, followed by her unit, the elite Queen's Guard. Then selected companies and their pipers from the regional forces would take up the rear.

Rua tried not to let her annoyance show when she heard about her role in the procession. She hated being made conspicuous, but it was an inevitable part of her duty and, in true Eiran tradition, made tactical sense if there was an attack.

There was a sudden hush as six men approached her. One of them was the drinker from earlier. He elbowed one of his friends and jutted his chin at her.

'D'you howl when you're in heat, bitch?'

Silas started to stand.

Rua pushed him back down.

'Hmph! I do, actually,' she said, jovially. 'But only with a man who's good enough.'

The innkeeper held up his hands.

'Hey, Davey, mate. Calm down, eh?'

The other men now stepped forward, glaring at Silas.

'Got a thing for tails, Elf? At least it's not one of our real women.'

'Thought we'd've butchered enough long-ears to teach you to stay out of Eira.'

Now she'd heard enough. Rua stood up, folding her arms.

'My, my, whatever has the world come to?' she lamented. 'You boys are so last century. Actually... wasn't that war three centuries ago, now? Positively primeval.'

'Filthy vermin!'

'We should hunt you down, just like your little brothers and sisters.'

She fixed them with a cold stare.

'I'd like to see you try,' she growled softly.

They all rushed at once, fists flying. She avoided every assault; ducking from their punches, weaving between their lunges, jumping back and forth with ease. She didn't even uncross her arms. They stumbled around, smashing into chairs and tables.

She caught the innkeeper's eye and gave him a reassuring nod; she would take this outside. With a swish of her tail to catch their attention, she hopped onto the bar.

'Is that seriously the best you can do? Maybe you need more breathing room.'

Rua somersaulted off the bar and began walking leisurely to the door. She made her way out, sidestepping their attacks and maintaining her slow pace, just to piss them off.

'Slippery eel!' they shouted. 'You're not a real warrior, with your fancy footwork!'

'You've got a point,' she noted. 'I tell you what – why don't I stand still for you?'

She turned around to their angry faces, washed out from the flickering light of the street lamps. She drew a circle in the dirt with her toes and stepped inside.

They now held back, looking unsure.

She pouted.

'Aw, there, there. I promise I won't kill you. Here, see?'

Rua scanned the gathering crowd of spectators, ignoring the gasps and whispers from the Vulpines who had recognised her. Waving at Silas, she unclipped her dagger and sheath, tossing them into his open arms. She bent her knees, shifting into a forward stance, her arms curled up to guard her chest, one leg in front of the other.

'No nasty knives. Just good ol' fisticuffs. Or am I still too scary?'

Enraged, one of them ran towards her and threw a punch.

She caught it with her hand, stopping him in his tracks.

His fist shook with exertion, but he couldn't push any further; her planted feet held her fast. Slowly, she dug her claws into his knuckles, making him cry out in pain.

She looked up into his eyes.

'Tell me again how I'm not a real warrior.'

She released his fist, sending him off balance. As he fell forward, she caught him on the chin with a swift uppercut. He flew onto his back, knocked out cold. Re-centring herself in the dirt circle, she extended one arm out and beckoned with a finger.

'Come at me, brothers.'

Two rushed at her this time. The first that reached her tried a jab to her solar plexus. She blocked it to the side with a inside forearm twist, then stepped into him and smashed his nose in with a backhand strike. The second tried to jump her from below, but she kneed him in the temple, knocking him to the ground. Then two more came at her from both sides at once.

She clicked her tongue, exasperated.

They approached with their arms outstretched to grab her. She leapt straight up at the last possible moment. They crashed into each other. She twisted in the air above them and dropped, the back of her heel catching one on the head. She landed on him daintily and cracked her knuckles, then stepped back and elbowed the other in the face.

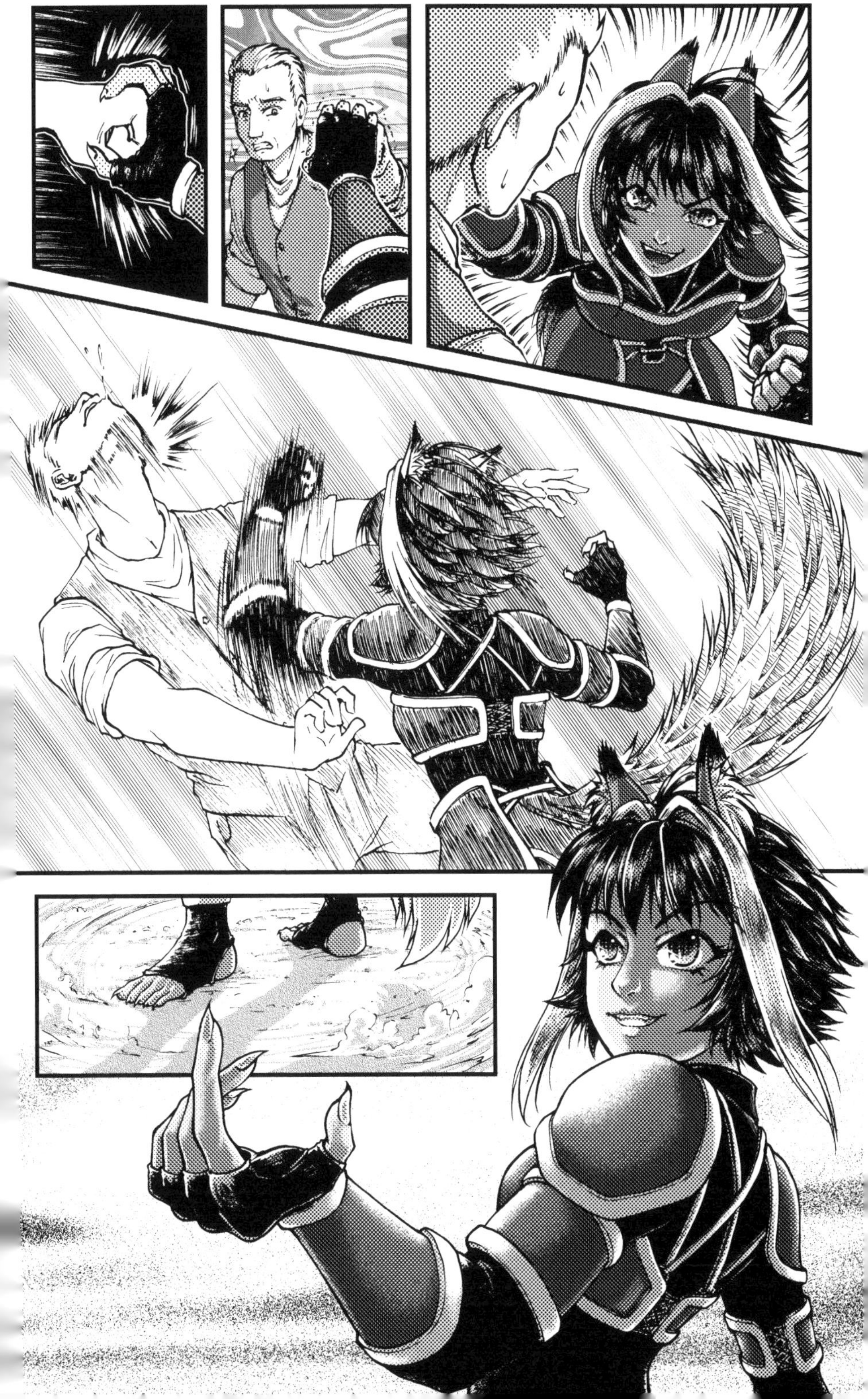

'Oi, Davey, give that back!' the innkeeper called.

The drunkard was shuffling towards her with a kitchen knife.

She straightened up and narrowed her eyes. She was beginning to lose her patience.

'Trust me, Davey, you don't want to do this,' she warned.

He hesitated for a moment. Then, he spat on the floor.

'I don't listen to beasts!'

He threw it at her clumsily.

She felt sad as she caught the blade and threw it back at him, impaling his hand.

'What did I do to you?' she wondered aloud, her words obscured by his screams.

III

Shrill whistles filled the night as the city guards arrived. The troublemakers were promptly arrested and taken away. The innkeeper came rushing over.

'I sent for the city guard, Miss. That lot are barred; I don't want none of their sort ruining things for decent folk! Neither does any other tradesman – Seacht Sisters won't have it. We're proud to welcome all travellers, whatever their kind!'

'I know you are, Dec. Sorry for causing a mess.'

'They broke the chairs, not you. I'll be sending them the bill once they're out of gaol. I must say though, it's strange... Davey grew up here, so you'd think he'd know better. He never used to have a problem with other kind.'

Rua rolled her shoulders, suddenly feeling tired.

'I think we'll be heading up now.'

'G'night, Miss. See you in the morning.'

She felt troubled as she took Silas's arm and went back inside.

'Dec had a point, y'know. It's been a helluva long time since the Great Wars; I've not seen that level of hatred from Eirans for over two hundred years. Nowadays, we might give Elves a bit of mild ribbing, but that was bang out of order. And as for how they spoke to me; that was even more off. We're a native race; there've been Vulpines in Eira at least as long as Humans, if not longer.'

Silas stayed silent until they entered their room.

'I knew I did not have to be, but I was a little worried about you, out there.'

She pinned her ears back, ashamed.

You stupid, selfish girl. You didn't even think about his feelings.

'I had everything under control,' she mumbled. 'Even so... I'm sorry, love.'

She put her arms around his waist and squeezed.

He hugged her back tightly.

'Thank you,' he said.

He bent down to kiss her, then leant back and stroked her ears affectionately.

'Would you like me to fetch your nightshirt?'

'Yes, please.'

He stepped back and drew a glowing square of Spirit energy in the air. He pushed his arm through the flap he created and rummaged through his Magus inbox. He handed a nightshirt to her, then turned his back as usual, to give her some privacy. She undressed quickly, pulling it on before getting under the covers.

'I'm done,' she called.

After a minute, she felt the bed creak as he got in with her. She twisted around to look at him. His silvery eyes crinkled as he smiled at her, his hair falling across his face.

He was so beautiful, so caring and selfless. She didn't deserve him.

He must have seen some of her unhappy thoughts swirling in her eyes; his smile faded into a look of concern and he gently gathered her into his arms.

'I will not love you any less for being yourself, Rua.'

She burrowed into his side. If only she could make herself believe it.

***

After breakfast, they waited at the roadside for the stagecoach with Nuala, her husband, her two children, her aunt and her two brothers.

Silas was keen to find out more about Rua's hometown.

'So can you tell me more about Sienna Vale?'

'Well, it was called Sinnach'Baile when I was born, but you can't expect everything to stay the same for six hundred years... except me, of course.'

'Indeed. What does it mean?'

'It's the oldest Vulpine settlement in Eira; it means "Home of the Fox". Over the years, the name was brought more in line with the Common tongue; Sienna Vale was a nice compromise, as most Vulpines in Eira have that colour in their fur.'

The stagecoach finally pulled up. They set off at a brisk pace across the undulating landscape of the Dess Downs; the little boy making a game of spotting old barrows dotted in amongst the hills. It was a full day's journey to the Vale on the busy thoroughfare; several coaches passed them coming from the opposite direction.

There was much talk about the Council taking place in their home country. Sienna Vale was throwing a week long feast, with a funfair full of games, crafts and performances. The Council itself would be held in Albanon's Guild Hall, with a public viewing gallery for invitees and lucky ticket holders. This would be followed by a series of cultural performances and concerts around the capital to showcase the traditions of Eira and of the visiting Vulpines from all over the world.

Rua knew loosely about the programme of events; although she was the official Chair, there was an organising committee who took care of most things on the ground. She had signed off on most of these very promptly over the past few months, thanks to Silas and his access to the enchanted postal system.

But she cringed when she heard about the queen's red-carpet reception for the Vulpine Council at the palace; an event that would require Eiran formal dress. And in the warrior-like mindset of Eira, the more formidable the fighter, the less they wore in ceremonies; to prove that they could emerge unscathed from any attack.

She really didn't want to have to wear that silly little dress again.

***

Sienna Vale could truly be described as being at one with nature. Vulpines had been in these woods since records began, their early houses fashioned after dens and burrows. The ancient settlement grew organically; but-and-ben cottages with dry stone walls and coppiced wattle willow fences built between semi-subterranean dwellings hollowed out of the root systems of great oaks. The larger buildings used the trees themselves as supporting columns or entrance halls.

Of course, the city was filled with Vulpine folk, but there were almost as many Humans, even a few Elves and Dwarves. Many were locals, having settled or married into life in Saint Leona's forest. There was a thriving tourist trade due to the natural beauty of its architecture and its convenient location between the coast and the capital.

The stagecoach pulled up in front of The Crown And Claw, one of the oldest coaching inns in Eira. A stablehand scurried over to their carriage and began helping everyone down. As the young fox took her hand, he looked up into her golden eyes, framed by the distinctive streaks in her hair peeking out from under her hood.

He gasped and bowed low.

Rua clicked her tongue in irritation. He must be a new hire.

'Don't fuss over me,' she muttered to him. 'I thought Meghan would've told you.'

'Forgive me, ma'am! I-I'll help the others with their bags.'

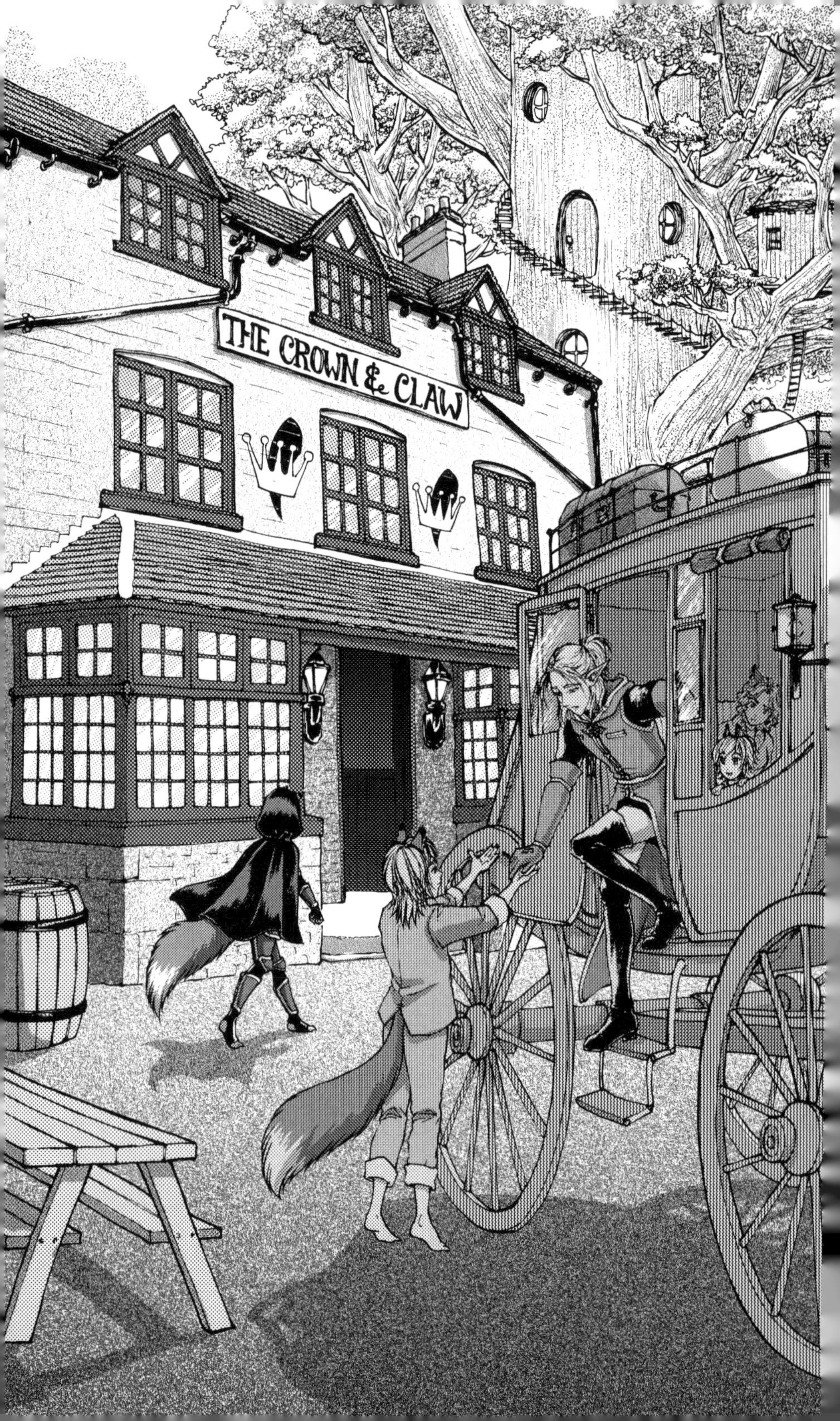
THE CROWN & CLAW

She nodded curtly then, throwing a glance back at Silas, hopped down and walked swiftly towards the inn. She threw open the doors and it was as she had feared; instead of the regulars, it was heaving with tourists who were here for the Council celebrations.

She wasn't going to hide in her own ancestral home.

She pulled down her hood and wound her way through the tables.

A hush rippled through the room as everyone with a tail stopped and stared.

She kept her face blank as she heard the same whispers all over again.

The living legend. The immortal assassin. Slaughterer of thousands. Wrath of Ciel. Ruler of all Vulpines. Demi-goddess. Death incarnate.

An old vixen stepped out from behind the bar. With her grey hair in a severe bun, her pocketed shirt and her trousers tucked into her flat-heeled ankle boots, she looked like a drill sergeant. She folded her arms, addressing the entire room.

'Hey! She may be *the* Dagger, but she's my cousin, and she's just as warm-blooded as you and me, so quit your ogling! If she's not in uniform, saving your life, or killing you 'cos you deserved it, you treat her no different! Else you're barred!'

Rua cracked up, her tension gone in a peal of laughter.

'Meg, you're supposed to be reassuring people, not threatening them! Come here.'

The old woman grinned and gave her a fierce hug as the seasoned serving staff continued briskly with orders, forcing the atmosphere back to normal.

Rua stepped back and took Silas's hand.

'Meghan is my cousin, twelve times removed,' she explained to him. 'She's my closest kin. Meg, he's the one I've been telling you about.'

'It is an absolute pleasure to make your acquaintance,' he said, performing his usual bow and flourish. 'I did not realise you would be running the inn.'

When he stood up, upon looking at her face, he startled slightly.

'Well? Spit it out, lad!' she snapped.

'Forgive my manners! Your eyes... they are like Rua's.'

Meghan puffed up with pride.

'No other Vulpines have this in their bloodline. Since Rua's blessing, our vixens have always had golden eyes, and we do not take husbands easily. When we do, the men know; their daughters will never have their eyes. They will have hers.'

Another golden-eyed vixen came running out of the kitchen. She was closely followed by a Human; he was carrying a Vulpine toddler, shyly clutching at her blanket.

'Speaking of daughters and their husbands...' Meghan said, trailing off.

'Rua! It's been far too long!' the young lady cried, launching herself at Rua.

'It has, Fiadh. You're looking well; motherhood suits you.'

Extracting herself from the cousin thirteen times removed, she looked down at the little one that was fourteen times removed.

'Now, Dwyer,' she asked the man. 'Who is this little girl I've been hearing about?'

The kit burrowed deeper into her father's chest, her own set of golden eyes peeking out over the blanket, making them look too large for her face.

'This is Gráinne,' Dwyer said, tenderly.

He whispered into the little vixen's ear.

'Why don't you say hello to Auntie Rua and Uncle Silas?'

The toddler flicked her ears back and forth, deciding.

Rua had just the ticket.

'Silas, love, could you fetch that present now?'

He nodded, accessing his inbox to pull out a stuffed toy; a fox, made from wool felting, with gold beads as its eyes. Exchanging a companionable smile with Dwyer, he bent down and made it scamper into her hands.

The girl giggled, cuddling it. She looked up at the both of them.

'Thank you, Auntie Rua... Uncle Silas.'

Her sweet, tiny voice made Rua's heart ache. As much as she loved meeting descendants of her line, it was tinged with sadness. They always died too soon.

Meghan touched her shoulder.

'I've tidied up the back room. Sorry, I couldn't replace the bed with anything bigger, we're totally stretched for them at the moment.'

'It's fine! Silas is skinny. We'll just have to snuggle, right?'

He blushed.

'Anyway,' Rua continued. 'I'm more interested in food. I'm starving!'

They were promptly seated at the bar; plate after plate deposited in front of their noses with military efficiency. Fish in a crispy beer batter sprinkled with vinegar, seasoned lamb mince topped with creamy mashed potato and cheese, pork and apple sausages braised with root vegetables in cider. Eiran comfort food was heaven to Rua. As they washed it down with ale and polished off the steamed bread and butter puddings, the conversations died down and a lone voice started singing.

'*Le grá dhuit níl radharc am cheann, Eibhlín a Riún.*'

It was Fiadh. Her voice was a rich, mezzo soprano, throbbing with emotion.

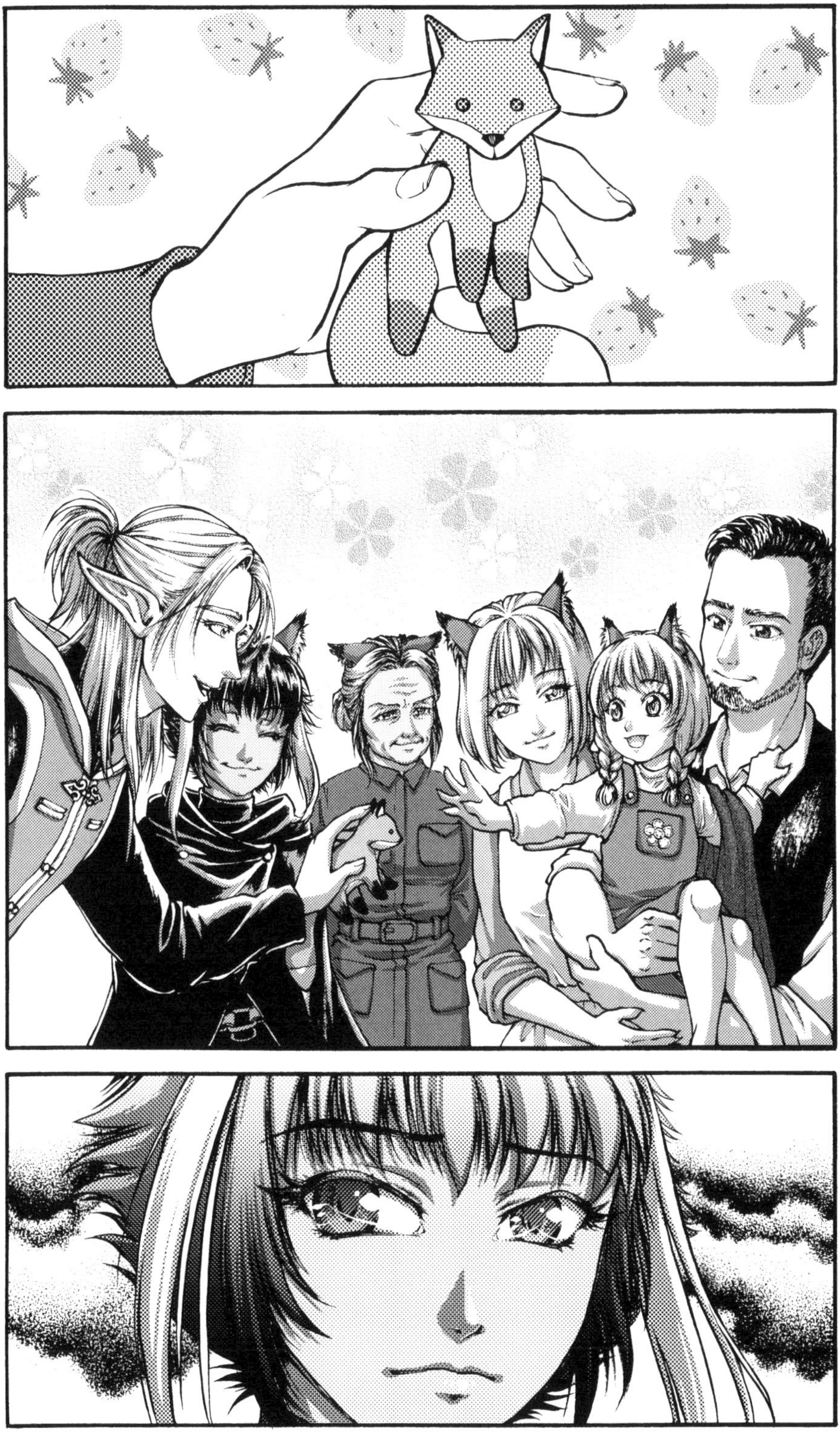

Rua loved this song; she stood up to watch.

'*Is trácht ort is saidhbhreas liom, Eibhlín a Riún.*'

Noticing Rua, Fiadh beckoned and nodded.

Rua grinned and joined in, walking over to her cousin. Their voices now rose in harmony; Fiadh singing the melody, Rua providing trills above it.

'*Ó mo mhórdháil ró-ghreidhnmhear thú, sólás na Soillse's tú...*

Ó mo lile thú, mo mheidhir is tú, mo bhruinneal thú go deimhin.

A's mo chlús dá bhfuil sa choill seo's tú.

As mo chroí 'stigh níl leigheas gan tú, Eibhlín a Riún.'

They finished to much applause, but Rua didn't care. She enjoyed singing solo, but singing in harmony with a loved one was one of the best feelings in the world. She skipped back to Silas, who pulled her close and sat her on his knee before she had a chance to feel self-conscious about it.

'That was beautiful,' he murmured into her ear.

Giddy from the beer and her impromptu performance, she swivelled around in his lap to kiss him with abandon, lingering on his lips long enough to make his heart race.

By Ciel, he tasted so good.

Just then, the stablehand she had scolded earlier came running in.

'Meghan! Another coach has come!'

The old vixen frowned.

'What? It's too early! Gavin, you start checking them in. Urgh, some of the beds still need making... and what about the next batch of food orders?'

'I'll look after the bar!' Rua suggested. 'Silas can help... with making the beds. Don't put him in the kitchen. Or the dining room. Use his hands, not his feet.'

He nodded vigorously in agreement.

'Okay then,' Meghan said. 'Fiadh, you show him how it's done.'

Meghan swept into the kitchen as Silas followed Fiadh up the stairs.

Rua leapt over the counter, cracked her knuckles and spread her arms wide.

'Come on, you lot. Who needs a refill?' she asked.

An elderly dog handed her his tankard first, twitching his ears nervously.

'Wasn't expecting *the* Dagger to work behind the bar.'

'Hey, I haven't forgotten my roots, y'know. Haven't we all been there, pulling pints for a bit of cash?' she said, pouring his drink.

'Haha, you're right, lass!'

A vixen now pushed her wine glass forward.

'I'm more impressed you've snagged a boyfriend who's willing to do housework!'

'Oh, he's willing, but he's not always able!' Rua said with a wink.

They laughed as Rua took their coins and counted up their change.

She worked her way down the line, bantering with customers as she went. When she heard the doors swing open, she ducked under the bar to bring out a tray of clean glasses for the new arrivals.

She stood up and nearly dropped the tray in shock.

'Rua, *ma chérie*. It's been a while.'

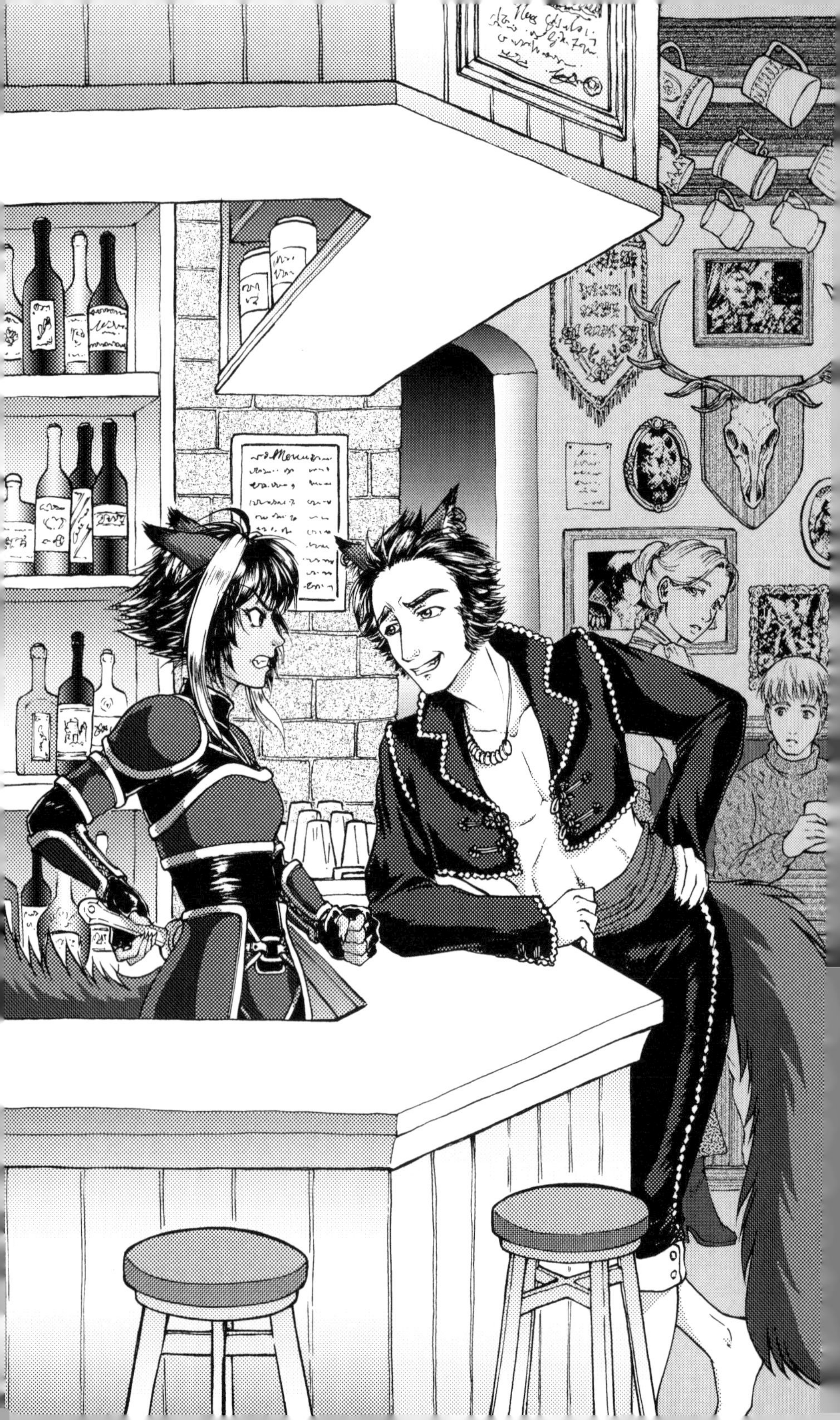

IV

Of course, he looked older than when she last saw him twelve years ago. His shaggy, dark hair was still a mess. He had a couple more gold hoops in his black-tipped ears. Save for a green scarf wrapped around his waist and the base of his tail, he was bare-chested underneath his cropped, red jacket. A gold chain strung with coins clinked against his collarbone. His green eyes blinked lazily as he gave her a crooked smile.

'What's the matter, *chérie*? Lost for words?'

Rua placed the tray down, her hands shaking as she tried to control her outrage at his presence. Then she straightened up and slapped him hard across the face.

She was marginally impressed that he didn't even try to avoid it.

'I suppose I deserved that,' he reasoned.

'You did.'

'For what it's worth, I was going to pay you back.'

'Money wasn't the issue. It was the lies.'

'Was it though? Or was it because you wanted an excuse to leave me?'

'You gave me so many excuses, it's a wonder I stayed with you as long as I did.'

Slowly, he leant forward over the bar, his nose just a few inches away from hers.

She could smell his musk, mixed with the cologne he was wearing.

'A wonder, yes? Well, I could remind you why...' he offered.

She narrowed her eyes and touched the handle of her dagger.

'Reynard, you never could take a hint. Don't make me pull my knife on you again.'

'Rua, are you alright?' Silas called from the bottom of the stairs.

How much did he see?

He made his way to her side, eyeing Reynard who held his hands up in truce.

'I'm fine, love,' Rua said, patting Silas on the shoulder. 'We were just... catching up.'

Reynard raised an eyebrow. He extended his hand to Silas with a lazy grin.

'Reynard Débonnaire, newly elected Vulpine Councillor of Vertcielle.'

Rua's heart jumped into her throat.

Oh, for the love of Ciel, no!

Silas politely shook his hand.

'Magus Silas L'Heritier. *Je suis très heureux de faire votre connaissance.*'

'*Enchanté,*' Reynard replied.

He turned to Rua again and winked.

'It seems you have a penchant for Vertciellen men, no? Perhaps I made a bigger impression than I thought.'

Before she could cover up her flushed face with a sharp retort, he turned away to walk upstairs to his room.

'See you tomorrow, *chérie.*'

'Don't flatter yourself!' she called belatedly as he disappeared from view.

She slammed her hands down onto the counter, digging her claws into the wood.

That vain, cheating, sly, son of a–

'Rua...' Silas began in a worried tone.

'Gavin!' she shouted to the stablehand, making him jump. 'How long is that bastard booked in for?'

'Th-three nights, ma'am!'

She raked her claws sharply over the bar, leaving lines and splinters.

'No,' she muttered. 'I can't stay here that long. Not with him around.'

She paced over to Gavin, her tail whipping back and forth.

'I want two horses saddled and ready to go in the morning,' she commanded.

He nodded nervously.

She stormed through the kitchen, past Meghan, who threw her a look of concern.

'I'll tell you tomorrow,' Rua growled.

The blood rushing in her ears didn't affect her sense of direction as she navigated through the dark. She pushed open the door to her bedroom.

It was small but cosy; the ceiling low enough for her to touch. A single window looked out into the forest, just large enough for her to jump through if she needed to make a quick exit. The curtains were open; moonlight streamed onto the bed.

Rua took a few deep breaths to ground herself; the smell of this unassuming room was the closest thing she had to a childhood home. Then her eyes suddenly felt hot as tears threatened. She felt betrayed, violated.

46

That bastard was in her home. Her sanctuary was gone.

She distracted herself by thinking about what she needed to get done before leaving. Drawing the curtains, she started unlacing her shin guards. She had pulled off most of her armour by the time Silas appeared, already with her nightshirt in hand.

Without a word, he gave it to her and turned around as they both changed into their nightclothes. When she was done, she reached behind her to tap his shoulder, before she crawled into her bed.

He got in behind her. Then she felt his tentative hand on her side.

She curled into a ball. She didn't want to be touched right now.

He moved his hand away.

'Please, Rua... when you feel able to talk about it, tell me.'

'... I will.'

***

In the morning, Rua rose early, leaving Silas still asleep in her bed. She slipped out and closed the door quietly. She tiptoed into the kitchen as Meghan and Fiadh were cooking breakfast for the guests. She was thankful their eyes were full of sympathy rather than anger at her outburst. Although they were family, she still felt ashamed telling them the whole story.

'... So I'm gonna have to cut my stay here short. I'm really sorry.'

Meghan wiped her hands on her apron and gave her a big hug.

'Rua, sweetheart, of course I understand. Just make sure you pop back soon.'

Fiadh took her shoulders and kissed both her cheeks.

'You don't need to feel guilty about anything. Not us, nor him... though you ought to say something to that Silas of yours. He's worried about you.'

Rua put a finger to her lips as she heard sounds from her bedroom.

'Later,' she whispered, before raising her voice, in a jovial tone. 'Can I help with chopping anything? How thinly d'you want these mushrooms sliced?'

Silas came in, all eyes, his hair still tousled.

Busying herself with the mushrooms, she forced a smile at him.

He didn't force the issue.

'Good morning, ladies. Should I help with boiling more water?'

'Aw, thank you darling!' Meghan said. 'You're a treasure.'

Sitting himself down near the stoves, he magically stoked the fires. Rua was pleased he had the sense to do something that meant he was rooted to one spot; she dreaded the thought of him tripping over customers. When the first rush of orders died down, they grabbed a quick bite before filling Silas's magus inbox with supplies. They said their goodbyes to her family and left on the horses Gavin had prepared for them.

Rua only began to relax once they were deep in the ancient oak forests of Saint Leona. She had purposely chosen a path that was well away from the main stagecoach route; she had had enough of unwanted chance encounters. Perhaps staying away from everyone for the next couple of days would be for the best. She cast her eye at Silas.

As expected, he was pretty awful at horse-riding; it took several attempts for him to mount, and when he finally got on, his seat was all over the place. At least his gelding was very forgiving; a big, placid horse that was content with following her flighty mare. And Silas hadn't complained at all about her change of plans. In fact, he had been exemplary since her outburst at Reynard last night.

She needed to address that.

'Thanks. For giving me room. And sorry for all of this. I... I'll try to explain.'

He glanced up from his reins and nodded.

She looked into the trees, trying to imagine she was just speaking to the birds.

'It was twenty years ago, in Fleurys. Remember that cult I told you about in Pas-Droit? Yeah, that. Nastiest job I had to deal with in ages. Involved children. Never could stomach it when kids got hurt.'

She shuddered.

'After I killed them all and... put some of their victims out of their misery... I met him that evening, at the inn where I was staying. He was a young troubadour back then. I knew I shouldn't have let him sweet-talk his way into my pants. But I felt so numb. I wanted to forget. I wanted to feel. Anything, even pain was better than nothing.'

'He hurt you?!' Silas said, breaking his silence.

'Oh, no! Well, not really. I kinda wanted... oh, never mind. Look, it wasn't a relationship formed in the healthiest of circumstances. And it didn't get any better. It lasted for years. I kept going back to him, even though I knew he was wrong for me.'

Because I didn't deserve any better.

She twisted around to face Silas, her expression completely deadpan.

'I finally ended it after he lost a large chunk of my bounty earnings on a racehorse. Owned by another one of his girlfriends.'

48

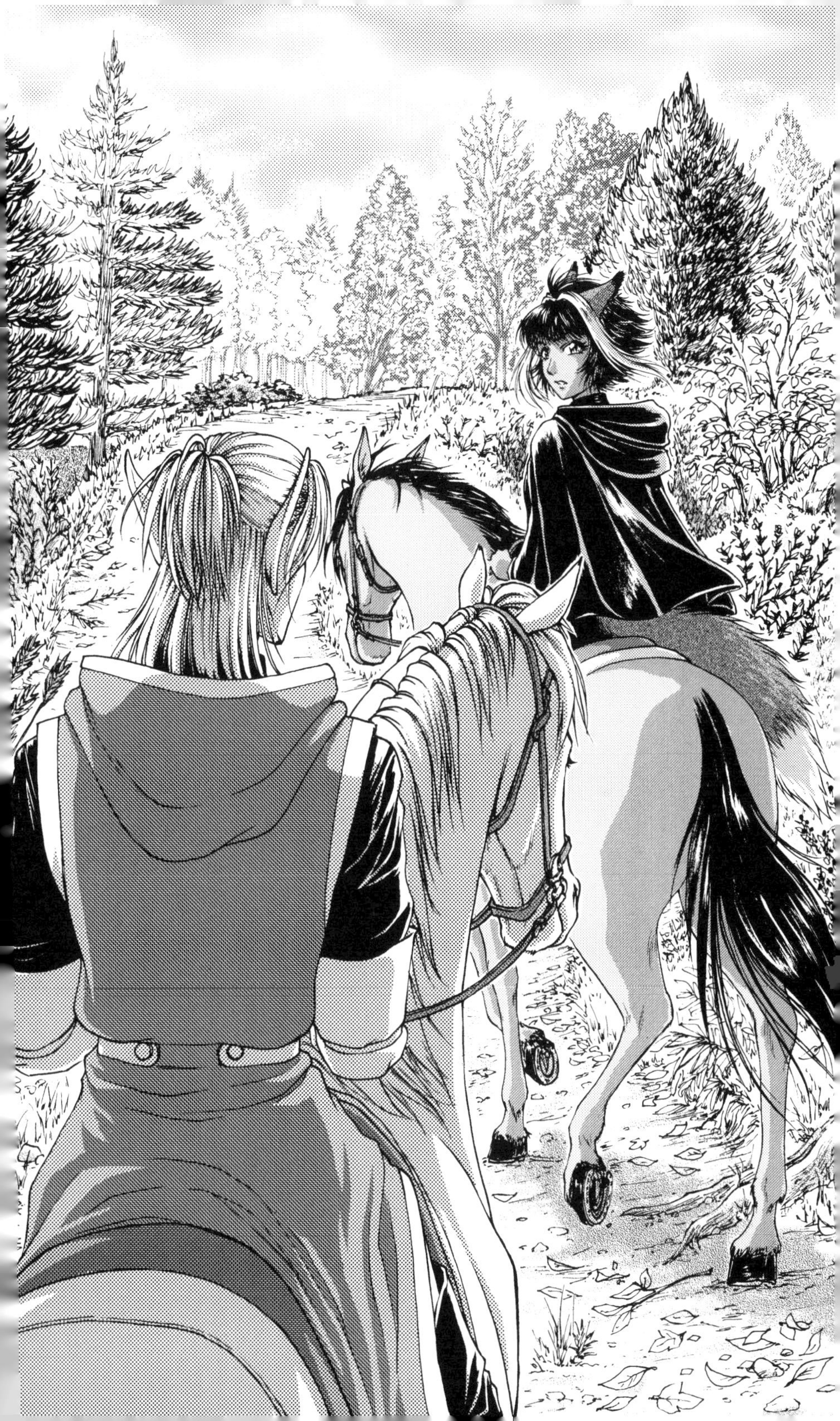

Silas cringed.

She turned back ahead.

'I'm gonna have to deal with him at the assembly, whether I like it or not, because he's a Councillor now. But in the meantime, I sure as Hell won't stand being near him any longer than necessary.'

They rode together quietly for a minute.

'Magus Code be damned,' Silas declared. 'I wish I had set his tail on fire.'

Rua burst out laughing; the image of Reynard trying to put it out jostled with the thrill that ran through her at hearing Silas curse.

She reined her horse in and gestured for him to come alongside her. When he pulled up, she stood in her stirrups, tugged him closer by the collar and kissed him.

'Silas, you're wonderful and I love you.'

'I love you, too.'

Their reconciliation was cut short by her horse suddenly shying off the path.

As she battled to get the mare under control, a huge shadow passed overhead. It flew over them, skimming the tops of the trees with its talons. Circling around in a wide arc, sunlight glittering off its scales, it lined up with them again for another pass. Its yellow eyes, not dissimilar to hers, eyed them hungrily, its wing span spread to the fullest in a swooping glide.

'DRAGON!' Rua shouted. 'With me, Silas, as fast as you can!'

V

Rua dug her heels into her horse's sides, urging it into a gallop.

Silas's gelding followed suit; its nose to her mare's tail.

The leaves shook like a tidal wave as the dragon passed above, the powerful downdraught of its wings carving a corridor of broken branches. Now high in the clouds, it circled and folded its wings to dive, accelerating as it dropped out of the sky. Just before reaching the ground, its wings spread wide, maintaining its breakneck speed as it headed straight for them.

Rua wheeled her horse around, making a run for the trees.

She heard a monstrous rasp as the dragon took a deep breath.

'SILAS! WATCH OUT–!' she shouted.

Their horses shied sideways as the fireball sped in between them, showering the path and the surrounding shrubs in flames.

Rua turned to see Silas fall off his horse, tumbling onto the ground heavily. The gelding took off into the dense bushes and the dragon loomed, back-beating its wings to land. The earth shook as the huge lizard dropped onto the ground, its muscular legs spread wide to distribute its weight. It fixed its hungry eyes on Silas, growling softly from deep within its throat; like thunder rumbling in the distance.

To Rua's relief, Silas stood up and with a wave of his hands, vanished from sight.

He must have used a Spirit Fabric to make himself invisible.

She leapt off her frightened mare, slapping its rump to send it running. She dashed in front of the dragon and drew her dagger, swishing her tail to catch its eye.

It baulked, surprised at how one potential snack disappeared only to be replaced by another. Then it lunged forward, maw open wide to gobble her up.

Rua sprung up and over its snapping jaws then plunged her dagger into its shoulder. The blade was small enough to slip between its scales and connect with flesh, but for a creature of this size, it would have been a mere scratch.

The dragon snarled in irritation and swivelled its head around to bite at her.

She dodged its teeth again, jumping off its shoulder in a back flip to lever her dagger out. Landing on her feet, she brandished her blade at it, staring it down.

It circled on her and backed up, now eyeing her more cautiously.

Then the sound of hooves filled the air along with shouts of familiar commands.

The Dragoons swept in on their steel-armoured destriers, their winged helmets decorated with claws from dragons they had dealt with prior. A huge net flew overhead, landing on the dragon and tangling in its wings. Rendered flightless, it roared in frustration, spinning and snapping at the knights as they surrounded it.

As one, they herded it up the forest path, taunting it and making it charge towards them before dodging out of the way. They drove it towards a tall structure being pulled out of the trees by heavy horses. It was a mini siege tower; just over two storeys tall, sparsely constructed from iron poles and wooden planks.

Two figures jumped out.

Unlike the others, their fierce faces were clearly visible. Fashioned from the horns and jaws of their quarry, their ornamental face guards merely held back their hair; his dark and cropped, hers long and wild in bright copper curls. Their fearsome armour was a mix of steel overlaid with dragon hide, teeth and horns.

Hefting a great axe from his back, the man started running.

Two knights led the dragon to him; as it chased after them, they held steady then split apart at the last second, leaving the axeman directly in its path.

He ducked under its jaws and rolled, planting the spiked handle of his axe into the ground so that its blade was sticking up. As the dragon passed overhead, the axe cut into it, grating all the way along its belly.

It threw its head up in pain and shrieked.

Now the woman hefted her huge claymore overhead, crashing it down onto its chest to crack its scales. Relentless, she sidestepped to counterweight her weapon and pulled the sword around in a colossal arc to unleash a sideways strike across its weakened chest. Knocking off several scales, the blow drew blood. Still caught in a spin, upon facing the dragon again she angled her sword vertically in an upwards slash, slicing deeply through its flesh. The tip of her claymore finally brought her devastating series of assaults to an end, embedding in the ground behind her.

Blood spurting from its chest wound, the dragon staggered back, roaring in agony. It took a deep, rasping breath.

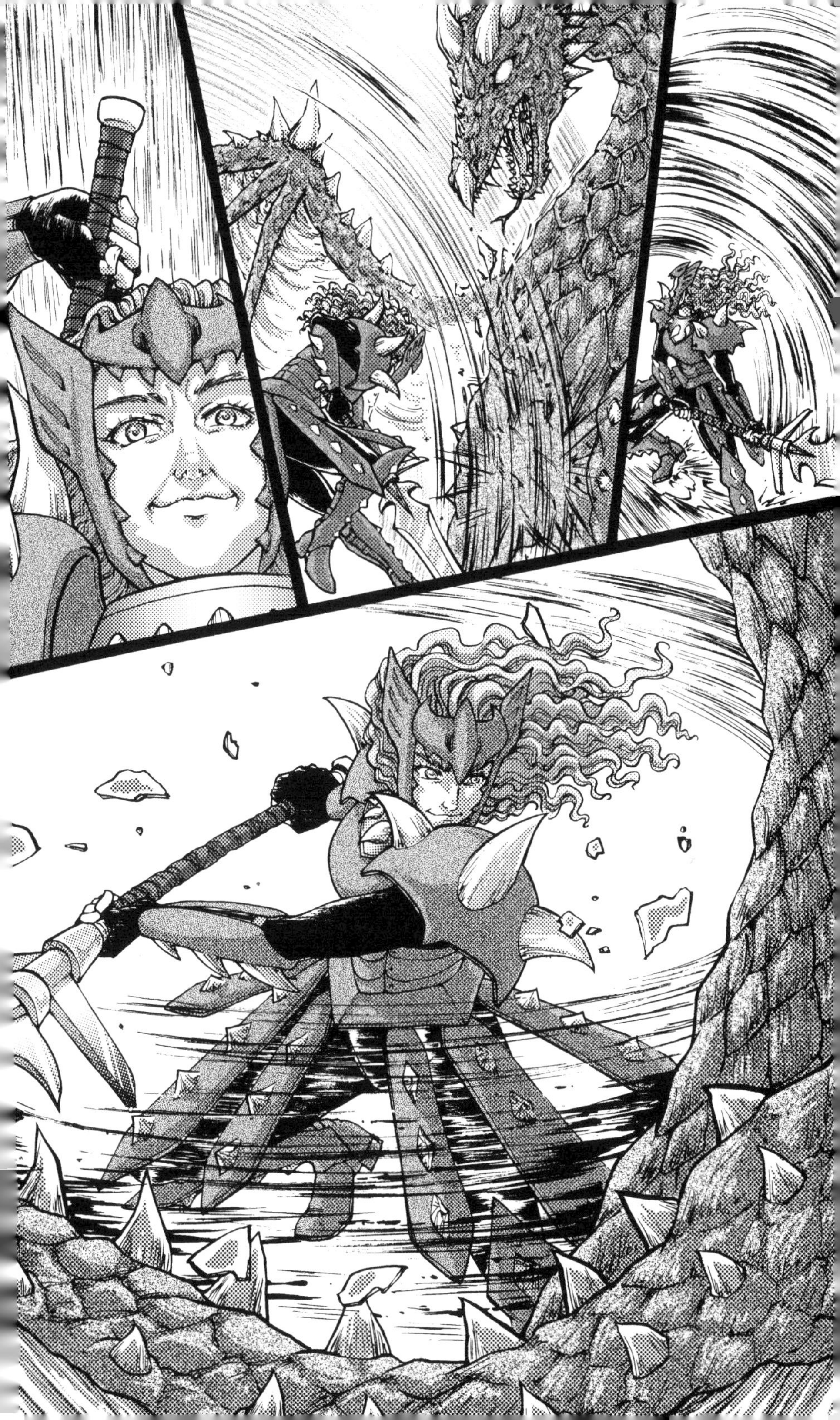

The woman instantly grabbed the long handle of her claymore and swung herself behind the flat of its huge blade to take shelter as the dragon released a continuous stream of fire at her. Her sword parted the flames but where the blaze licked at the edges of her body they didn't catch, the dragon hide on her armour was fireproof.

The siege tower swung around; the man with the axe had climbed it halfway. He yelled at the driver and they raced towards the back of the dragon. As the tower drew level with the huge beast, he jumped and sliced the dragon's tail off.

The dragon lurched forward, thrown off balance by the loss of its tail. Enraged, it thrashed about, shooting several small fireballs at the man to no avail; just like the woman, he could roll through the flames and emerge only slightly singed.

His flashy dodging was all in aid of distracting the dragon from the woman, who had now climbed up to the very top of the siege tower. As if commanding an enormous chariot, she pointed her blade at a spot about fifty yards in front of the dragon's trajectory and the siege tower lurched into action. As they raced towards a side-on collision with the dragon, the woman held her sword behind her in a crouch. Then she ran and swung her blade out in front of her as she leapt off the tower, which veered away sharply to avoid crashing into the dragon. The weight of the sword and the former momentum of the carriage flung her clear of the platform and over the approaching dragon. As she flew through the air, she pulled herself in close to the blade, aiming the tip straight down and placed her feet in the grooves partway down the cutting edges to secure her foothold.

The claymore landed squarely in the spine of the dragon, right between its upper set of shoulder blades. The weight of the sword, the woman and their fall from a considerable height all combined to drive it straight through the protective scales, embedding the enormous blade in all the way up to her feet, over three feet deep.

Rua grinned in appreciation; at that level of penetration, it was sure to have pierced the heart. A textbook kill by a mistress of the art of dragonslaying.

The dragon ground to a halt. Releasing its last breath in a death rattle, it staggered forward. The woman held on by her embedded sword. The dragon swayed and finally collapsed, its nose just a few feet away from Rua's toes.

Now that the forest was silent, her ears picked up the sound of familiar footsteps. She turned to face them and Silas finally revealed himself, shaking off his Spirit Fabric.

The Dragoons formed an orderly line on either side of the pair. Bolt upright in their saddles, the men and women held their lances high, standing to attention.

The copper-haired woman peered down at Rua from the dragon's back.

'Rua? Is that you? Wasn't expecting to see you until Friday.'

She released her sword and navigated her way down one of the dragon's front legs, sliding off its knee to land on the ground. She nodded at the two nearest Dragoons, who immediately dismounted and started climbing up the dragon to extract the giant claymore for her. She clasped Rua's forearm warmly.

'What are you doing out here, anyway?'

Rua rolled her eyes.

'You're one to talk! Isn't there this thing going on, like, the Silver Jubilee?'

'Och, not you as well. It's been months of prep already; it's practically taking care of itself! So I thought I'd sort out this dragonslaying request *and* get out of the capital for some fresh air. Kill two birds with one stone, so to speak.'

She turned to Silas, sizing him up.

'Are you the boy taking up my itinerant Champion's time? She's home rare enough as it is! Can't believe I have to compete with yet another person for her attention.'

Silas looked a bit dazed and confused.

Rua cleared her throat. Maybe he needed a clearer introduction.

'Éilís, you've no doubt gathered that this is Silas L'Heritier, otherwise known as the Weaver. Silas, love, this is Her Majesty, Queen Éilís the Enlightened.'

Silas finally found his tongue, hurriedly bowing low with a rushed flourish.

'F-forgive me, Your Majesty, for being such a drain on your subject's time!'

Éilís cackled.

'Hah! I was jesting, lad. Rua's always been free to come and go as she pleases.'

She breezily threw an arm over his shoulders, but pulled his ear close to whisper.

'Her obligation to the royal family ended five hundred years ago with Queen Liadán the Grey. Rua remains Queen's Champion for as long as she deems us worthy enough to serve... and so far, we've all been sensible enough not to piss her off. Even so, I only summon her when it really counts. I know that she is, first and foremost, Ciel's Dagger.'

She unhooked her arm from Silas and turned to smile broadly at the man with the great axe, who had finally caught up with them.

He clasped Rua's arm, dropping to one knee.

Rua acknowledged his gesture of respect with a nod, then pulled him to his feet.

'Long time no see, Owyn,' she said.

'Well met, Champion,' he replied.

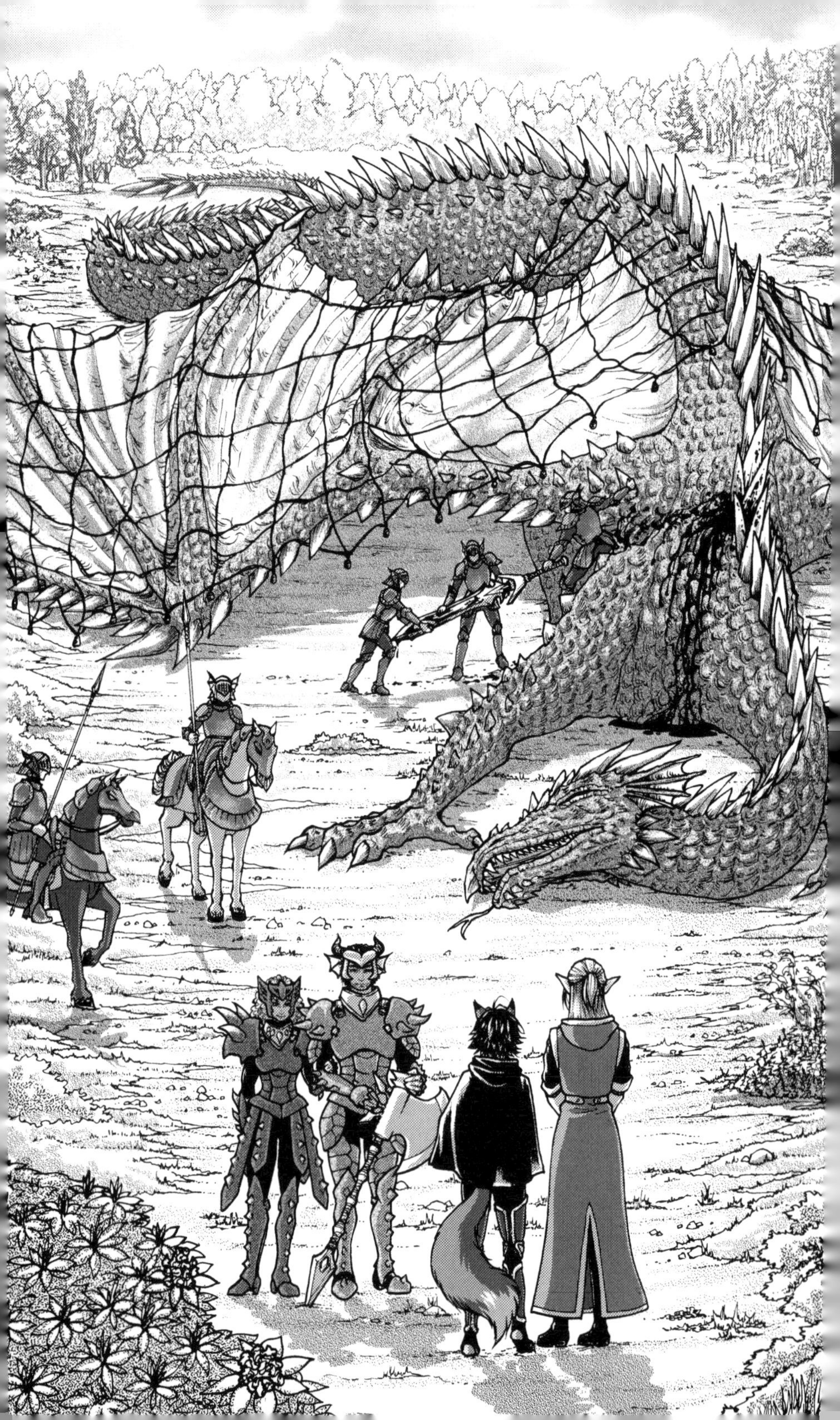

He faced Silas, offering his hand.

Silas tried to clasp it in the same manner he had seen Rua do it. His ears dipped slightly but otherwise he gave no other outward show of experiencing any pain; Owyn must not be holding back with his grip.

'Owyn. Prince Consort. Well met.'

'Magus Silas L'Heritier. Pleased to meet you.'

Éilís went to Owyn and put an arm around his waist, kissing his cheek.

'Nice tail cut.'

He grunted.

She turned to Rua.

'Now that the introductions are over, I ask again; what are you doing out here?'

'We... decided to make our way to Albanon early, to show the Silas the sights. But given how our horses have run off, we may end up taking 'til Friday on foot.'

'Och, Rua, I'm sorry. It's probably my fault you lost your horses; we'd been chasing this dragon all morning so it must have been eyeing you up for a snack. We'll give you a lift back to ours. Your room's ready anyway.'

An open top carriage pulled up. Owyn opened the door and bowed.

Éilís climbed in and flopped down with a sigh. She raised an eyebrow at Rua.

'Coming?'

VI

The forests gradually gave way to heathland, then into cultivated fields; dark with exposed soil from tilling after the harvest.

To pass the time, Éilís gave Silas a history lesson.

'Albanon has been our capital city for several thousand years. Now, my line wasn't from these parts; we Eirans are a fiery lot, so we've had a fair few civil wars. All the Duchies of Eira were quarrelling over who should lead us as a nation, way back when invaders started landing on our shores. This was well before the Great Wars, mind you. Whilst everyone squabbled down south, the dragon population got out of control, feasting on cadavers left on the battlefields. My clan, the Fiag'Arachs, ruled over the Duchy of Celidon in the Highlands. And true to our name, dragonslaying is in our blood. When dragons started attacking Albanon, my ancestors, led by Duchess Úna, defended the capital and drove them back. Since then, Eira has always had a queen, and the crown is passed down through our daughters. And for all the pageantry that comes with royalty, we've never forgotten our duty to hold dragons and other beasts at bay.'

'Hey, Silas,' Rua said, tapping him on the shoulder. 'Look.'

He turned around and his eyes went wide.

The wheels rattled as they drove onto a magnificent bridge. Suspension cables led up into two soaring towers, holding up the wide thoroughfare spanning the river.

'Liadán's Leap,' Éilís said proudly. 'One of the largest suspension bridges in Ciel's Cradle. The water barriers at the base of the towers also divert water to the surrounding farmlands and control the flow of the river Tamesis. It keeps the water level consistent for the docks further downstream, no matter what tides come.'

Noticing the Dragoon outriders and the royal carriage, curious city folk gathered on the pavements; they waved and cheered when they realised it was the Queen who was passing through. She waved back with a smile. Éilís was well-loved by her subjects, proud that their queen wasn't afraid to get her hands dirty.

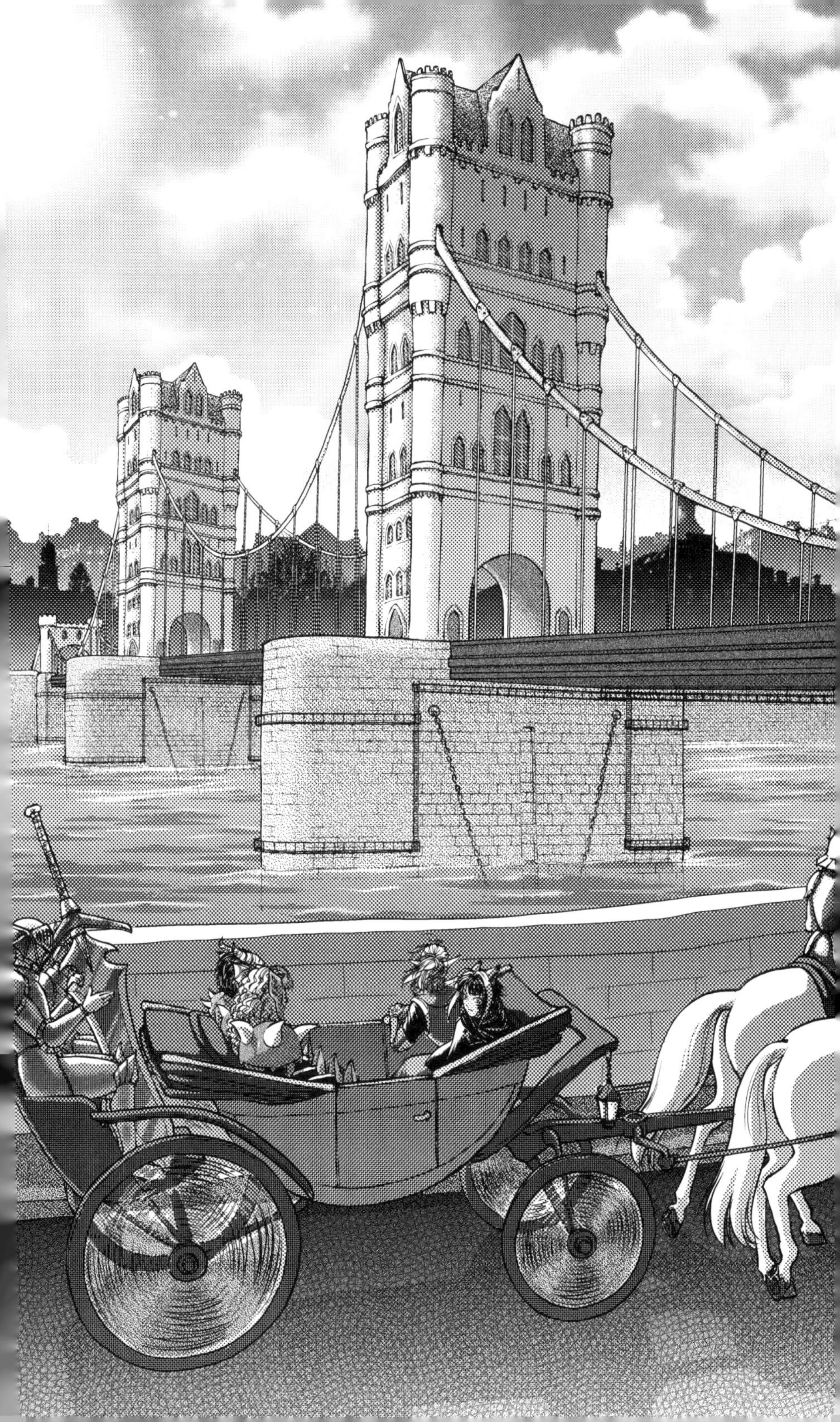

Several onlookers also noticed Rua in the carriage with her. Their jaws dropped and they turned to each other to confirm it, not quite believing that they had caught a glimpse of the elusive Queen's Champion.

Rua squirmed from the recognition.

They rode down a bustling avenue, flanked by impressive townhouses with fine restaurants and shopfronts at street level, filled with crowds on the pavements.

'We're almost there,' Rua said to Silas.

'Really? But we are right in the middle of the city!'

Éilís grinned.

'Dúnragnhailt Palace isn't situated far out of the way. When we're in Albanon, we like to be in the middle of things. Our city has built up directly around us.'

The road widened out more and they circled a large roundabout; atop the central island was a bronze statue of a warrior queen wielding a giant sword against a dragon with its wings outstretched. They had reached the palace.

A mix of red brick and sturdy stone columns rose up into the sky; the narrow windows and battlements giving the impression of an imposing fortress. Like every ancient Eiran building, the palace was originally built for war and defence. Over the years, its side walls blended into the buildings next door, blurring the lines between where the royal residence ended and where other institutions began.

The portcullis was already raised. Their carriage drove through the enormous gatehouse, the clip-clop of hooves on the cobblestones echoing in the long archway.

'This is one of the longest gatehouses I have ever ridden through,' Silas noted.

'Longest in Ciel's Cradle,' Éilís confirmed. 'My ancestors liked having plenty of time to trap any enemies trying to escape.'

He swallowed gingerly.

They pulled up in the first courtyard. As footmen helped them down, a young woman came out of the building. Her auburn hair was pulled into intricate braids along the sides of her head before falling in loose waves over her back. Dressed in the flowing robes and tartans of traditional Eiran court dress, her bare shoulders looked muscular and the silver torque around her neck was embedded with gemstones. A mixture of dragon scales, teeth and dragon claws hung from its piercework.

'Niamh, look who I've brought home!' Éilís shouted.

The young woman stood up straighter, now looking carefully at the carriage. As soon as she clocked Rua, her face lit up and she ran straight over.

'You're early! Oh, I've missed you loads!' she said, giving Rua a hug.

'And I, you. Hey, there's more claws on your torque, nice! Were they recent kills?'

The princess blushed.

'Oh, they were from last year! I've not had time lately, I've been so busy preparing for mum's Jubilee, all the craftsmen and caterers... but enough about me!'

Niamh grabbed Rua's hand and started pulling.

'I've got to show you your new room! I've redecorated it!'

'Niamh!' Éilís barked. 'Manners!'

The princess dropped her hand and stood ram-rod straight, arms by her side.

'Our apologies, ma'am! We are thankful you have had a safe hunt, Ciel be praised.'

Éilís walked right up to her nose, her face stern. Then she cracked a grin.

'At ease, girl. I know you're excited. But I need to introduce you to her partner.'

She waved to Silas, who had been trying to get out of the carriage without falling.

'Silas, this is my daughter, Niamh, the Princess Royal. Niamh, this is–'

'Eh? *You're* the Weaver?! Hmm...' she paused, assessing him. 'I suppose you'll do.'

'NIAMH! What did I just say?! MANNERS!'

The princess bowed to Silas so low that the ends of her braids touched the floor.

'My apologies, Weaver. Rua means a lot to me and to this country. The Dagger has been waiting a very long time for Ciel to provide her with a partner. She deserves the very best. And I trust you must be, because Ciel has chosen you.'

Silas blinked. He crouched down and looked up to meet Niamh's eyes.

'Then you and I feel exactly the same way. I ask myself everyday if I am doing enough for her. Rua is everything to me.'

Rua felt a lump in her throat. Why did she feel so guilty about his devotion?

Niamh grinned and clasped Silas's wrist. She thumped Rua on her back companionably before jogging into the reception room and waving for them to follow.

Rua didn't really need to be led; despite its irregularities and additions over the past few hundred years, she knew the layout of the palace by heart, all fifty-five rooms of it. In order to give Silas a tour, they took the long way around, going to the end of the central corridor before ascending an impressive staircase to the first floor.

Although Rua's official residence was within Dúnragnhildt Palace, she was never comfortable staying in that big, draughty room. She preferred something cosier, like the back of the pub in Sienna Vale. At least the palace itself wasn't too fancy; Eiran castles were more practically built than those elsewhere, prioritising defence over looks. Even

Silas's villa was breathtakingly beautiful in comparison. But he gawked over the things she felt were normal. Weapons covering the walls. Suits of armour bristling with horns, claws and scales. Trophy heads and taxidermy of the most dangerous beasts to roam Ciel's Cradle.

As they passed the palace guards along the way, each of them saluted and received a warm forearm clasp from Rua. Many of them were old soldiers, transferred from the more active positions in the Queen's Guard.

They finally stopped outside Rua's door. Her room was in the middle of the palace complex; above the entrance hall and below the Queen's own chambers.

'Are you ready?' Niamh asked. 'Welcome to your new room!'

She pushed the door open and stepped back.

Rua's eyes went round and shiny.

The fireplace crackled merrily, framed by a granite surround so polished, it looked freshly hewn. The stone walls were covered in oak panelling and rich tapestries; some she recognised as belonging to former queens. Around the edges of the room were custom built weapon racks to house the assortment she had built up over the years.

She scrunched her toes into the deep pile of the rugs. Running her hands over the leather armchairs, she admired the marquetry on the side table before heading to the double doors of her balcony. She pushed them open, peering down into the formal gardens of the second courtyard, bustling with activity from the Jubilee preparations.

She turned around and marvelled at the stairs beside her door, housing books under every step. They led up to the mezzanine, filled with large floor cushions in forest greens and autumnal reds. She could see the evening sky through a large porthole window above the first courtyard; an additional point of entry for herself that she had requested four hundred years ago at the start of the Great Wars.

She looked at the bed. Twice as large as the one before, it was made from solid oak in a clean, rustic style. Piled on top were a multitude of chunky knitted throws and cushions in heather, moss and russet tones. By her bedside was one last weapon rack.

Glinting softly, the twin crescent blades stood side by side, their central handlebars newly wrapped in supple strips of leather. Their continuous cutting edges were a true feat of master smithing, curving outwards then inwards before ending in cruel looking barbed hooks. She touched their backs, the cool steel reminding her of the thousands of lives she took in defence of her nation three centuries ago.

'Na Deirfiúracha...' she breathed. 'You found The Sisters? I thought I'd lost them.'

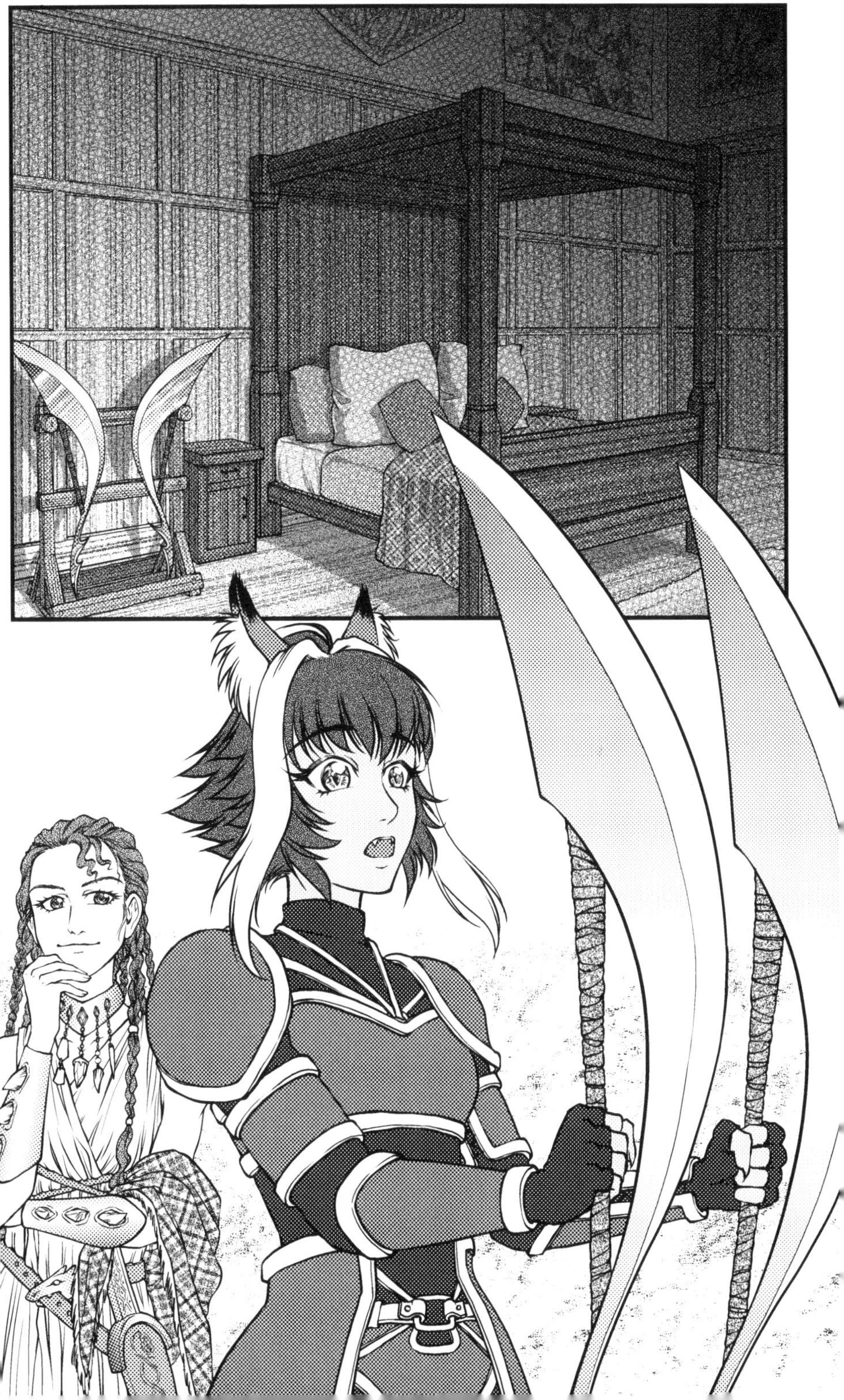

'It was a recent gift from King Xavier IV of Vertcielle,' Niamh explained. 'After finding out about their history, he returned them, out of respect for Eira's warriors and to launch the Eiran-Vertciellen military exchange programme.'

'So they went all the way over there as spoils of war...' Rua wondered.

She pulled them out of the rack. Whirling them around to test their weight, she spun them over her wrists a few times, then caught the grips with their tips pointing straight up. She closed her eyes and brought them together, touching their backs to her forehead in reverence.

'*Failte Abhaile,*' she whispered, welcoming them home.

'So... d'you like it?' Niamh asked as Rua placed the blades back in the rack. 'I know you don't like things too fancy, so I tried not to go overboard. Are the colours–OOF!'

Rua had thrown herself at Niamh, giving her a fierce hug.

'I love it. Thank you so much.'

'You're welcome. Now, I need to get back to all the paperwork mum left me. I'm sure you'll want to enjoy your new room, so I'll be seeing you later. If you're eating with us, be sure to let the cooks know before six.'

'Aw, thanks, but don't worry about us, we've got plans!'

Niamh waved and backed out of the room, closing the door.

'We do?' Silas asked.

Rua nodded brightly.

'Yup! I have an entire army to catch up with.'

VII

Rua guided Silas through one of the side corridors of the palace, passing ministers carrying papers and petitions for the queen. It was a reminder that Dúnragnhildt was a busy, working environment with government offices as well as residences within its walls. Their route ended at a heavily studded door guarded by two soldiers; their slanted caps, light cuirasses and daggers marking them as members of the Queen's Guard.

Upon seeing Rua, their eyes widened. They clicked their heels and saluted smartly.

'Permission to speak, ma'am!' one of them said.

'At ease, soldier. Permission granted.'

'...Welcome home, boss.'

'Thanks, Lynette. Remind me to get you both a drink when you're next off shift.'

'Thank you, boss!'

They both took hold of a door handle each and pulled it open.

Rua and Silas stepped through. In the open forecourt, soldiers walked, talked and sparred. They had entered the North Barracks, which housed and trained the Queen's Guard, the nation's elite fighting force.

'The Queen's Champion!' someone shouted. 'Attention!'

Every single soldier in the square dropped what they were doing and spun about to face her, stamping their feet together and placing their arms rigidly by their sides.

'Salute!'

As one, they raised their right hands to their foreheads.

Rua saluted back, then prowled between them with a stern look on her face.

'At ease. I know it's been a while since I was last here... so I hope none of you are slacking in your drills! I intend to personally test each and every one of you new recruits. You are the Queen's Guard. You are the best in the world. Prove it to me.'

She stopped and broke into a grin.

'But that can wait. It's good to see you all again. Dismissed!'

'Yes, ma'am! *Fáilte Abhaile!*'

The soldiers milled around her, thrilled at seeing their legendary general back. She tolerated the attention for a few minutes, then eventually shooed them off, complaining about her rumbling tummy and headed for the officers' mess with Silas.

As they walked across the forecourt, Silas chuckled.

'Hmm? What is it?' Rua asked.

'I remember your unease at seeing the serving staff of House Heritier bow and curtsey... it really is not much different from the way these soldiers salute you, no?'

'But it's just... different!'

The corners of his mouth twitched in amusement as she twiddled her ears trying to think of a better comeback and failed miserably.

She sighed.

'...Okay, maybe not so different. Still, I'd much rather deal with mine than yours.'

They walked into the officers' mess and joined the queue for food. Rua didn't want a formal dinner in the palace with Éilís and whichever duke or ambassador might be visiting. Tonight, she just wanted to catch up with her comrades-in-arms.

She took her tray of food to a corner table where several officers were sitting.

They started to stand and laughed when Rua puffed up her cheeks.

'But you're the most senior officer in the isle! Should we bow instead?'

'Aoife, don't wind her up! How about a whisky? I've owed you one for three years!'

Rua was delighted to be treated as a fellow officer again. She hoped they would treat Silas similarly. She plonked her tray down, gesturing at him and glowering at them.

'Now, before you lot start misbehaving... this is Silas L'Heritier. He looks as fresh as a daisy, but let me assure you – this battle mage can take out sixteen men at once and defended me against the Dark Goddess herself. He is the Weaver, the only mage in the world who can wield all five elements. He is now my partner. Ciel made him my equal...'

Silas squirmed uneasily as the officers raised their eyebrows, clearly impressed.

Rua continued.

'...but only insofar as the raw ability to kill bad guys. Aside from that, he's clumsy, and has very little common sense. But, by Ciel, can he handle his drink!'

Now Silas turned red as the officers cheered and whooped. She hoped he understood; trading insults was the traditional Eiran way to make friends.

As they sat and ate together, she soon had plenty of her own medicine when the officers recalled that time she got drunk and challenged a statue to a fight; or how she accidentally broke one of the Queen's vases in an impromptu arm wrestling match during a formal reception at the palace.

When a few Elves stepped into the mess, Rua heard a loud gasp.

'*Oh, la vache, c'est vrai?*! Silas? Is that you?'

Rua started reaching for her dagger as a particularly large, broad-shouldered Elf came running at them but stopped when she saw how familiar his smile was. A full head taller than Silas, he was powerfully built; the black knitted jumper he wore stretched over his bulging muscles. His hair was platinum blond, pulled into a messy braid that ran down the back of his head. He put Silas in a headlock and ruffled up his hair.

'What are you doing here? Your letters said Friday!' he crowed.

'The same can be said of you!' Silas sputtered from behind a brawny arm. 'I thought you were based in the South Barracks?'

'I am, but the wine here is better, and visiting commissioned officers can go to whichever mess they choose. Now, come here!'

The burly Elf stepped back with arms wide, cocking his head.

Silas got up and gave him a hug.

'*C'est si bon de te revoir,*' Silas said.

'Good to see you, too,' the Elf replied, exchanging kisses on both cheeks.

Keeping an arm around the man's waist, Silas turned to Rua and the other officers.

'This is my older brother, Gildas. He is the Chevalier in charge of the Eiran-Vertciellen military exchange programme.'

Gildas flashed a smile at the table, then his sunny blue eyes came to rest on Rua.

'So this is the famous woman who has captured my little brother's heart.'

He stepped away from Silas and standing to attention, clicked his heels together. He thrust his fist to his chest, then got down on one knee with his head bowed.

'I am sworn to King Xavier IV of Vertcielle but so long as it does not go against my king or country, I promise to serve you the best I can. Yes, you are Ciel's Dagger and the Queen's Champion... but most importantly, you are family.'

Rua's heart felt full. She lifted Gildas to his feet and pulled him into a hug.

'My thanks, brother. Please, sit with us.'

She motioned to the other Elves who had been hanging back to give them space.

'You lot, too! Plenty of room! Here, we can spread out onto this table as well.'

The wine flowed and there was soon a bit of a party atmosphere in the officers' mess. After swapping a few stories, Rua wanted to know more about the programme.

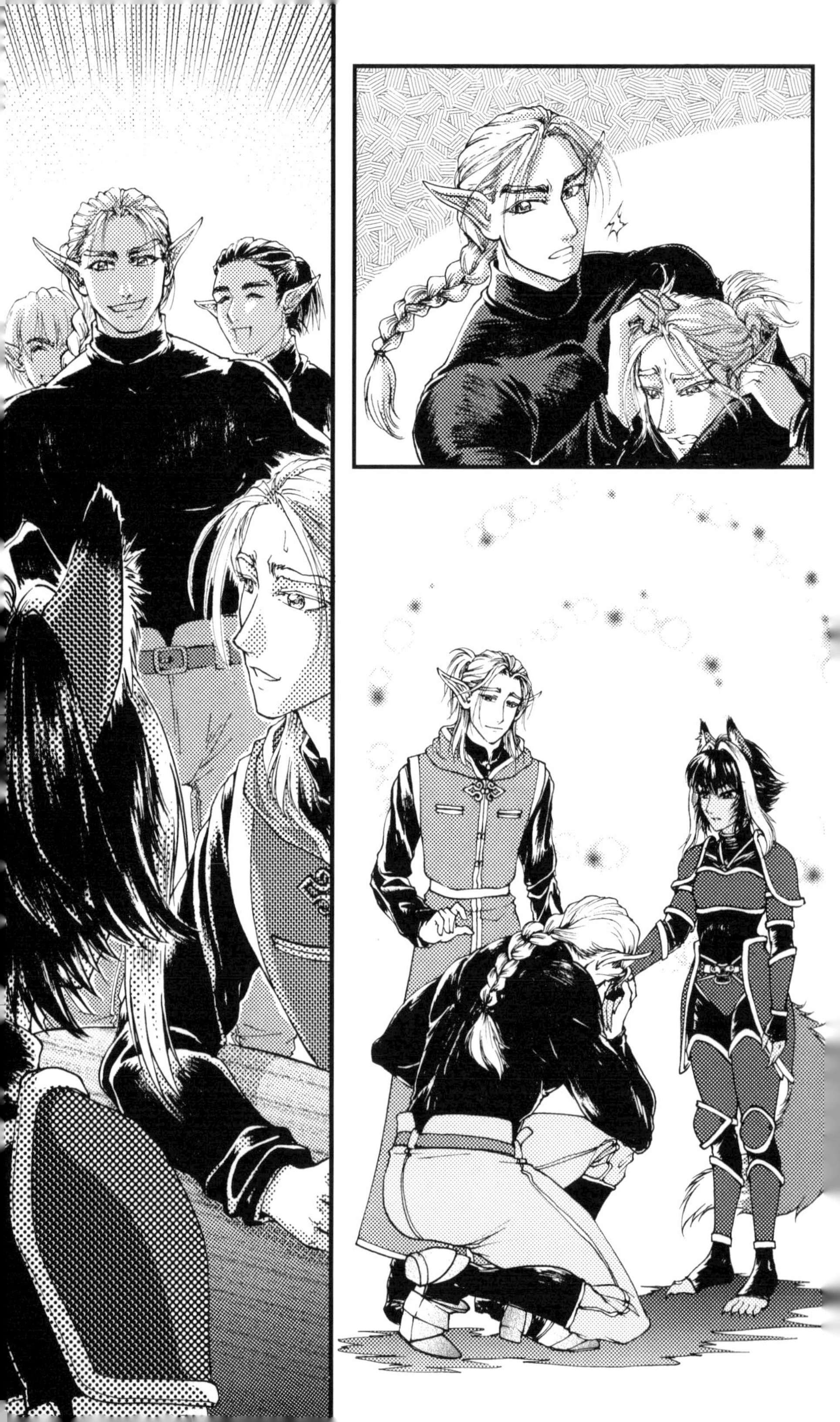

'It's partly a cultural exchange, but mainly about improving intelligence, military skills and techniques on both sides,' Gildas explained. 'Although we have clashed in the past, Eira and Vertcielle are closer than ever and King Xavier IV is keen to keep it that way. He has great admiration for your queen and the Eiran approach to battle. Even I will admit that your warriors, particularly the Queen's Guard, may best me in a fight.'

He grinned, wagging his fingers at the Eiran officers.

'But you all must admit that it is the Vertciellens who excel in better manners and diplomacy, no? At the very least, our looks get us further than yours.'

The Eirans roared with laughter, aware of their rough exteriors.

The rest of the evening passed quickly. After discussing tourist spots for Silas to visit, the officers retired early to avoid hangovers during morning drills. Rua and Silas went back to her room, where he couldn't resist her staircase library. They fell asleep with books in their laps and bedside candles burning out harmlessly in their holders.

***

They rose early for breakfast with the royal family. Éilís, Owyn and Niamh were already in the morning room, but it was only after Silas and Rua made their order that the last royal showed up. A young man came into the room, still yawning, his ginger hair sticking straight up in spikes. He was a whole foot taller than Rua recalled.

'Catching flies, Teagan?' she shot at him.

As if a steel rod was shot through his spine, the prince leapt to attention.

'Yes, ma'am! I mean, no, ma'am!'

She snorted trying to hold in her laughter and patted the seat next to her.

'S'alright, lad. Sit here, I haven't had a chance to catch up with you yet.'

He soon reverted to the mischievous boy she knew; teasing her about her new boyfriend, bickering with Niamh over her last dragon hunt, then being told off by his mother for being rude, whilst his father stayed silent, glaring his disapproval.

Their Eiran-style full cooked breakfasts arrived; Silas seemed unsure if he could finish it but he did admirably, washing it down with tea before Rua bid the royals farewell and impatiently ushered him out of the room. She had a busy itinerary planned.

Donning her hooded cape once more, she took Silas to Albanon's most famous attractions. Their first stop was the covered Northbank Market to soak in the noisy clamour of greengrocers and fishmongers bargaining with customers.

Then they went to the quiet Galleries to contemplate art. Rua cringed when she spotted herself in a painting titled 'Fire on the Weald' depicting one of the key Eiran victories of the Great Wars; the Queen's Champion astride a horse, leaping over a burning bridge to aid the Twelfth Company of the Lowlands Regiment.

Opposite the Galleries was Taliesin's Hall, Eira's largest concert venue and school for bards. They arrived just in time to buy cheap tickets to listen to a rehearsal of a Cambrian male voice choir perfecting their routine for a Jubilee performance. Silas was amazed by the sound; he had never heard this sort of close harmony before.

They walked down to the banks of the Tamesis and took a river taxi to the Southbank Docks, settling in for afternoon tea and watching the lofty masts of the merchants' clippers come in. Silas discovered that rustic Eiran scones slathered with clotted cream and strawberry jam were just as delicious as delicate Vertciellan pâtisserie.

Reinvigorated, they hopped onto a horse-drawn omnibus to Liadán's Leap. They admired its architecture and looked down onto the concentrated streams gushing out of the edges of the water barriers below, set to maximum closure by the city's mages due to the high autumnal tides threatening to come in through the mouth of the Tamesis.

They returned to the South Barracks, home of the Dragoons. Clangs filled the air as knights in armour clashed; Gildas was in a sparring match with a Dragoon.

Rua was impressed. He could have improved a few of his strikes and blocks by going for efficiency rather than form, but that was down to style. He definitely had substance, stamina and strength in droves.

With a powerful swipe throwing his opponent off balance, Gildas threw a kick and knocked him over, pinning him down to finish the fight. There was a ripple of applause. Gildas helped him back up and shook his hand. When Gildas removed his helmet, he finally noticed Rua and Silas were watching, and hailed them.

'I was just finishing up here; I know a great place nearby for pies...'

'The Duke Of Weolingtun?' she interjected. 'They're so good!'

'That's the one! I'm meeting an old friend there; do you mind if he joins us?'

They left the barracks and walked two blocks away to a bustling pub, plates of piping hot pies gliding around the tables. It was obviously as popular with the soldiers as Rua remembered; several diners were still in armour, just like Gildas.

A Dwarf raised his tankard high as they approached his table outside the entrance.

'*Hej hej*, Gildas! I hope you don't mind me starting, I was parched!'

'I'll get you the next one, friend. Morten, this is my brother, Silas, and his lady, Rua.'

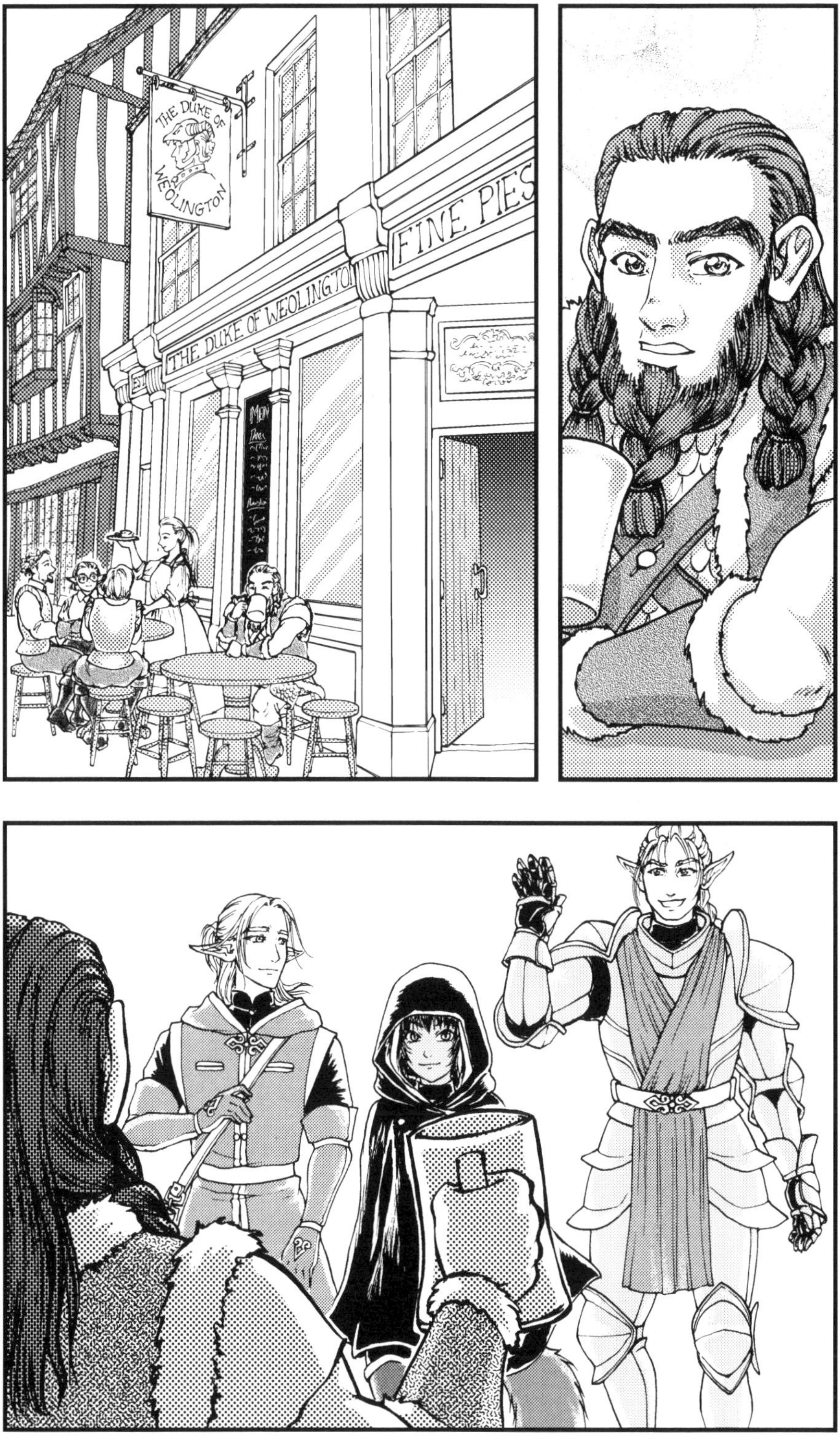
THE DUKE OF WEOLINGTON
FINE PIES
THE DUKE OF WEOLINGTO

'Well met!' the Dwarf said, standing up and shaking their hands. 'Morten Anderssen, Caravan Guard for the Beneficial Society of Iskarian Mining Capital.'

Gildas pulled off his gauntlets, clanking them down on the table. He pointed at the chalkboard on the wall.

'I already know what I want; steak and kidney with mustard mash! I'll get it, my treat. Ales all around, I assume? What are you after?'

'Beef and mushroom, horseradish mash!' Morten grunted.

'Chicken and tarragon! Spring onion mash!' Rua said gleefully.

'Oh! Umm... the fish pie, please, with cheesy mash,' Silas requested.

As Gildas went inside to order, Morten grinned at Silas.

'I first met Gildas in Fleurys, when I delivered some gemstones to the Palais des Étoiles. Your brother took me out one evening and, by Ciel! Never thought an Elf could outdrink me. Since then, whenever my shipments brought me to Fleurys, I'd always look him up. Imagine my surprise when I came to Albanon with a special order of jewels for Prince Teagan's new torque and I heard that Gildas was knocking about!'

Gildas returned with drinks and their pies soon followed. They argued over the differences between Eira and Vertcielle with Morten playing referee; tea versus coffee, whether beer was better than wine, and how thinly one should slice a potato into chips.

Then Rua noticed a group of men lingering in the street, glancing at their table.

'See lads; foxes and foreigners! None o' them on that table should be here.'

They were Human, locals, from their accents. This irked her; one race-related incident was bad enough, but two in a matter of days?

She stood up and stared straight at them. She dropped her hood.

The men's faces dropped as well.

'You think I don't have a right to be here?' she purred, advancing on them slowly. 'When my ancestors have personally defended your queens and country for centuries?'

Some cowered. Some stood straighter, swallowing nervously.

'*Fág a' Bealach!*' she growled. 'Or aren't ya Eiran enough to understand? It means...'

She stopped right in front of them.

'... "Get out of my way." '

Someone from the back of the group flung a bottle at her table.

Rua whirled around but she needn't have worried; Morten smashed it out of the air with his arm bracers. He pulled a piece of glass out of his beard and grinned.

Gildas stood up, cracking his knuckles and nodded to Rua.

She turned back to the men.

'There's always gotta be one fool, eh?'

Without giving them a chance to reply, she headbutted the one in front of her. He fell to the floor and she followed, dropping low to avoid a swipe from another man. She spun and kicked his legs out from underneath. He landed heavily on his back, wincing in pain. She looked up to check on the others.

She had started a full-on pub brawl; all the other customers joined in to grapple with the gang. Gildas blocked and smashed his way through every punch they threw. As for Morten; they kept running at him and they kept falling down. A security professional, he deflected and countered with an air of inevitability, like a mountain that wasn't to be moved. Silas's eyes glowed red; a small ball of fire floating above his palm convinced the men to leave him well alone.

The gang had had enough; those that were still able to stand helped up the ones who had fallen and legged it.

Gildas looked at Rua with a frown.

'The Vulpine Council is tomorrow, yes?'

Rua nodded.

He smoothed the hair out of his eyes.

'I think we had better up security.'

VIII

The overcast sky reflected Rua's mood. The crowds were much more jolly; cheering and waving at their legendary warrior as she waited with Silas on the red carpet leading to the grand entrance of the Guild Hall.

She shifted from one armoured foot to the other. Although this occasion called for formal wear, she really didn't want to put on that dress. And given the recent troubles following her, she wanted to be better prepared. Not wanting to disappoint the crowds, she compromised by wearing the full battle armour of the Queen's Guards. Fairly light in comparison to other regiments, the highly polished metal of her half-cuirass, layered shoulder pauldrons and hip guards still gleamed despite the grey clouds. Her dagger hung from a fancy jewelled belt on her hip, giving her room to carry her magnificent twin crescent blades, The Sisters, on her back.

'Urgh, how much longer are they gonna be?' she complained to Silas. 'I swear, they always do this to torture me, they know how much I hate this part.'

'Please try to smile, Rua, everyone here really is so happy to see you.'

She sighed and managed to stop herself from pouting.

Gildas strode towards her. He saluted.

'Ma'am, my Chevaliers have doubled up with the Dragoons. They will watch each other's backs. So far, everything seems normal; nothing further to report.'

'Thank you, Gildas. Some of the Queen's Guard are in plain clothes, watching your kind and mine. Adding Elven soldiers on top of this Vulpine ceremony will be a slap in the face to those bigots. This may well tip them over the edge and if they attack, we'll be ready. One more thing – once all the Councillors are here, I want you inside with me. I need another set of eyes I can trust. Dismissed.'

He saluted again, then marched back to his post by the doors.

She felt a finger stroke the back of her hand.

'You know that I will be by your side,' Silas said. 'What shall I do?'

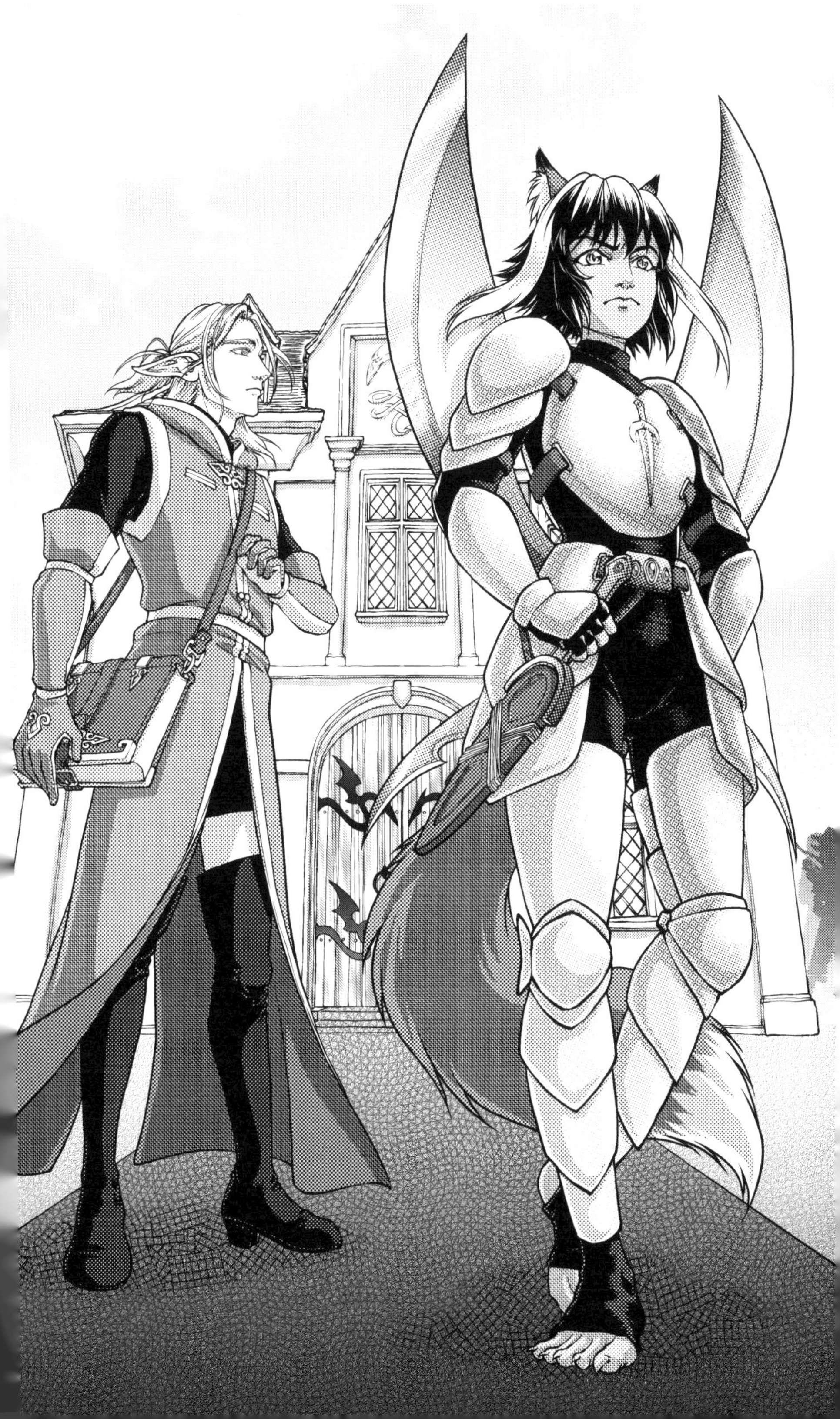

'What you always do. Protect those that need it.'

A fanfare heralded the arrival of two large coaches, escorted by Dragoons. One by one, the Vulpine Councillors processed down the carpet to a very excited public.

First came the motherly Giovannuzza of Pontiazza, the largest of the southern city-states of the Azure Basin. Her ears and tail were dark brown like her curly locks, tumbling over her shoulders. She hugged Rua, having known her for many years.

Then came the huntress Rävenstål, the Iskarian representative. Her fur was snowy white, her hair fashioned into a sleek bob. Her narrow eyes regarded Rua in an icy blue gaze, assessing her for the first time, before offering a cordial handshake.

From Hesperia, Azzenar, a fox with flame-red fur she had met once before. A merchant by trade, he was scowling before his turn to exchange kisses with her, confessing that he found the Eiran climate rather cold.

The petite Teumissia was next. The Alekhandrian vixen had dark fur, olive eyes and a nervous disposition. She had never travelled north of Heaven's Ring before.

The second carriage opened and out stepped Zerda, a sandy-coloured dog from the deserts of Ifriqikah. His particularly large ears suited his love of gossip.

A cheer went up from the dogs in the crowd as the voluptuous Daji wiggled out of the coach, her robes exposing her shoulders. Her long, black hair made a startling contrast with her pale yellow ears and tail. She fluttered behind her folding fan. The beauty from Shuntien was almost as famous amongst Vulpines as Rua herself.

The Amligan Councillor slowly came to Rua, his eyes kind and wise. This being the third time Rua had received Komekwan at a Council meeting, she thought he had aged well, his silvery braids finally matching with his grey fur.

And lastly, the one she had been dreading.

Reynard swaggered up the carpet, one hand on the hilt of his ornate rapier, the other blowing kisses to swooning vixens in the crowds. His cropped jacket was embellished with gold cord, showing off his figure in a ruffled shirt and high waisted breeches. He bowed before her with a flourish, then kissed her reluctant hand.

'As always, Rua, you look ravishing,' he said. 'But this is not fair; the rest of us have made more of an effort with our outfits! I was hoping that you would be in Eiran formal dress. It has... quite the reputation.'

She retracted her hand quickly.

'As this is your first time as one of my Councillors, I will say this only once. This is *my* Council meeting. I can wear whatever I want.'

She stepped aside and gestured for him to go in.

He winked at her, then obeyed.

She glanced at Silas.

Oh, he had that look on his face. The one which meant he was barely holding back the lightning bolts he wanted to cast.

The Councillors filed into the chamber and took their seats. Scribes and servants rushed about with wine, water jugs, quills and sheets of paper. Rua walked to the head of the table. Gildas shut the doors and nodded at her.

She spread her arms, appealing for silence. A hush fell over the room. She addressed the table and the audience in the public viewing gallery above.

'My honoured guests. I am Ruaidhrí'ogan, Queen's Champion, Dagger of Ciel and Honorary Chair of the Vulpine Council. It's a pleasure to meet some of you for the first time, but also to see familiar faces once again. Allow me to welcome you all to the grand Council meeting of 2360. This year's Council is dear to my heart because Eira is my homeland. I hope you all have been enjoying the festivities in Sienna Vale, where I was born? And there will be plenty more activities in the capital, for you and the general public. I recommend having a go on the bagpipes; they're always a bit of fun.'

There was some polite laughter before she continued.

'We offer our sincere thanks to Queen Éilís the Enlightened for her gracious hospitality. She has very kindly provided venues, accommodation and transport for this Council. She has even planned a reception at Dúnragnhildt Palace, all whilst dealing with the complexities of her own Silver Jubilee. So may I please propose a toast to her Majesty, the Queen.'

'The Queen,' the Councillors murmured, taking a sip from their wine glasses.

Rua swallowed and tried to sound matter-of-fact for this section of her speech.

'A final general safety announcement; in case of any emergencies, my battle mage Silas will provide support and directions on exiting the building. Those in the public galleries should obey any instructions from him, the Dragoons and the Chevaliers.'

She sat down and picked up her notes.

'Now, addressing the first item on the agenda... Giovannuzza, you seem to be having an issue with land rights and the local pear tree farmers?'

'*Mamma mia*,' the matronly vixen sighed. 'They are fixated on a variety of pears with golden skins, but their cultivated trees don't seem to be taking well in their usual orchards. They have, however, noticed the wild trees in our ancestral hunting grounds flourishing. They are petitioning the Principe of Pontiazza to enforce the sale of our lands for the city-state's financial interest, as the pears are fetching very high prices.'

Rua pursed her lips thoughtfully.

'Perhaps there is a way to satisfy all parties. First, surely if a product is over-produced, it will lose its rarity. A case could also be made that if the woodland were converted to orchards, whatever special quality they had for growing this fruit would be lost. A well-managed forest can have multiple uses.'

Giovanuzza raised her eyebrows.

'So are you saying we should share?'

'Quite simply, yes. What you use the woodland for has little to do with the wild pears. You need to work out the specifics... maybe arrange times when they can access the woods, plant these pears in moderation and harvest them, in exchange...'

'... for a cut of the profits!'

As Giovanuzza started excitedly working out the details with suggestions from Teumissia, who had some experience in forest management in a similar climate, Rua hoped that the rest of the points on the agenda would go as smoothly. Sadly, it didn't. Azzenar brought up the possibility of an international sporting event, which started a shouting match over which sports to include; Rävenstål was offended that he hadn't considered any skiing events, but Zerda was quick to point out how all winter sport was irrelevant to any Ifriq. Then Daji wanted to combat the misinformation about sexy fox spirits in popular literature. The irony of her complaint seemed to be lost on her.

Rua listened to all of this, and much more, whilst having to deal with being in close proximity to Reynard's smirking face as he watched the proceedings with amusement. He was sitting next to her, but at least that made it harder for him to stare at her outright. Surprisingly, he refrained from talking or speaking to her much at all. His lack of interest seemed out of character. Had he learnt how to behave?

She glanced behind her.

Silas had the most thunderous expression on his face.

Had he been glowering at Reynard the whole time?

Her thoughts were distracted by the final topic on the agenda; where the next council would be held. As the younger ones bickered over the prestige of hosting it, Rua decided to put her foot down and recommend the obvious choice, in her eyes.

'If I could beg silence for just one moment?' she said.

Turning to the Amligan Councillor, she spread her arms wide.

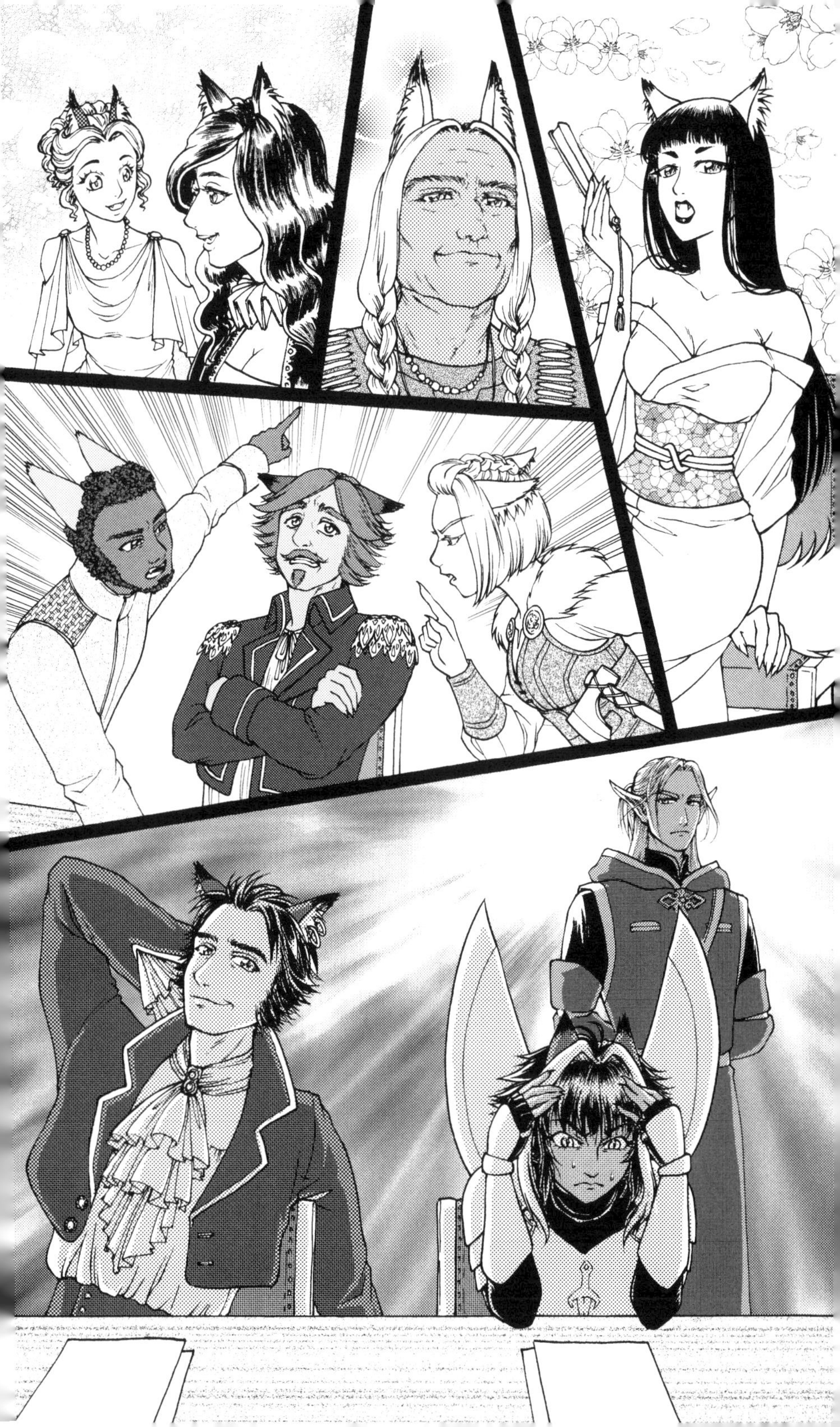

'Komekwan, you've been attending these meetings for thirty six years. You've always been a calm and wise influence in these discussions. In twelve years' time, I would value your presence more than ever, and I don't want to put you through the hassle of such long distance travel again. Please, may we come to you?'

The old dog's eyes shone with tears.

'You are a true friend, Rua. Thank you for your consideration, it would make things easier for me. I would be most honoured to welcome you all to my homeland.'

Cowed by the realisation that they had been acting selfishly, the young Councillors started mumbling in agreement.

'Well, that settles it then. The next—'

She cut herself off as she heard shouts from outside. Then she detected the sound of a crossbow ratchet from the public gallery above.

She leapt out of her chair as a bolt shot past her face, landing in her seat cushion.

She looked up and into the cold, blue eyes of the hooded Human who had fired it.

'For the Righteous Order of Purity!' he declared.

IX

Rua dashed along the board table and leapt high, grabbing the bottom edge of the balcony and pulling herself over into the viewing gallery. The man with the crossbow was gone, but there were screams of panic all around her as several hooded men stood up from their seats with bloodied knives. More armed men were still coming up the stairs. She drew her crescent blades.

'Gildas! Secure the bottom of the stairwell!'

'As soon as I can, ma'am!' Gildas called back. 'We are also under attack! Silas, get those hostages in the gallery down here and shield them. Councillors, stay with him, or if you can, defend yourselves!'

'With pleasure,' Rävenstål snarled, already with her axe and buckler in hand.

'This sword isn't just for show,' said Reynard, drawing his rapier and main gauche.

The other Councillors went to Silas, whose eyes had started glowing green.

Rua swiftly herded the assassins in front of her and the hostages behind, defending them with parries and counters until Silas established a steady pipeline of Air cocoons to transport them down. Then she switched tactics, aggressively driving the men back down into the narrow confines of the stairwell. Aware that the hostages could no longer see what she was doing, she smiled viciously.

Now, she could slaughter these terrorists in a place where they couldn't get away.

Corpse after corpse fell and blood flowed down the stairs like a fountain. When they tried to run, they were trapped by an iron grate at the bottom; Gildas had locked them in, as instructed. They screamed as she butchered them, flailing desperately through the grate at the equally terrified soldiers on the other side. Only when they were reduced to a silent pile of mutilated remains did she command her troops to open it.

A trembling Dragoon unlocked the grate before rushing away to retch outside.

She caught Gildas's eye. He looked pale, but otherwise fine.

'Status report,' she barked, sheathing her blades.

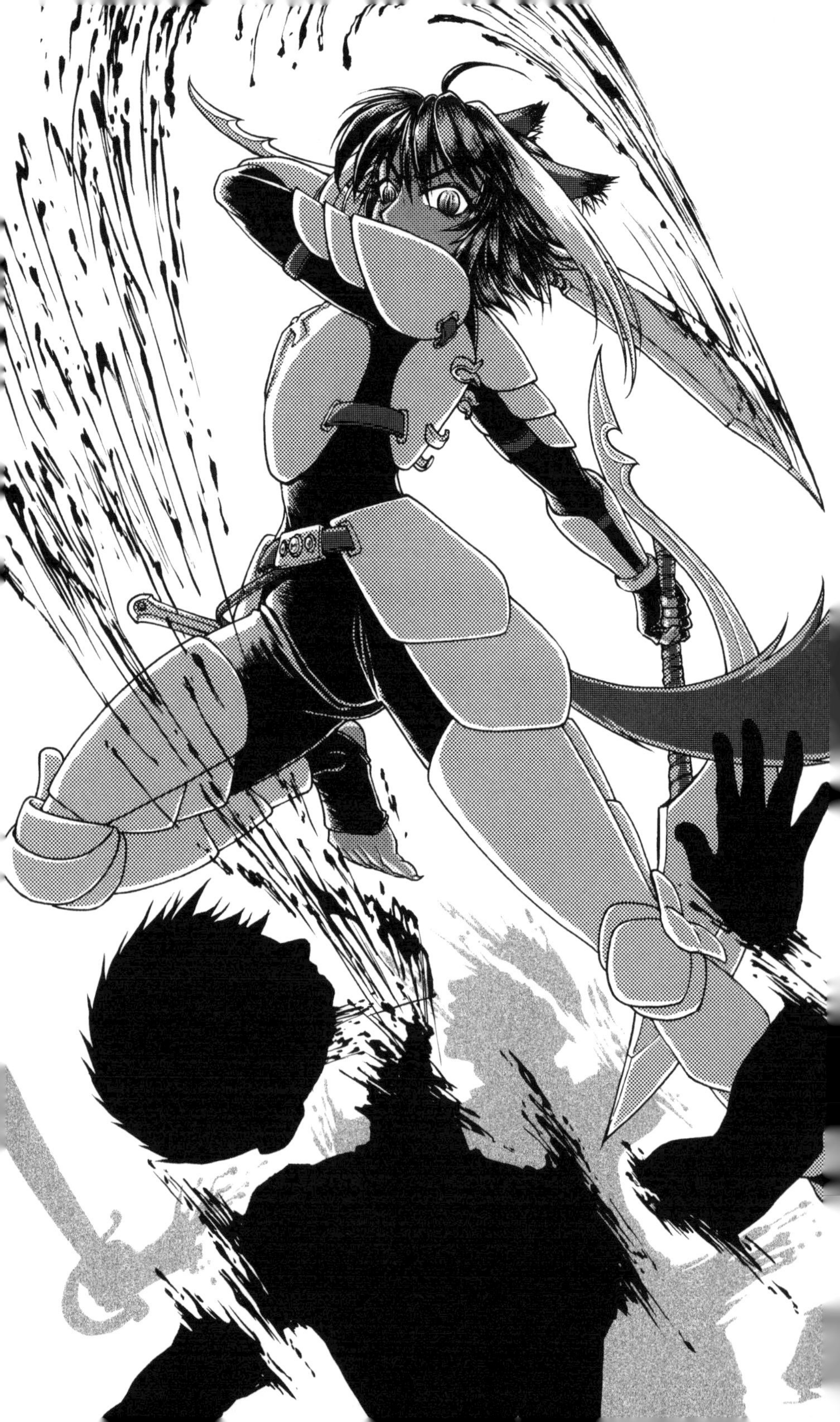

'Yes, ma'am! The Councillors and I dispatched the men who got into the main chamber. Silas relocated all the hostages down from the gallery. Councillor Giovanuzza is applying first aid to those hurt in the initial attack. With luck, they will all survive.'

'No sign of the one that shot at me?'

'No, I'm afraid I could not get here in time.'

Another Dragoon came running into the reception room, saluting Rua and Gildas.

'Ma'am! Sir! The streets around the Guild Hall are now secure. All units accounted for, three Chevaliers will need healers. Five Vulpine civilians dead, eight wounded.'

Rua's heart sank. Five people who were here because of her.

'What was the nature of the attack?' she asked.

'At five o'clock, five Vulpines were stabbed in unison, causing panic in the crowds. Corporal Lynette observed one of the assailants lifting a sewer grate to allow several men to emerge from within. This occurred across several locations, two of which were next to the Guild Hall entrance, hence why some made it past us. We made sixteen kills, two captures. The rest retreated; the plain-clothes Queen's Guards are tailing them.'

'My thanks, officer. Please ensure the Queen gets a full report. Gildas, please go with him. I need to stay here a little longer. You are both dismissed.'

They saluted her and left as Dragoons started leading out the frightened hostages. She shifted in front of the stairwell, trying to hide the mangled mess she had left inside. The Councillors followed, along with Silas. He broke away from them to rush to her.

'Rua! Thank Ciel you are safe!'

She recoiled, making him flinch.

'Rua... are you... alright?'

Ignoring the hurt in his voice, she looked past him at the Councillors' faces.

'Five Vulpines have been killed.'

Their faces contorted in fear, anger and shock.

'These men are also after Elves, Dwarves, even Humans if they're foreign. Whoever doesn't fit their idea of Eiran *purity*... well, to Hell with that! Come now – with me!'

They emerged to a tragic scene. The pavements were smeared with blood. Soldiers carried away cloth-covered bodies. Vulpines were huddled in groups, crying and wailing.

The people quietened as the Councillors stood together with their heads bowed.

After a minute of silence, Rua spoke.

'I am so sorry for what has happened. This despicable act was committed by cowardly men. They call themselves Eiran, but they are nothing like us.'

83

She started walking down the stairs into the sparse remains of the crowds, her golden eyes defiant as she looked into their faces, channelling her outrage with her gaze.

'Where was their honour? What did they want to achieve by attacking a celebration, one supported by the Queen herself? Did they want to terrify us into leaving our Isle, our home for thousands of years? Did they think they could get away with it?'

In a flash of steel, she drew The Sisters, holding them high as the late afternoon sun broke through the clouds. Fresh blood still dripped from the cutting edges.

'These blades have killed thousands of enemies, to protect Eira. They were used, in the past, against foreign invaders. I used them again, today. The men I have just killed were not foreign by birth. But their way of thinking was.'

She lowered her blades, but raised her voice.

'Whether you are Vulpine or not... from Eira or elsewhere... it doesn't define your worth. You are defined by what you do. And Eira will not be defined by terrorists! I will hunt down every single last member of this group, personally. That is my duty. But we will live! We will not give in to hatred or fear! That is the duty of us all!'

The people erupted with cheers as she spun her blades around and sheathed them in one fluid motion. She turned to face the Councillors.

'Rua, *cherie*, what can we do?' Reynard asked her softly.

She frowned, reassessing him. Perhaps he had grown up after all.

'Keep calm and carry on.'

***

Word soon spread about the attack on the Council, but her speech made the rounds too. Crowds still turned up for the concert at Taliesin's Hall that evening. The Vulpine Councillors were the guests of honour for the performance by the best young talents in Eira. As the strains of an old love song was plucked in intricate polyphony from a harp, Rua sat next to Silas in the Royal Box with the Councillors, but she felt alone.

She had lived through so many wars and conflicts; she knew this was how they all started. The weak-minded are fearful. Fear becomes suspicion. Allusions are made, conclusions reached, justifications found. That's when Ciel's children start killing each other and when Ciel's Dagger has to clean up the mess.

She was repulsed by Silas's relief that she was safe. Unlike her, those five people would not come back. And she hated herself for it.

He hadn't spoken to her since; he didn't dare ask her again if she was alright. But his eyes did. As did the way he shadowed her as she exchanged small talk with Eiran nobility. And the way he touched the back of her hand when no one was watching.

That night, she sat on the bed watching him potter about, tidying the books away. She thought about how normal it seemed, these night time rituals. How those grieving families would no longer see their loved ones go through these motions.

Her eyes began to fill with tears; they fell into her lap in big, wet splotches.

All at once he was there, holding her tightly and rocking her, shushing in her ear. He snuffed the candle and pulled her under the covers with him, nestling her onto his chest. She cried until she had no more tears left to give, falling asleep from exhaustion.

***

Three hours later, Rua sat up. For a minute, she watched Silas's peaceful face as he slept. She couldn't resist running a finger over his messy hair, allowing herself a tiny, tactile goodbye before getting dressed and slipping out of the room.

Stalking through the corridors, she arrived at the doors to the South Barracks. She nodded at the Dragoons on duty, who saluted and let her through. She made her way through the empty forecourt and down a spiral staircase. Voices echoed through the subterranean tunnels. She followed them into a large cell.

Two prisoners in shackles were knelt on the floor before Gildas and Reynard.

She had expected the Chevalier, but was a bit surprised by the fox. Then again, maybe not. It was their kind who were targeted, after all. Perhaps what was more surprising to her was that it meant he cared.

'Have they said anything yet?' she asked.

'*Non, cherie*,' Reynard replied. 'Although I have learnt a few new swearwords.'

Perhaps a softer touch would do the trick. She crouched in front of them.

'The Righteous Order of Purity,' she said, testing it on her tongue. 'A very grandiose name. Probably a little difficult for these poncy Vertciellens to pronounce, eh?'

The prisoners looked at each other, a little unsure.

'D'you know, my great-great-great-grandma was the Queen's Champion during the Battle of the Bridge? She single-handedly slaughtered an entire squadron of long-ears.'

Their eyes widened in admiration.

Gildas started towards her, but Reynard held him back.

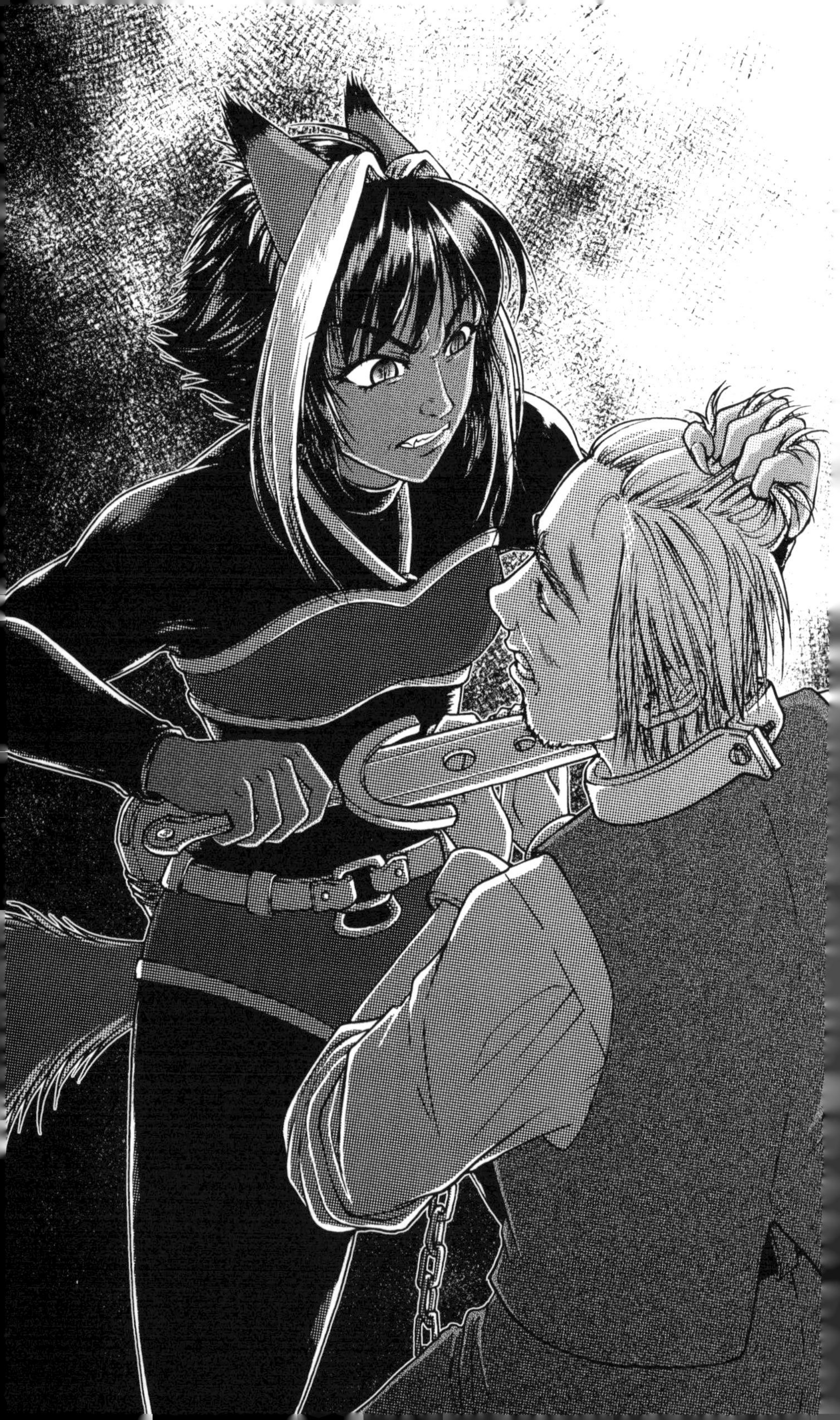

'Come now, boys,' Rua continued in honey-sweet tones. 'The enemy of your enemy is your friend. We foxes know our place... we serve the Humans. We can help you kick out these foreigners. We don't want them taking our jobs any more than you do!'

The two prisoners started nodding.

'We all want to keep Eira strong. But we've gotta get the public on side, see? So you need to make sure you keep true Eirans safe. You hit too many Humans and you lose any support you've gained. You're not... planning anything that might do that, are you?'

They looked uneasily at each other and started arguing between themselves.

'What if she's right? Maybe that would just make things worse...'

'The Queen is part of the problem too!'

'The tourist spots, yes, but the procession crowds... wouldn't they be mostly Eiran?'

'No, the Queen and her supporters are the ones letting the long-ears in!'

'You know,' Rua said quietly. 'If your Order are planning something for Sunday morning, there is still time. You can save a lot of Eiran lives. This is your last chance.'

They clammed up. They knew they had already said too much.

She sighed and stood, turning to a grim-faced Gildas.

He knew the truth; that she was the Queen's Champion during that battle.

She took his hands and squeezed them.

'I'm sorry for saying that, brother,' she whispered. 'And I'm sorry I had to do it, too. That was then, and this is now.'

His blue eyes still looked hurt as he looked into her solemn face, but he nodded.

She looked back at the prisoners and drew her dagger.

'I suppose I ought to leave them alive. Do they need to be walking?' she wondered.

'Ideally,' Gildas confirmed. 'So they can march to the gallows on their own feet.'

'They probably won't need their hands,' Reynard suggested.

She crouched down in front of them again. Grabbing one by the hair, she tilted his head back, tracing the tip of her dagger along his neck shackle.

'By the time I'm done, you'll be begging to tell me everything you know. I hope you don't mind the sight of blood. There's going to be a lot of it.'

X

Throughout Saturday Rua's face flitted from forced smiles in public to a stony mask in private as she went to the many functions she was obligated to attend. After what she discovered from interrogating the prisoners last night, she was hardly in a celebratory mood. She wasn't looking forward to what she needed to do.

Silas, unfortunately, had to bear the brunt of her bad temper. She wanted him near, but couldn't bear him getting too close. Every time she flinched from his touch, or gave him a brusque reply, she knew she was hurting him, but she couldn't stop herself. She was building up those barriers once more. Cruel work needed a hardened heart.

She prayed that he would forgive her.

When the stagecoach brought her back to the palace after she had officially opened a Vulpine-themed exhibition at the Galleries, they silently made their way to the second floor. They knocked and let themselves into the Queen's private sitting room. Éilís and Owyn were there, along with the Princess Royal and Prince Teagan. Then Gildas poked his head in, followed by Reynard.

The war cabinet could begin.

'Who are these men, Rua?' Éilís asked. 'And what is their purpose?'

'The Righteous Order of Purity, they called themselves. Now I've personally not seen such hostility in our lands since the Great Wars against Vertcielle ended. But prior to the Guild Hall attack, I'd been harassed in public twice by gangs of men with similar attitudes. Has this been building up in the three years I've been away?'

'I can't say for sure. King Xavier IV and I launched the Eiran-Vertciellen military exchange programme two years ago; that meant more Elves visible on our soil…'

'Your Majesty,' Gildas jumped in. 'I have been subject to mild teasing in the two years I've been living here, nothing serious, but only in the past six months have things got physical, with some arrests for public order offences. Yesterday's attack, however, was unprecedented.'

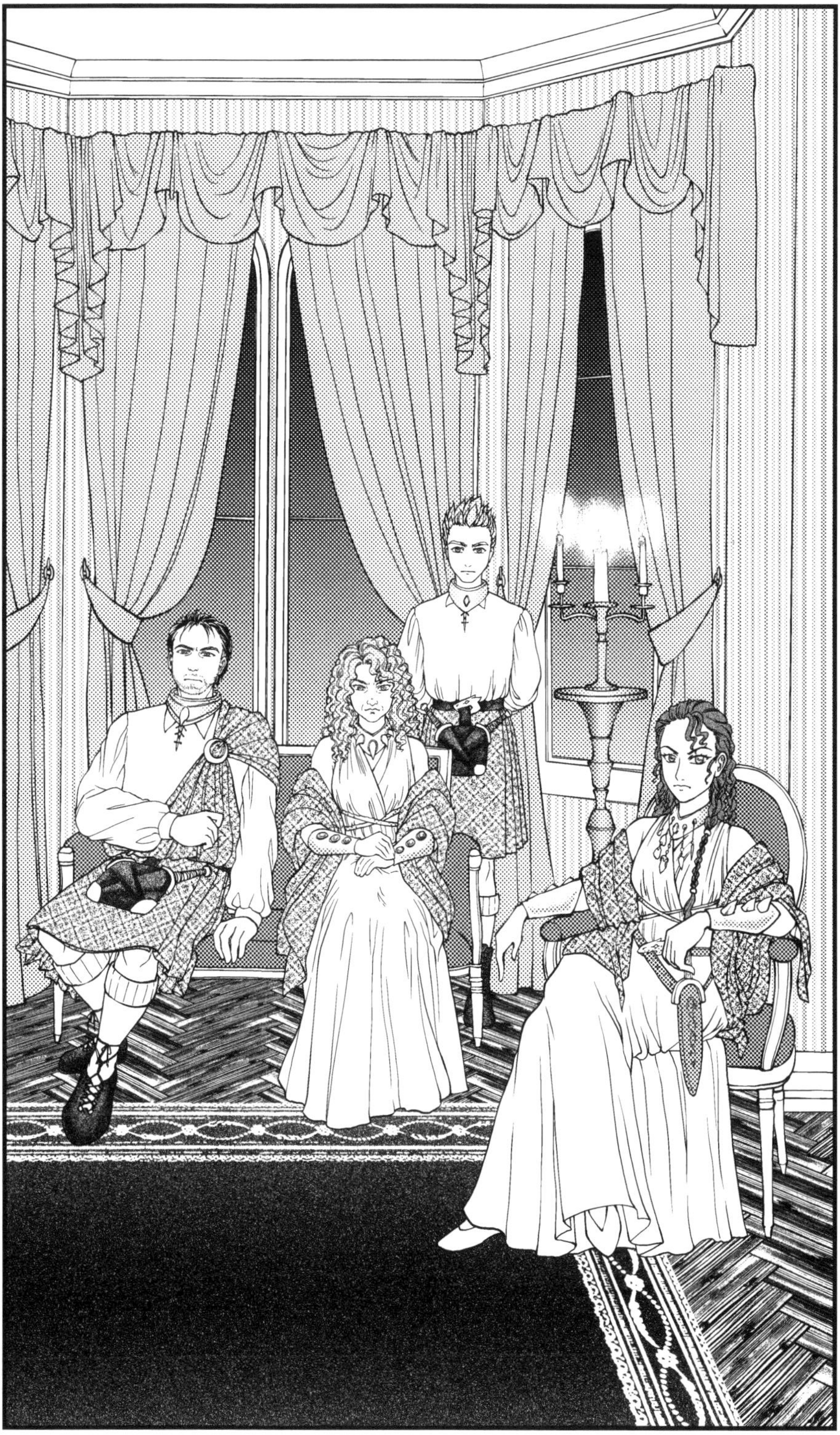

'The gang of men in Seacht Sisters...' Silas said, frowning. 'One of the men was a pub regular, someone who had grown up on the coast. The innkeeper mentioned that it was very much out of character.'

'It screams of a cult to me,' Reynard growled. 'Things seem fine and normal, and then a few people go missing or change all of a sudden. Like that time in Fleurys, Rua, *n'est-ce pas?*'

It was as if her heart had iced over. The horrors of what she had to do back then came flooding back. It seemed inevitable that she was going to have to do something similar now; and this time around, hundreds more lives depended on it.

Éilís frowned.

'So the nature of this problem is strongly suggestive of a relatively small group of men rather than a change in the general public's opinion. We can take heart in that, at least. Now, according to your report, Rua, there is a planned terrorist attack during my procession tomorrow morning? I know the details, but please summarise for the others.'

'Last night, I was able to extract from the prisoners the location of several bombs that are to be situated in the sewer systems to cause damage and panic along the procession route, as well as in a couple of tourist locations.'

Aside from Rua's fellow interrogators, everyone else in the room was shocked. She avoided Silas's eyes; he had had no idea of her midnight excursion.

'Which is why,' Éilís began. 'Much as it pains me, I approve Rua's plan of action.'

She rose and paced over to the fireplace before continuing.

'The Queen's Champion is excused from the procession tomorrow. At two o'clock in the morning, she is to descend into the sewers. Alone.'

Everyone began talking over each other at once in protest, but Éilís raised her hand.

'Given the scale of losses they suffered on Friday, they likely need every member they have to carry out their plans on Sunday morning. It is an opportunity to catch the majority of these culprits in one fell swoop. If I organise a mass raid on the sewers any earlier with my troops, those men might call the whole thing off; then we would risk a future attack where we would be less well-informed!'

She pointed at Rua.

'We need someone who can sneak in, gather intelligence, defuse bombs, kill silently and hide bodies. Taking them out one by one in a quiet manner means they may be fooled into thinking everything is going as planned. Plain-clothes officers will be positioned around major entry points to the sewers if she needs assistance. She is to report or send word once all the bombs are taken care of. As a safeguard, I will send in a large force of my troops exactly one hour before the procession is due to start, to flush out the last of the men and bombs on the procession route. They can then report to the troops managing the crowds, who can arrange a quick cancellation if necessary.'

Éilís placed her hands on Rua's shoulders.

'This would be an impossible task for anyone else, Rua. In reality, my final safeguard is you. No one else is guaranteed to survive a solo mission such as this.'

***

Rua nodded to the plain-clothes officer, then slipped out of the alleyway and dropped down into the large storm drain. It had obviously been used as an entry point by the Order recently; the grate lay about the entrance in broken pieces. She ducked her head and slipped into the sewer tunnel. As she ran along the relatively clean brick walkways, skipping over the odd rat; she remembered one year when the Tamesis backed up with so much raw sewage, the entire city had stunk for the whole summer. Thankfully, the city had upgraded its sewer systems since. Tunnels were enlarged, access points increased and filtration systems put in place, all managed by the Municipal Mages specialising in Earth and Water.

But there was one mage she really wasn't happy with right now.

'Silas. I know you're there. You can come out now.'

She heard him sigh and with a quiet rustle, he appeared in front of her.

'Please... do not be angry with me, Rua.'

She clenched her fists. All this tension had been building up in her since Friday's attack. But down here in the sewers of Albanon, away from the palaces, the VIPs and the adoring public, it strangely felt like it was just the two of them again, out on just another adventure. And she finally let it go.

'TOO LATE FOR THAT! You stubborn brat! What in Ciel's name were you thinking?! You've just disobeyed a direct order from myself and the Queen! Do you have any idea just how dangerous this is?! You're gonna get yourself killed!'

'I apologise, but I... could not stay away. I want to help.'

She harrumphed. He had guts, she would give him that.

'Fine! But when I said this was dangerous, I meant it. Keep up with me and watch your footing. You can use a small Spirit lamp, but nothing else. And stay quiet.'

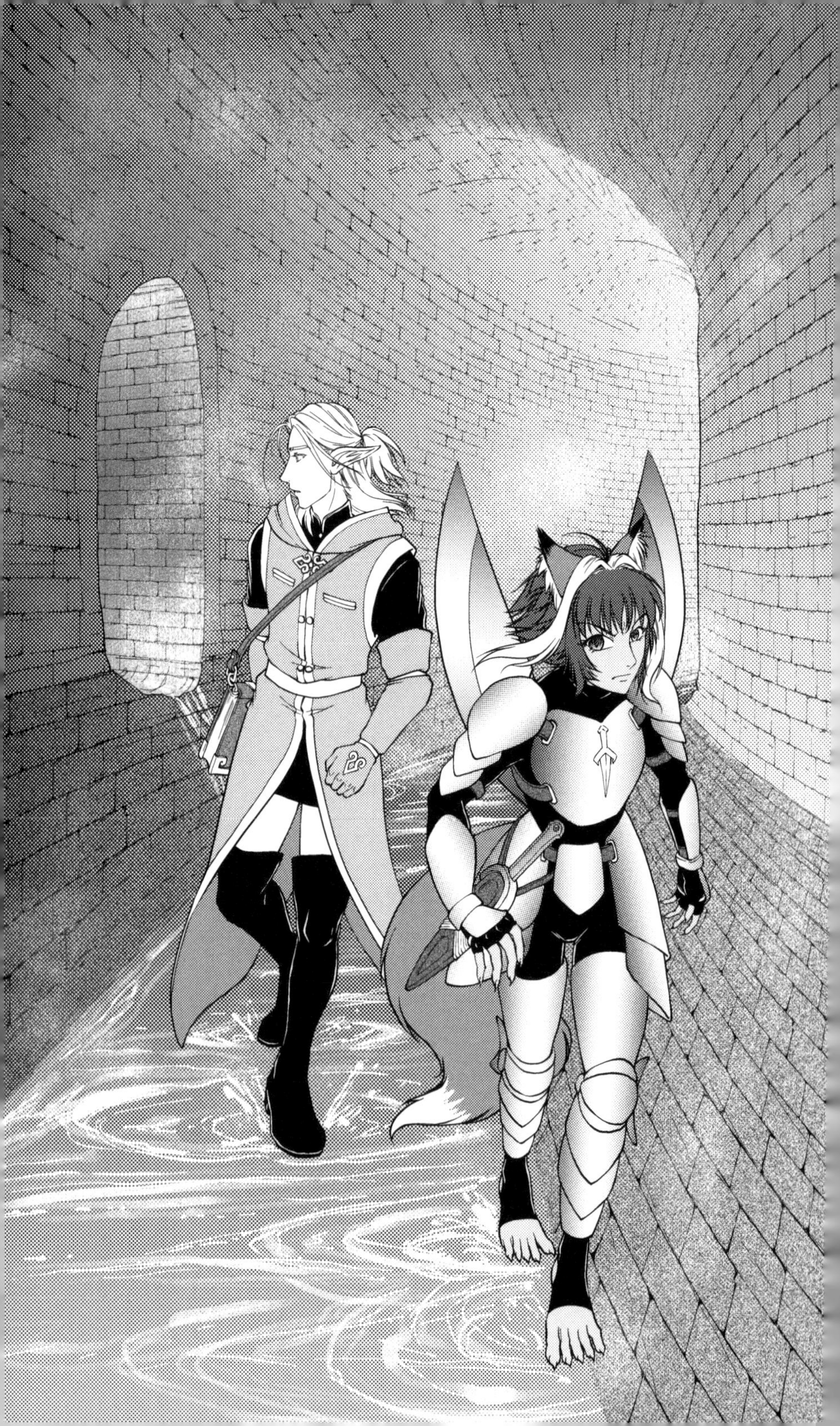

They descended further into the tunnels, her superior night vision allowing her to lead them confidently into the darkness. She had spent the past few hours memorising the layouts of the sewers, particularly the tunnels beneath the planned procession route.

As her sensitive nose became accustomed to the damp, she picked up a clean, metallic tang with a hint of sulphur and oak. Black powder. She followed the scent, turning off the main tunnel and climbing into a smaller, older section. Stashed under an archway were three large barrels joined by a long fuse that trailed all the way along the side of the wall. She gently pulled the fuses out of them.

'Silas, can you soak the black powder inside the barrels? And the ends of these fuses? Then no one will be able to tell from a distance that we've tampered with them. They could even light the fuse and it will work like normal until they reach the barrels.'

He obliged, his eyes glowing blue. He didn't even need to incant; he simply pointed at the canal flowing next to them and water rose up in a swirling thread. He pointed down the holes at the top of the barrels and the water went in until they were filled up.

She smiled at him and he smiled back proudly.

They retraced their steps back to the main tunnel and continued to follow the path of the procession overhead, Rua picking up the smell of two more bomb stashes and Silas rendering them harmless.

Whilst they were finishing off the third stash, Rua heard the sound of footsteps. She tapped Silas on the shoulder and put a finger on her lips, then pinched the fingers of her hand together. He dismissed his Spirit lamp and crouched next to the barrels.

She tiptoed to the end of the side tunnel, pressing her back to the wall. The light of a flickering torch bounced around the tunnels, getting brighter as it got closer. She listened to his steps. One man. She drew her dagger silently, choosing to save The Sisters on her back for another time. As he rounded the corner, she pounced, smothering him with one hand and stabbing him in the kidneys, before pulling her blade out and drawing it across his throat. She released him and he fell forward, twitching. She bent down to stab him again behind his ear, just to make sure. She dragged him into the side tunnel, then retrieved his torch, extinguishing it in the canal.

'Silas,' she whispered. 'A little light here please, I want to search him.'

He came out from his hiding place and summoned his usual ball of glowing white Spirit, tossing it over the body where it stayed, hovering.

She rifled through his pockets and withdrew a crumpled scrap of paper. Smoothing it out, she peered at it for a few moments and clicked her tongue.

'I'm afraid, my love, we'll have to cut our underground explorations short.'

'What is the matter?'

'There's no way we can handle this many bombs on our own. Look – there are at least fifteen more on the procession route, but there are six more under Albanon's tourist hotspots as well. The prisoners must have only known about some of them. It's taken us an hour just to deal with three, and some of these new ones are pretty far. We'll need some backup.'

After dragging the body behind the barrels, Rua led them back into the main tunnel, trying to get to the nearest exit with an assigned plain-clothes officer. But after ten minutes of walking, her ears picked up the distant sounds of echoing footsteps.

'Silas, we're being followed. Take the map. Get in front of me now. Cast a Spirit Fabric. The exit is just two straight sections ahead, then it's a left, you should see the ladder at the end. Reveal yourself then, and the officer will come to you.'

'Wait, Rua – are you coming?'

'No, I... I have to stay back and allow myself to be captured. If I don't, they'll know whoever they're following has escaped and they might pull their plan entirely. They have to think it's working, all the way until the last possible moment.'

'What?! But–'

'No buts. You have to reach the Queen. Tell her to leave me be and focus on defusing all of the bombs in one large morning raid. That is what matters. Everything will be fine. I can take care of myself.'

'Rua, I cannot possibly leave you–'

'Silas! You must, everyone is depending on you,' she whispered, taking his face between her hands. 'Trust me. I will always come back. Always. No one else does.'

She kissed him and touched her nose to his.

'Now go. I love you.'

'I love you, too.'

His eyes flashed and flickered between white and green as he quickly created a Spirit Fabric and muffled his footsteps with a cushion of Air. He took one last look at her, then threw the Fabric over himself and disappeared from sight.

She couldn't hear or see him, but somehow, she sensed that he was still there.

'Go!' she scolded.

After a few seconds, she finally felt she was alone. She turned down a side tunnel, splashing through the puddles as loud as she could to lure them. It worked; she could hear them whispering amongst themselves. She waited, wondering how many she had to kill before she allowed them to capture her.

Three rushed at her from behind, with two more coming from the front. She put up a decent show of a fight; ducking and dodging, cracking a few skulls. Then as she picked up the sounds of more coming from around the corner she broke away, feigning retreat, and ran straight into the newcomers. She raised her arms in surrender, but one of them threw a punch at her cheek, knocking her to the ground. They piled into her, kicking and stamping, pulling The Sisters off her back and taking her dagger.

She pretended she was out cold as they picked her up and carried her through the tunnels. She couldn't pinpoint their location; the fight had made her lose all sense of direction. She would have to beat it out of them later.

After half an hour, she was flung onto the floor. Her wrists were tied together in front of her with rope then she was lifted up again, the rope pulled tight, her hands high above her head. They kept pulling until her feet were off the floor.

Then, someone chucked a bucket of water over her.

She coughed and sputtered, shaking her head.

She opened her eyes to see that she was in a dark chamber. A couple of torches lit the space, wedged into the rusty old pipes and levers on the walls. An old pumping station, perhaps? In front of her were a dozen men, some a little worse for wear from their short tussle, judging from the nosebleeds and split lips.

Someone started clapping, slowly.

'Well done, brothers,' a voice called from the dark.

He came into view. Short, dark hair. Stocky build, sword at his side. His pale eyes, full of contempt, were familiar. The man she saw at the Guild Hall. The one who fired his crossbow at her.

The edges of his lips curled up into a cruel looking smile.

'I really was hoping that it would be you. I was rather annoyed that you dodged my bolt. But that's not going to be a problem now, is it?'

He turned to one of his cohorts.

'Was she alone? You're all looking rather battered for a fight against one animal.'

'Give us a break, Bricriu! Vulpine or not, she's the Queen's Champion, she didn't go down easy. And yes, we didn't see anyone else.'

He came up close to look at her, studying her expression.

She gave him a good show of snarling, trying to show a hot temper.

'Bit off more than you could chew, eh?' he smirked. 'It's always frustrating when things don't go as planned.'

He backhanded her across the face, the force of his blow making her whole body swing sideways on the rope. He watched her wincing and laughed.

'See, brothers? Even the Champion can cry!'

Two more men came into the chamber.

'Bricriu, we've placed the last of the barrels in position.'

'Excellent. That part of town is the smear on the purity of Albanon. The waters will cleanse our Isle; it will wash them away. We still have a bit of time before we need to light the fuses, but I want all of you in your positions by seven o'clock. It has to happen right at the start of the procession, so the crowds are all in place. We need to make sure they all go off mostly at the same time, about nine. Now get going.'

As the men milled about, he gestured to the two that had just come in.

'I know you both have just come in from a little further afield; why don't you have a rest? I was just about to start having a lovely conversation with this beastie here. We could take it in turns, even.'

They grinned.

'Sounds like fun.'

Rua listened to the drops, biding her time.

Drip... drip... drip.

The sound of her own blood falling into the pool below her finally stopped. She was still so numb from their last torture session, that the surest way for her to tell that her body had started healing was when the scabs had formed.

Her armour had been pulled off; her clothes and skin torn to shreds under their whips. Then they had started breaking her toes, one by one. The burns weren't as bad; once the torch got through the upper layer of skin and damaged the nerves, she couldn't feel them any more. All the blood and scorch marks covered up the healing process quite effectively. Her throat ached from all her screaming though.

Squinting through only her left eye – as the right was still too puffy – she swiftly closed it again so as not to attract attention. She wanted them to think she was already dead. In that glance, she had committed to memory the scene in front of her.

Bricriu hadn't come back. He had left halfway through the whipping, when he realised she wasn't talking. Only two of his men remained in the chamber, drunk on power and ale, judging from the empty bottles on the table. Even though it was dark in the depths of the sewers, the solitary torch cast enough light for her to see her crescent blades and dagger lying in the corner of the room.

She made a few calculations; it had been roughly four hours since she had handed herself over to the Order. That should have been enough time for Silas to have returned to the palace and ready the troops to take care of the rest of the bombs on the map. But there was something Bricriu said. Something that made her think that there was a piece of the puzzle missing. Something very big.

'I think she's bled out, now,' one of the men said.

'Good. I want her tail as a souvenir; it'll be easier to cut it off without it spurting everywhere.'

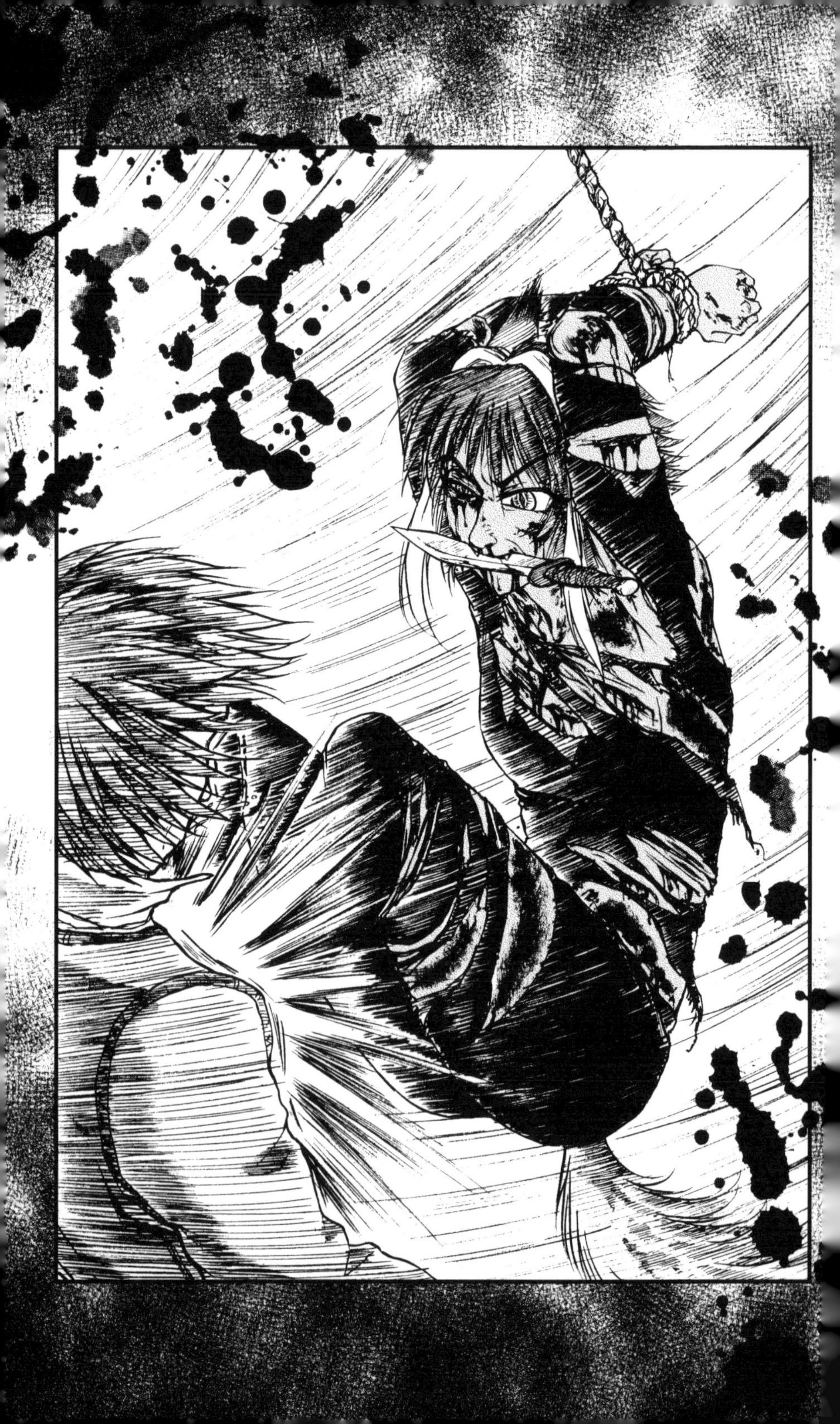

She heard him get up, draw a knife and shuffle towards her. She held her breath.

He stopped in front of her and cupped her face in his hand, turning it to look.

'Y'know, she'd've been quite the looker if she weren't half-beast. She's still warm... maybe if we cut her ears off too, then we could– GAH!'

She had opened her eyes wide, staring at him with murderous intent.

The knife he was holding was right there, next to her cheek. She threw her head forward, biting on the blade and pulling it out of his hand. Raising her knees up, she kicked him square in the chest, pushing off him to swing back high and spit the knife into her hands. He staggered back and fell onto the table, smashing into the bottles.

She frantically sawed at the rope she hung from, trying to cut herself down.

Nope, not enough time, the other one was on his way over.

As he lunged for her legs, she curled them up, swinging out of the way. She swung back down and caught his head between her thighs, then twisted violently and snapped his neck. Like an anchor, his added weight was what she needed to sever the remaining frays of the rope, and they dropped onto the floor. She winced as she landed on her toes; a couple of them were still healing.

The first man had picked himself up and was trying to get away. She threw the knife into the back of his legs, planting it in his hamstrings. He went down screaming.

Good. Now she could take her time with him.

She kicked him over onto his back. As she pulled off her ropes, she stamped on his thigh, pushing it down onto the knife. He screamed again, his expression pleading.

Rua was clean out of mercy.

'You have no idea how much I can make you hurt. You'd better start talking.'

***

She tracked through miles of tunnels, ruthlessly executing any members of the Order she found. She had no time to spare and no one to turn to; they had taken her to a pump room far away from the planned procession route, so the nearest undercover officer was further for her to get to than Liadán's Leap. Panic started rising in her heart. It had taken her over an hour so far. The procession would start soon.

He was planning something much bigger than just bombs beneath the procession route. He was going to blow up the foundations of the suspension bridge. This would have disastrous consequences, not just for the people who could die from the explosion and the collapse of the bridge, but also because the Leap partly functioned as a dam, controlling the water level at the central river docks, further downstream. The sudden release of water would flood that entire part of town, which was highly populated with tourists and expatriates.

That bastard was planning genocide by location.

She shielded her eyes from the sunlight as the open air and the sounds of cheering crowds assaulted her senses; she had come to the end of the sewers where they opened out onto the steep banks of the river Tamesis, just beside the bridge. From the looks of it, it was mid-morning, and the happy crowds mean that the procession had gone ahead as planned because the rest of the bombs had been defused. Ahead, the first suspension tower rose high above her, swelling with members of the public, eagerly awaiting the arrival of the Queen. She didn't know where to look; all around her were so many archways, raised walkways at different levels and scaffolding holding it all together. But she could smell the black powder in the air.

As luck would have it, she spotted him below, climbing up the scaffolding towards her. She walked up to the edge and stood, waiting for him. As he neared the top, he looked up and almost lost his grip when he saw her bloodied face, peering down at him.

'Where are the bombs?' she purred.

His shocked face soon turned into a sneer.

'It doesn't matter. The fuses are lit; there's nothing you can do.'

'Oh, there's still a helluva lot I can do.'

Jumping over the edge, she crashed into him, sending them tumbling back down, ricocheting off the criss-crossed poles of scaffolding before landing in a heap on the mid-rise walkways. They both struggled picking themselves up.

'You're not getting out of here,' she panted. 'Until you tell me where they are.'

'I'd rather die than let Eira be taken over by foreigners and animals!'

They drew their weapons and lunged at each other, clashing on the walkway.

She was still recovering from the torture that had been inflicted on her over the past four hours, and their tumble just now hadn't helped things. A couple of her toes were still broken and whenever she tried to twist or dodge out of the way, the scabs that had formed on her back and sides were being torn open again.

He was fresh and quick, swinging his hand-and-a-half sword with considerable force, making it painful for her to block and brace against strikes.

Think Rua! He's not going to talk. Where would he place the bombs?

Then she saw them, sparking and hissing in the gloom below her.

Her heart sank. Far below them, along the walkways, he had lit two fuse trails, both leading in opposite directions. She followed them with her eyes, steadily fizzling to their destinations. There was a mound hidden under a sheet next to the foundation base of the first tower and another at the anchorage block.

If either of them went, the whole bridge would go.

Rua broke away from him, running towards the anchorage point first. There wasn't enough time to get down there and stop the fuse by hand. She carefully took aim with one of The Sisters, and with all of her might, threw it.

It spun through the air like a bolt of steel lightning, planting itself firmly into the wooden walkway, cutting the fuse trail clean in two. And with the full height of the blade squarely blocking one side from the other, she was satisfied the sparks couldn't jump high enough to carry on.

She turned back to Briciu's enraged face.

'You might've stopped one, but you won't stop the other!' he shouted.

She sliced at him weakly to try and get him to move, but he parried again and again, stubbornly standing in her way. She was getting increasingly desperate; that fuse was burning up fast and if she couldn't stop it within the next thirty seconds, that bomb would go off.

She feinted to the left, then as he took the bait, darted right, dashing past him. She ran towards the tower until she was almost in line with the live fuse trail. She looked down and took aim with the remaining Sister.

As she swung her arm down to throw, Briciu's sword caught her in the shoulder.

Her blade fell aimlessly below, clanging as it bounced off the walkway.

She had missed.

The enormity of what now awaited them was not lost on her. Her mind raced through the possibilities, but they all led to the same conclusion.

She was going to die today. And no one else needed to.

She took precisely two steps left, turned around and leant back on the railing, spreading her arms wide.

'Go to Hell, bitch!' he yelled.

Briciu's blade went straight through her chest, buried up to the hilt.

His look of triumph turned to dismay as she wrapped her arms around him.

She smiled.

'Believe me, I've tried.'

She pitched back and took him with her.

The forty foot drop shattered her back on impact with the floor, cracking her spine and ribs in several places. Bricriu landed hard on her, rupturing her insides. She hoped that was enough to break his fall; she wanted to stop him escaping, but she also wanted him to survive and face justice.

With one final effort, she turned her head.

Good; she had landed right on top of the fuse trail. With any luck, the tip of the sword in her chest had cut it, and even if not, the blood that was now pouring out of her would soon put any sparks out.

Everything was growing darker. As she lay there waiting for Ciel to bring the welcome relief of death, she heard voices coming closer. She recognised one of them. She didn't think her heart could hurt any more, but it did.

'Rua!'

Her eyes were open, but she couldn't see him.

One last breath. Better make it count.

'See you soon, love.'

And with that, she was gone.

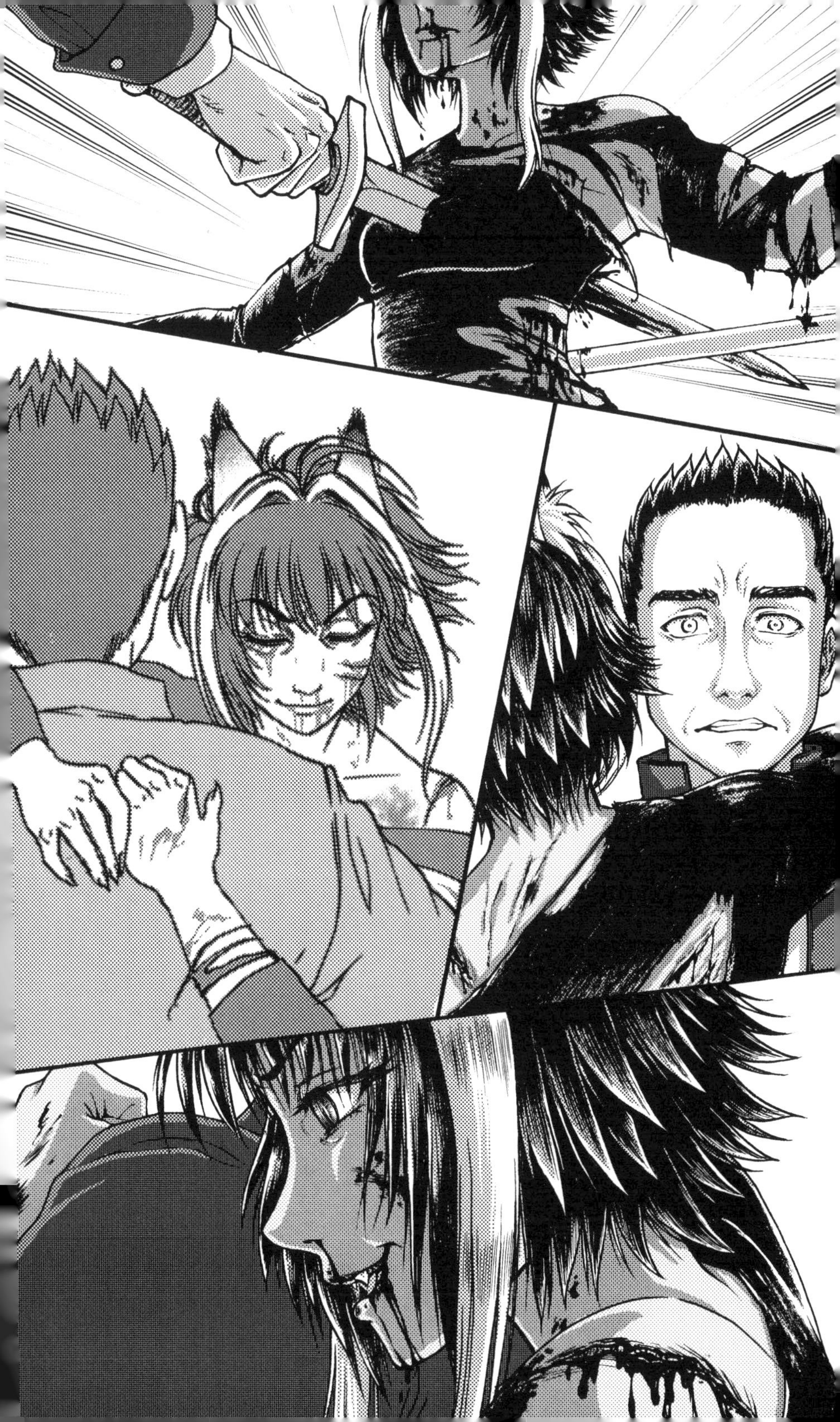

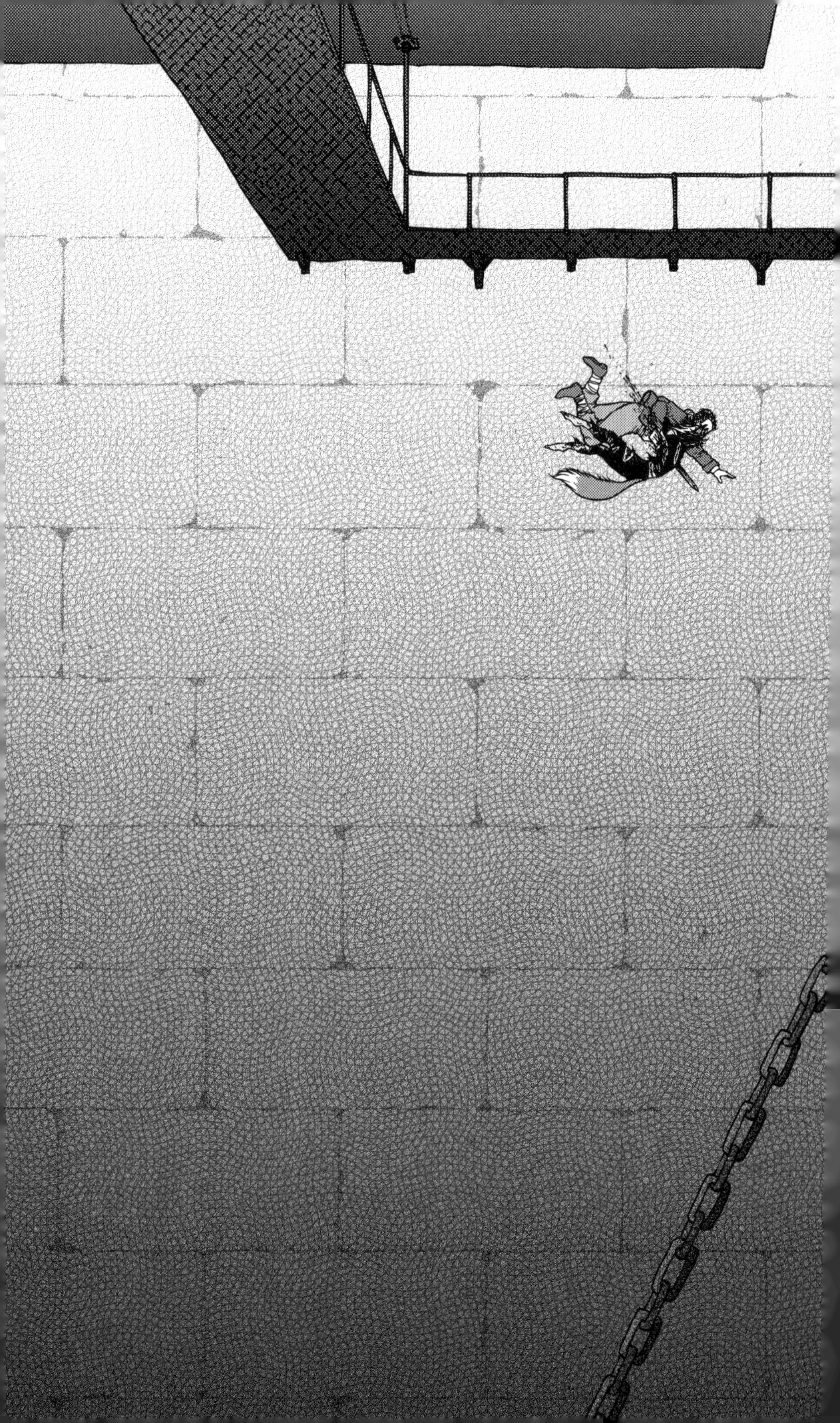

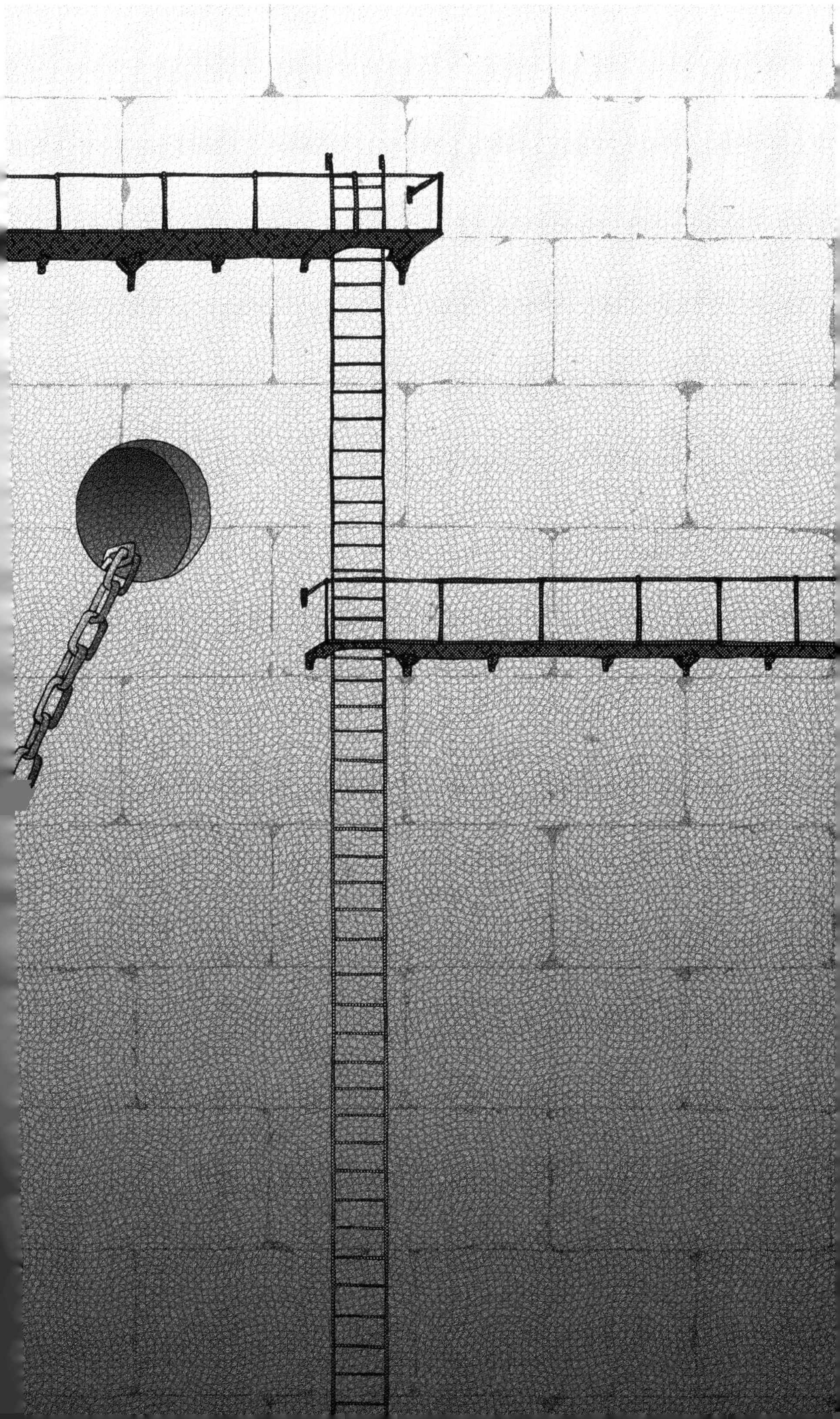

XII

'Rua, *cherie*, are you awake?'

Her eyes fluttered open and she sat up with a gasp.

Hearing Reynard's voice was a shock; for a moment, she thought she was in that small room at the top of the inn in Pas-Droit, in Fleurys.

Her eyes darted from the paisley rugs to the windows and then to the leather armchairs where he was sitting, by the fireplace. Her fireplace. Her room.

Reynard got up and opened the balcony doors, letting the cool air of the early evening wash in. He went back to the fireplace, poured a glass of water and gave it to her, crouching by her bedside.

She accepted it gratefully, swigging it down with ferocity. She gave him the empty glass back and leant back on her pillows, feeling exhausted.

'Status report,' she croaked, her throat still dry.

He raised his eyebrows at her, then shrugged and grinned.

'All the bombs were defused. With the new information, the Queen's troops stormed all of the locations an hour before the procession was due to start and captured or killed most of the Order members who were waiting to set them off. When they started finding members who were already dead in the sewers, they followed the trail to where you... where you were.'

Oh. Judging from his reaction, she must have been in quite a state.

She could hear the clinking of glasses and people chattering.

'Is it Wednesday evening already?'

He nodded as she got out of bed slowly and walked over to her balcony to observe the second courtyard below, staying behind her curtains and shutters.

'Where is Silas?' she asked.

'Probably with the Queen. She's been babysitting him these past few days.'

She shot him a frown.

'What do you mean by that?'

'Hmph. First, he tries following you into the sewers when he wasn't supposed to, then it was his fault that you got captured, then he didn't find you fast enough to stop you getting killed...'

Her hackles rose.

'Watch what you're saying, Reynard.'

'...And all he can do is weep when I speak the truth. What use is a boy if he cannot handle himself in a fight?'

'You have no idea what he is really capable of.'

'Why do you even put up with him?'

She motioned to the door with a tilt of her head.

'Get out.'

Reynard stood up and spread his hands in a peace making gesture.

'Rua, *cherie*, I was only trying to—'

'I said, get out.'

He was silent for a few seconds. Then, like a truant schoolboy, he stuck his hands in his pockets and slunk towards her, his tail low. Cracking a roguish grin, he raised his hand up to her face to cup her cheek affectionately.

'We were good together, once,' he said. 'Alas, I wasn't good enough for you.'

Her eyes softened, but she only offered a shake of her head in response.

His eyes narrowed.

'Is that boy good enough?'

She snarled.

How dare he.

She grabbed his hand and with the strength of incandescent rage, spun around and flung him out of the balcony doors.

He sailed through the air and landed on his backside with a huge splash in the courtyard fountain below.

'Sod off, Reynard!' she bellowed.

He hastily got up and made his way out of sight, leaving small puddles as he went.

Rua was so intent on glaring daggers at him, that it took about a minute for her to register that she had a large audience. The courtyard was teeming with people in formal dress; Vulpine Councillors, Eiran Dukes and Duchesses along with foreign dignitaries. They were staring open mouthed, halfway through their sparkling wine and canapés.

The rush of rage-fuelled adrenaline left her at this point and she wobbled slightly, clutching at the door frames to keep herself standing.

'Rua!'

His familiar voice buoyed her up. Straightening, she scanned the courtyard for his strawberry-blond head and saw him step out of the crowd.

'Silas,' she breathed, walking to the edge of her balcony.

She hopped over the rail and delicately dropped down to ground level, rushing towards him. Her eager steps broke into a run. He spread his arms wide and she leapt into his embrace, knocking him onto the ground. They sat up and knelt there, arms locked around each other like they would never let the other go.

'You are back,' he whispered into her hair.

'That I am,' she replied, nuzzling his neck.

He held her tightly for a few moments longer before pulling away and taking her by the shoulders. He looked down at her sadly, his eyes welling up.

'And I am so sorry.'

'What—'

'I failed you. I promised Ciel that I would do anything for you. I am your sheath, your shield. Yours. And when it came down to it, I was not enough. I tried...'

'Shush, love,' she soothed. 'You, of all people, would've done everything you could. You can't save them all and if you had to lose one, it may as well be me because... well, I always come back.'

'I know. Logically it makes sense, but I...'

His voice caught in his throat. When Silas started to speak again, it shook.

'When I saw the light go out in your eyes, it felt so final.'

Rua stayed silent. She had seen enough lights go out to know how it must have appeared to him, but she couldn't bring herself to think about what she would do if his eyes lost their light. Her grief and vengeance might bathe the whole world in blood.

His tears began to fall.

'In that moment, all I wanted was to take your place. If I had reached you sooner...'

'But we won because of what you did. What we did. What I told you to do.'

'I could not save you...'

'I didn't need saving!'

'I am not good enough—'

She slapped him hard across the cheek. He stared at her in shock.

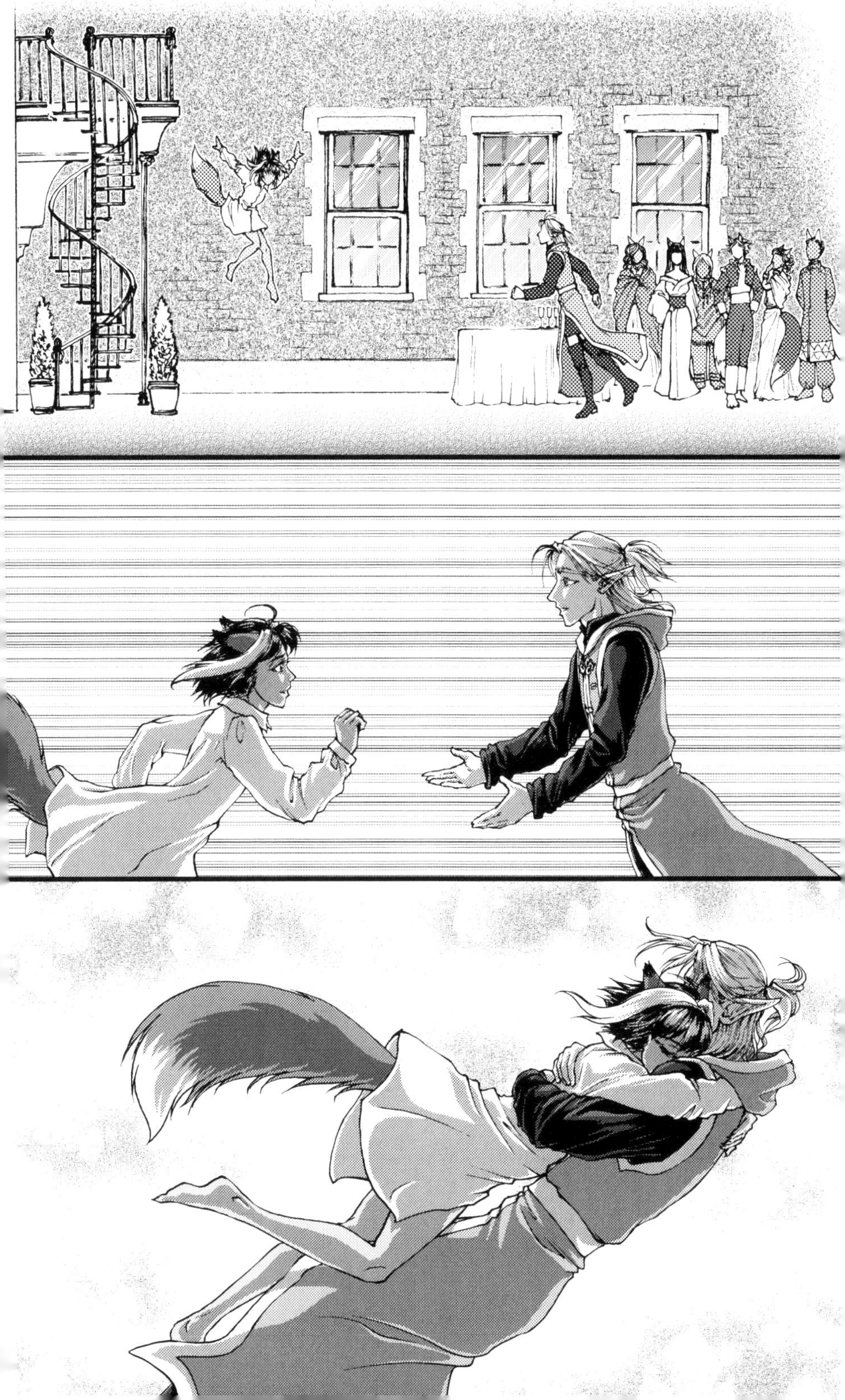

'Don't you ever say that again, Silas L'Heritier.'

Suddenly she was kissing him, urgently, hungrily. She had had enough of doubts, fears and hesitation. He needed her. And she needed him; all of him. She ground her lips against his, pressing her body close enough to feel his heartbeat quicken.

He shivered, his fingers digging into her back as his arms encircled her fiercely.

'Ahem.'

Their mouths parted and they both looked up at Éilís, whose expression was somewhere between admonishment and approval.

'You do realise you're in the middle of a garden party, right?' she said, raising an eyebrow. 'I think you'd better take this inside.'

The pair blushed furiously and helped each other up. Rua threw Silas a shy smile, then turned around and led him up the spiral staircase to her balcony. There was much cheering and clapping by the time they closed the curtains.

'I apologise if I have embarrassed you in any way,' Silas said.

Rua hardly registered his words because she had only one thing on her mind.

'Get on the bed.'

'But... I still have my boots on.'

'Get your boots off.'

He obediently sat down on the bed and bent over to pull off his boots.

'I suppose that you must still be very tired after your regeneration,' he surmised, concentrating on the task at hand. 'Do you want me to fetch anything for...'

He looked up and his words trailed off as Rua undid the last button on her nightshirt and let it slide off her bare shoulders.

'Rua, I... what? But... you,' he sputtered. 'Not...wearing...'

'I'm completely naked, yes,' she agreed, sitting beside him.

He stared at her body and swallowed. He was so adorable when he was nervous.

'What are you going to do?' he asked, under his breath.

She shuffled behind him, her hands snaking around his sides to unbutton his tunic and slide her fingers in.

'What I should have done weeks ago,' she replied.

She stroked the bare skin of his chest and trailed kisses along one of his pointed ears, making him tremble.

'I'm going to make you feel things that you've never felt before,' she clarified.

She nipped at his neck.

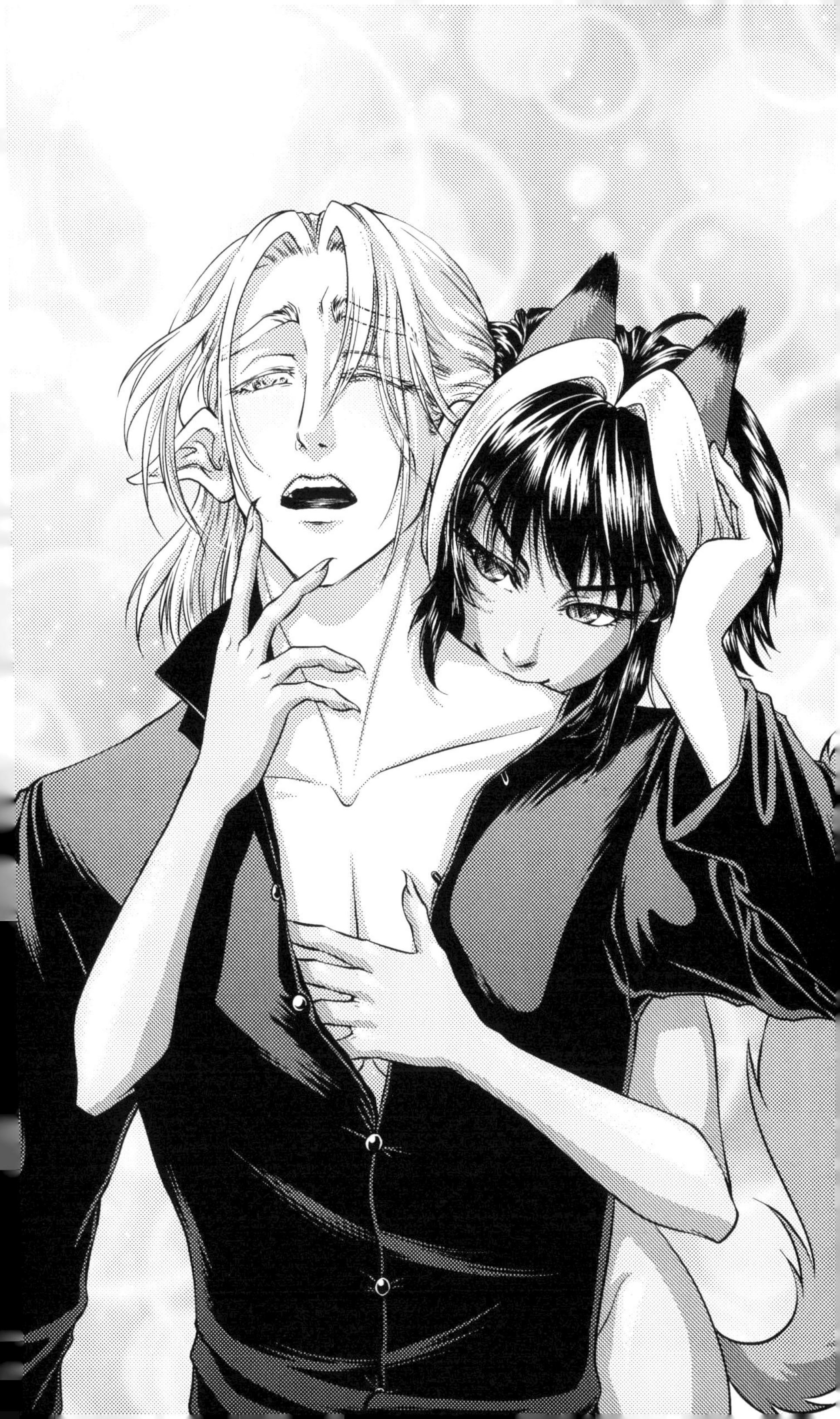

He gasped and reached behind him to run his fingers through her hair. She pulled his tunic off and ran her hands further down his body to pull down his hose. She breathed into his ear.

'I'm going to make love to you all night,' she confirmed.

Silas groaned and twisted around to brush his lips against her mouth, her chin, then her throat as he pushed her onto her back, then pinned her to the bed with a deep kiss.

She writhed beneath him, revelling in the feel of his weight on top of her, his bare skin rubbing on hers and his warm, spicy scent. She wanted him; now.

But then he stopped and propped himself up on his arms.

'Rua,' he panted. 'I... I have never... done this before, so is there... anything in particular that you like?'

She blinked. And then she giggled. Ever the gentleman.

'No, love, nothing fancy. I would just like you to do...'

She shifted a little, grabbed his hips with both hands and guided him.

'This.'

'A...aaah!'

'Mmm! Yes... now keep moving.'

***

She was woken up by the warm sunlight on her face, streaming in from her porthole window. That, along with the delicious waft of fried bacon, coming through the balcony shutters from the kitchens. She wiggled her nose, trying to catch more of that scent.

Silas chuckled.

Rua opened her eyes.

He was lying in bed with her, propped up on his elbow, his silver eyes warm with mirth. How long had he been watching her?

She gave him a sleepy smile. Then her eyes widened.

His arm was bare; he wasn't wearing a nightshirt. In fact, he looked naked. She lifted the covers to peer underneath.

Yes, he was. And by Ciel, so was she. Their lovemaking wasn't a dream.

'You are very cute when your nose wiggles like that,' he murmured.

'Well, I can't help it if bacon smells that good.'

She snuggled into his side, breathing him in. His smell was much better than bacon. She gave him a peck on the lips before reluctantly sitting up and stretching her arms. She looked at him, quizzically.

'Don't you usually get up before me?'

He stopped admiring her body and sat up as well.

'I am not usually this tired in the morning,' he said, wryly.

She blushed.

He got up to stand in front of the mirrored door on her wardrobe. He peered at his reflection with a slight frown and started finger combing his hair.

She didn't know what he had to frown about. She couldn't stop smiling.

Silas was perfect in her eyes; with his slim waist and hips, he cut such an elegant silhouette. His tall figure was lightly muscled and lean, the sharp shoulder blades on his bare back and his long, silken hair adding a fragile beauty to his form.

Then she realised what was making her so happy. He seemed so comfortable with walking around naked in front of her. Like he was always meant to. She had endured so many years alone that by the time he came into her life, she had convinced herself that she didn't deserve him. She kept pushing him away, to the point where he started questioning whether he was actually worthy of her. The absurdity of it all made her feel ashamed. Despite all of her shortcomings he trusted her, loved her and wanted her.

It was time she allowed herself to do the same.

She slid out of the bed and crept up behind him. She pressed herself to his back, enjoying the feel of his skin.

'I could brush your hair for you?' she offered. 'Seeing I'm the reason it's mussed.'

In the mirror, she saw his eyes had taken on a lustful glaze. It thrilled her.

'If you keep touching me like that, it will only get mussed again,' Silas growled.

She giggled, trailing her claws down his belly in response.

He swiftly turned around and kissed her, his fingers digging into her hair.

There was a sharp rap on the door and the handle turned.

They leapt apart, scrambling for the nearest available cover.

Éilís strode in.

'I trust you've...' she paused on seeing them, raising an eyebrow. 'Slept well?'

Rua had jumped into the bed, pulling the sheets up over herself.

Silas was still standing, with only a small cushion in front of him.

They both nodded.

The Queen walked to the other end of the room to look out of the balcony. She kept her eyes fixed on the second courtyard as they hurriedly dressed themselves.

'Now that the Jubilee celebrations are finally over, my family and I are taking a well-earned break. We're heading up to Bàrrathair Castle next week. It's a little later in the year than usual, but at least there won't be any midges. I also received a petition from the Highland shepherds for a dragon cull; it seems their numbers are getting out of control. We could use another experienced warrior, or battle mage.'

She turned around slowly.

Rua and Silas stood to attention, mostly clothed, save for the odd button undone.

Éilís continued.

'Which was why I called on you this morning. We're now packing and sending the supplies ahead, so we need to know in advance. Would you like to join us?'

The pair saluted.

'Yes, ma'am!'

~Interlude~

Highland Fling

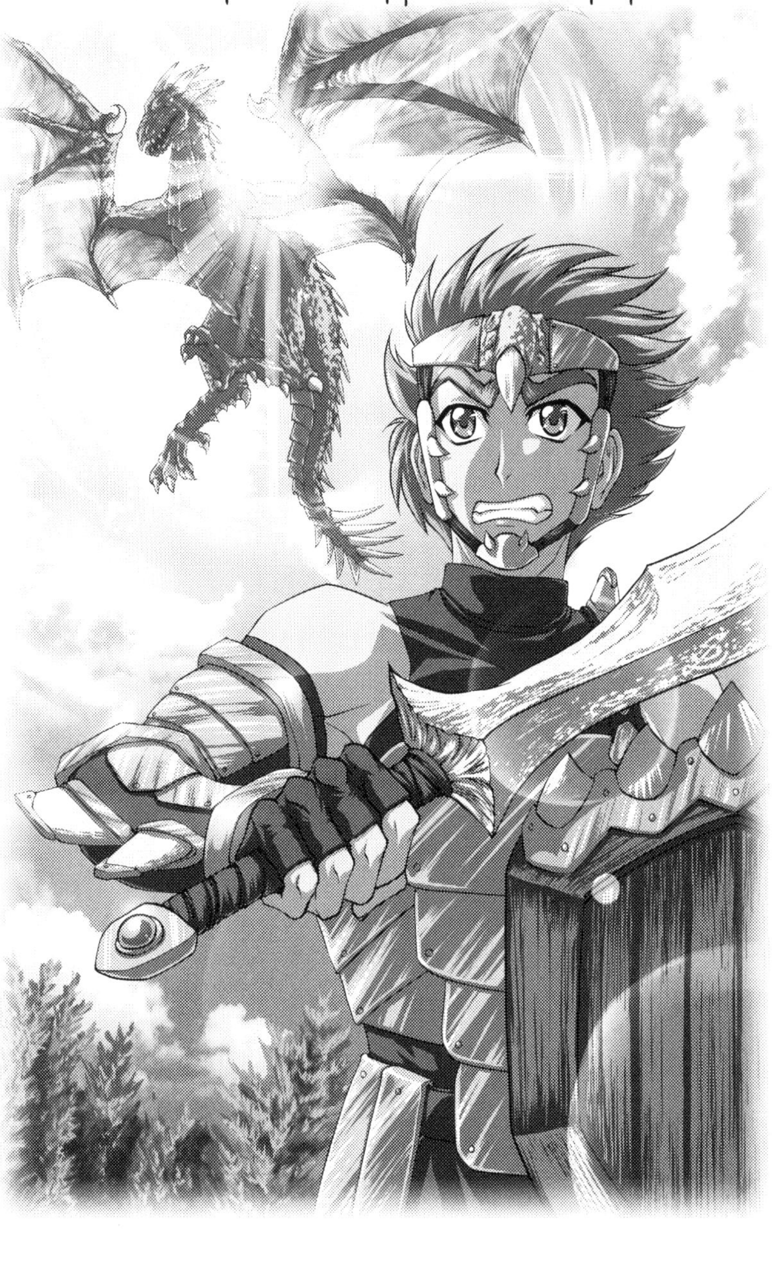

I

'Urgh, why does this journey always have to take so long?'

'Oh, grow up, Teag! You may as well be crying "Are we there yet?" like a child!'

I stuck my tongue out at my sister.

'See?' she said. 'You're only proving my point!'

Ciel's sake, why did she always have to win every argument?

I looked out of the carriage window. I didn't want to look at her smug face.

Surely I had a right to complain. We left Dúnragnhildt Palace two and half days ago, and we still had another hour to go. At least we stayed at the Duchess of Warrewyck's castle last night; she had the most amazing trebuchet that was still used to scare off dragons from time to time. I also liked Matilda, her daughter. Not only did she have a cute smile, but she also knew how to use the trebuchet. It was great fun seeing who could throw boulders the furthest. Well, until Niamh told on us. Such a spoilsport.

I pulled the window pane down lower and stuck my head out.

'Hey, get back in, you'll catch your death of cold! Dad, tell him!'

I never liked the length of this journey, but once we came far enough north, I liked the look of the mountains. In the summertime, they'd always be dark; solid, black crags above the mustard-coloured plains. The Silver Jubilee meant we couldn't head up until autumn kicked in. This time, the peaks were dusted in snow.

Ahead of us, the other carriage rattled and shook over the rough road. I used to love it as a child, getting bumped about the Highland roads. It was all too smooth riding down in Albanon. But at least it hasn't been boring lately.

Last week beggared belief, what with the Guild Hall attack and the Procession Plot – that's what the soldiers were calling it. Things could have ended up so much worse if it weren't for Rua.

No wonder Mum's been so stressed recently. Bad enough dealing with all the red tape, but the real threat of hundreds of people actually getting killed probably added a fair few grey hairs to her head.

Niamh has been tetchy too. She's had to pick up all the paperwork when Mum's had to go off to all those parties. I'm so glad I haven't had to do much of that, yet.

And Dad, well he's just... being Dad.

I leant back inside the carriage to check on him. He still wasn't saying anything, he'd not said a word since the last stage stop. He was just looking at his book.

On the other hand, Niamh was glaring at me.

'What?' I asked her.

'Nothing,' she replied.

I hated it when she did that. Why couldn't she be more upfront, like Rua?

'I bet it would loads more fun in the other carriage,' I complained aloud. 'I wanted to talk to Rua, I still haven't had a chance to show her how much better I am with a sword and she promised she'd spar with me.'

'Mum told you to give her some space. She wasn't long ago dead, y'know!'

'I know, I know... but she's all healed up now, right? Didn't she throw that Vertciellen Vulpine out her window?'

Niamh burst into laughter.

'Ahaha, I can still see his face! That, Teag, is the power of love... or lack thereof!'

Of course. I'd heard rumours that he was Rua's ex-boyfriend. He probably deserved it, then. Who would be stupid enough to piss her off? She was *the* Dagger, for Ciel's sake. She could hang your guts out to dry before you'd even realised you'd been gutted. She'd be the most terrifying girlfriend in the world. And now she was with that Elf.

'Well, Silas is... alright, I suppose. He did help to save a lot of people at the Guild Hall. And he helped defuse the bombs that morning. But I don't get what she sees in him, really. I mean, don't get me wrong, battle mages are great, but he's just so... clumsy... and... fluttery.'

Niamh gave me *that* look. The one like our old governess did.

'Teag, people have different strengths. Remember, the Goddess Ciel made him specifically for Rua. She's the strongest warrior in the world. She doesn't need another warrior as her partner. And he's not just any battle mage, either. He's the Weaver.'

I still found myself frowning. I wasn't convinced yet.

'You're not... jealous, are you?' she asked.

That cheeky cow.

'No way! Rua's like a big sister to me; in fact, I'd say she's better at it than you!'

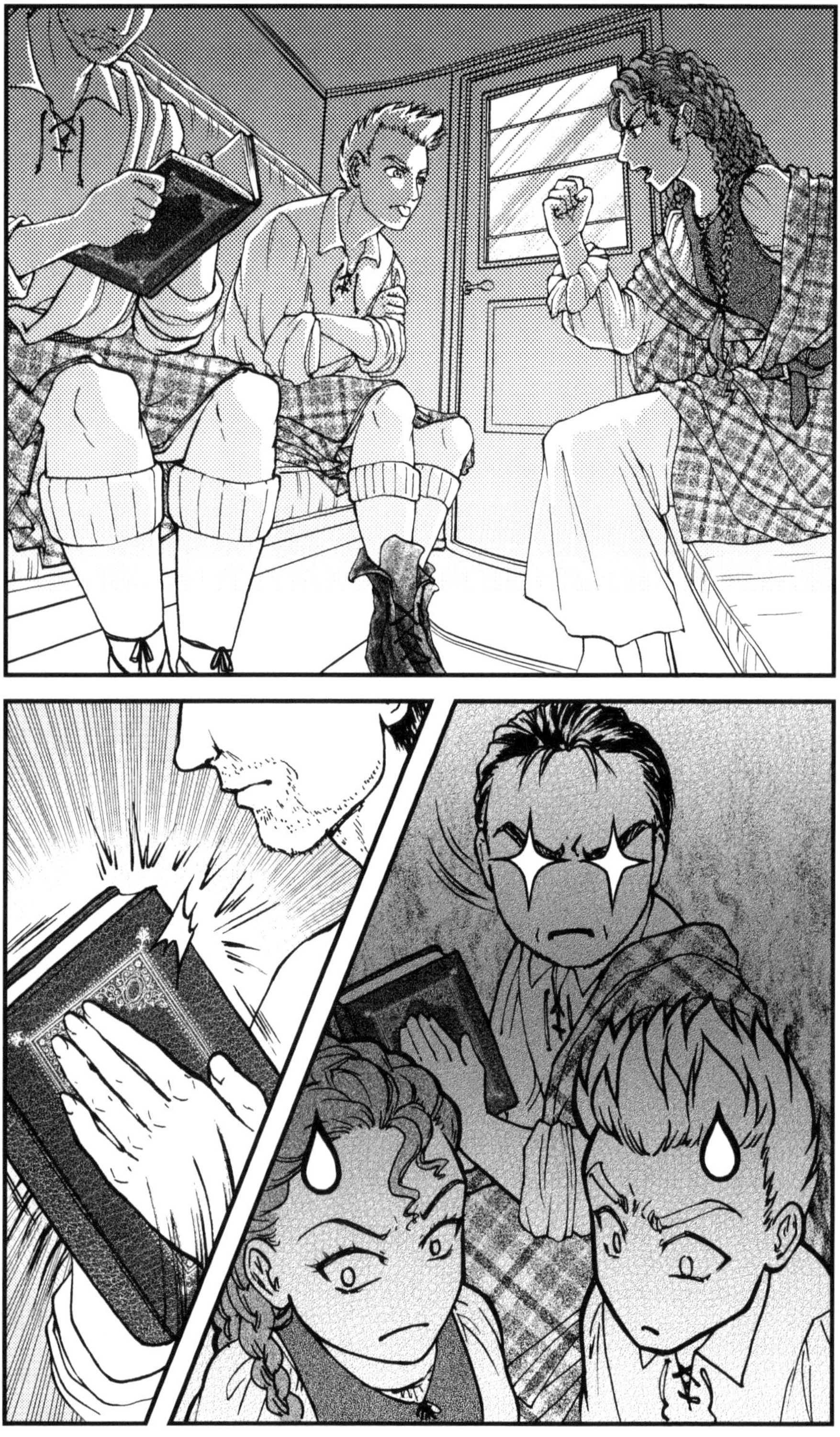

'You take that back, this instant!'

I stuck my tongue out at her again.

Dad slammed his book shut.

'Hey, kids. You're giving me a headache.'

I didn't want to carry on arguing. I looked out of the carriage window and into the clouds. I started thinking about the whole reason we were travelling up here in the first place. It wasn't just a holiday. It was also a job. And this was the first year I would be allowed to take part in the family business.

This time, I was going to slay dragons.

Thankfully, the last few miles of the journey flew by and I soon recognised the approach to Bàrrathair Castle. The river Bandhéa flowed parallel to the road, which curved into a wide stone bridge crossing its swift waters. We passed the old church on the corner where we always joined in with the locals during their harvest festivals and dedications to Ciel. Over the bridge and we didn't have to wait long at the gatehouse as the guards pulled the iron bars apart.

Then, the part I loved the most. I stuck my head out of the window again.

We came out of the trees just as the sun was setting. There was that familiar tower, rising high above the rest of the keep. Although it was our holiday home, it was originally a fortress, sturdily built by our ancestors not only to withstand armies, but dragons as well.

The carriage stopped and I didn't bother waiting for the footman; I opened the door myself and jumped out. Then I immediately wished I hadn't; pins and needles were shooting up my legs. I hid my grimace and hoped no one could tell.

As the tingling faded away, I looked over the waters of Loch Dearg just a little way down the hillside from the castle. My legs needed a stretch and I reckoned it would take another hour before the light completely went.

'Hey, Niamh, d'you want to come down with me to the shore?' I asked.

'Nah, I'm heading upstairs. I'm gonna make a start on redecorating my room.'

Ever since her work on Rua's room in Dúnragnhildt, she'd got bitten by the interior design bug. She'd taken it upon herself personally to refurbish many of the rooms at the palace. I didn't think she'd do the same to Bàrrathair.

'You're no fun.'

'Teagan!' Mum shouted. 'Don't forget this!'

She lobbed my daggers and sheath at me. As I caught them, she raised an eyebrow.

'You arm yourself when you go out there on your own. Remember that time?'

'Urgh, you won't let me forget! Alright, already!'

It wasn't such a big deal. I came across wolves when I was wandering along the shoreline once and I'd left my daggers back at the castle. I was only ten; it was way too risky to try getting past them without a weapon. I climbed a tree and ended up coming back home quite late after the Dragoons were sent out to look for me.

I clipped the daggers onto my belt and ran down the path leading to the Loch. It took me out the back of the estate. Once through the pair of stone dragons flanking the archway in the back wall, I made my way down to the shore, stopping when my boots touched the water.

In the twilight, the still waters of the Loch looked like glass.

Were there still Water Wyrms in there? I'd heard they'd died out in Eira, but they were still fairly common in Tianxia. What would it take to rouse a dragon?

I picked up a pebble from the shoreline and tried skimming it. I only got two skips. I tried another. That time I got three.

Then I heard the sound of boots crunching over stones.

With my hands on my dagger hilts, I turned around; it was the Elf, Silas.

'May I join you?' he asked.

I scrunched up my mouth.

'Well, sure, I won't stop you,' I muttered.

He gingerly picked his way over the rocky shoreline, lifting the hem of his long robe to stop it catching. Then he crouched and sifted through the stones. He finally selected a pebble, tossing it up and catching it a few times, testing its weight. He took a big step back and flung it, spinning it sideways. Twelve skips.

My jaw dropped.

'How d'you do that? Did you use magic or something?'

He chuckled.

'I am hopeless with my feet, but I am good with my hands. Mages need to be, in order to draw spell patterns. And I spent much of my childhood in Drachenheim. The Vertciellen Ambassadade was quite close to the Bridge of Mists so I often wandered down to the White Lake's shores by myself.'

His eyes looked sad for a moment. They looked like they belonged to someone much older. I wondered what happened to him to make them that way.

'Niamh told me you're only nineteen. Not much older than me, then.'

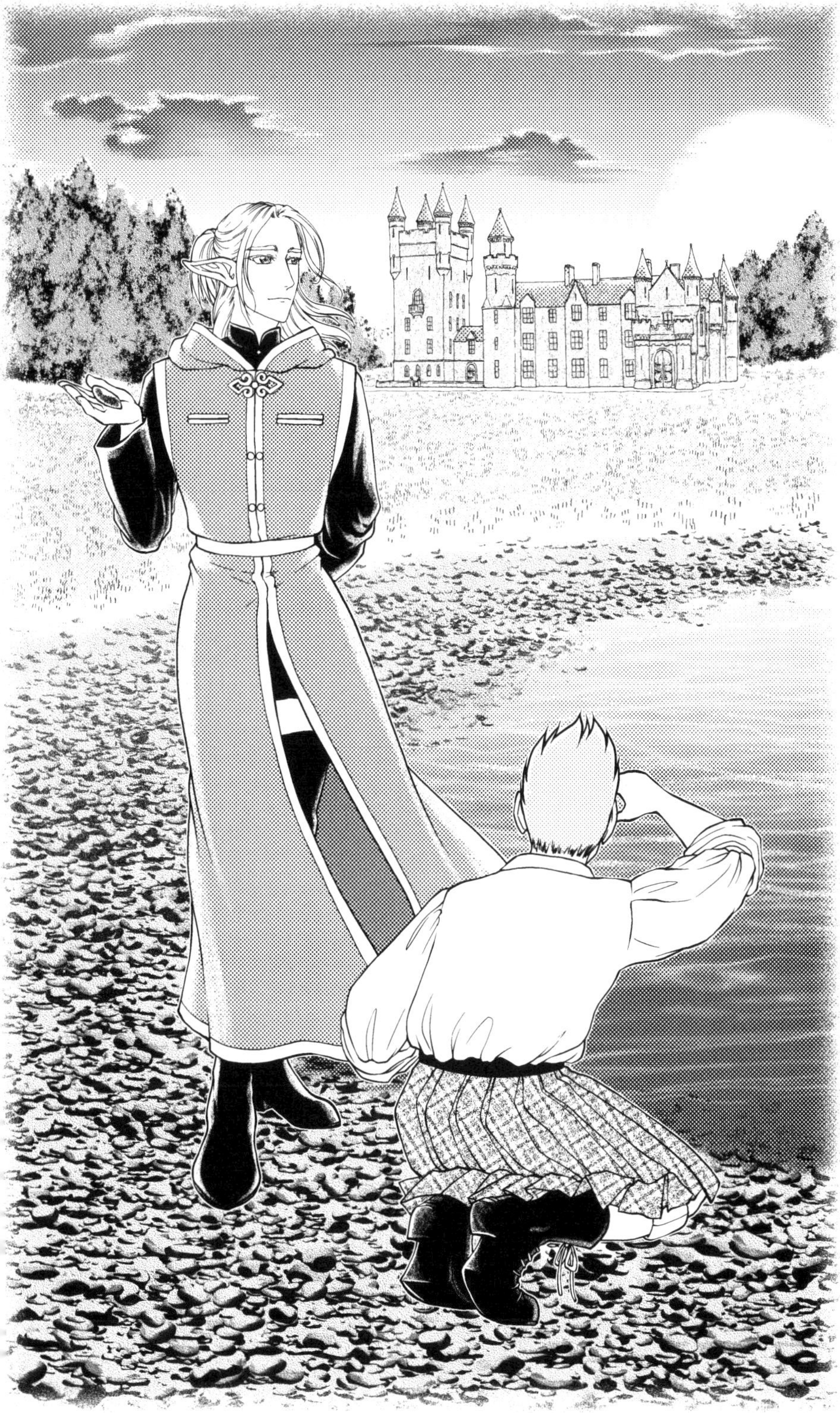

'Indeed, not.'

I watched him as he watched the ripples disrupt the near-perfect mirror image of the mountains reflected in the water. I'd met Elves before, of course, but only briefly at formal events. None of them were my age – well, as far as I could tell.

'Are all Vertciellens like you?' I found myself asking.

He smiled, shaking his head.

'No, absolutely not. Chevalier Gildas is my brother; you have met him?'

'Oh, yeah! I see your point. Sorry... that was a silly question.'

The waters of the lake stilled again. He selected another two stones.

'Not at all. I was the same when I met Rua; I had not spoken to many Vulpines prior. My foot was in my mouth so many times, it is a wonder I am still talking at all.'

'Hey, why didn't Rua come down here with you?'

'She was feeling hungry.'

I laughed. Of course she was.

He placed a stone in my hand.

'Use your thumb and forefinger to spin it as you throw,' he advised, demonstrating his grip on his own stone. 'Go in at a low angle, around twenty degrees.'

I followed his instructions.

'Six skips! I've never managed that many before. Thanks!'

'You are most welcome.'

II

'Teagan, what time do you call this? Brighde! He's here!'

I tried not to look at Mum as I sat down at the breakfast table and yawned.

'Too early, whatever it is,' I managed.

The cook came into the room with a tray.

'I thought I'd heard ye come down, laddie. Here – I kept these warm for ye.'

I grinned.

'Thanks, Biddy,' I said, scooping some sausages onto my plate.

'Oh, are there any left?' Rua asked eagerly.

She took the last sausage. This was probably her third helping.

I looked over at Silas; he sipped at his black coffee and scribbled away on a letter he was writing. There were some bacon scraps on his plate, but mostly lots of crumbs. That explains why there was only one piece of toast left in the toast rack. I grabbed it and started spreading butter on top.

'Honestly Teag,' Niamh said, rolling her eyes. 'I'd have thought you'd make an effort today. You're going out on your first dragonslaying in an hour.'

I almost choked on my toast.

'Wh– wait, WHAT?'

Mum sucked the air in through her teeth as she looked through her pile of papers.

'That's right, Teagan. Nothing quite like learning on the job.'

I swallowed. I'd trained for this my whole life; sparring in the South Barracks, reading all the manuals. But I'd never been up close to a real, live dragon before.

'Och, sonny, don't look so worried. I'll start you on an easier one, first. Here.'

She shuffled the papers and picked one out, passing it to Niamh.

'It's a Lesser Wyvern that's been picking off sheep from the neighbouring duchy. Teagan, you'll ride out with Niamh and six Dragoon knights. She'll be in charge of this hunt; so do what she says and learn.'

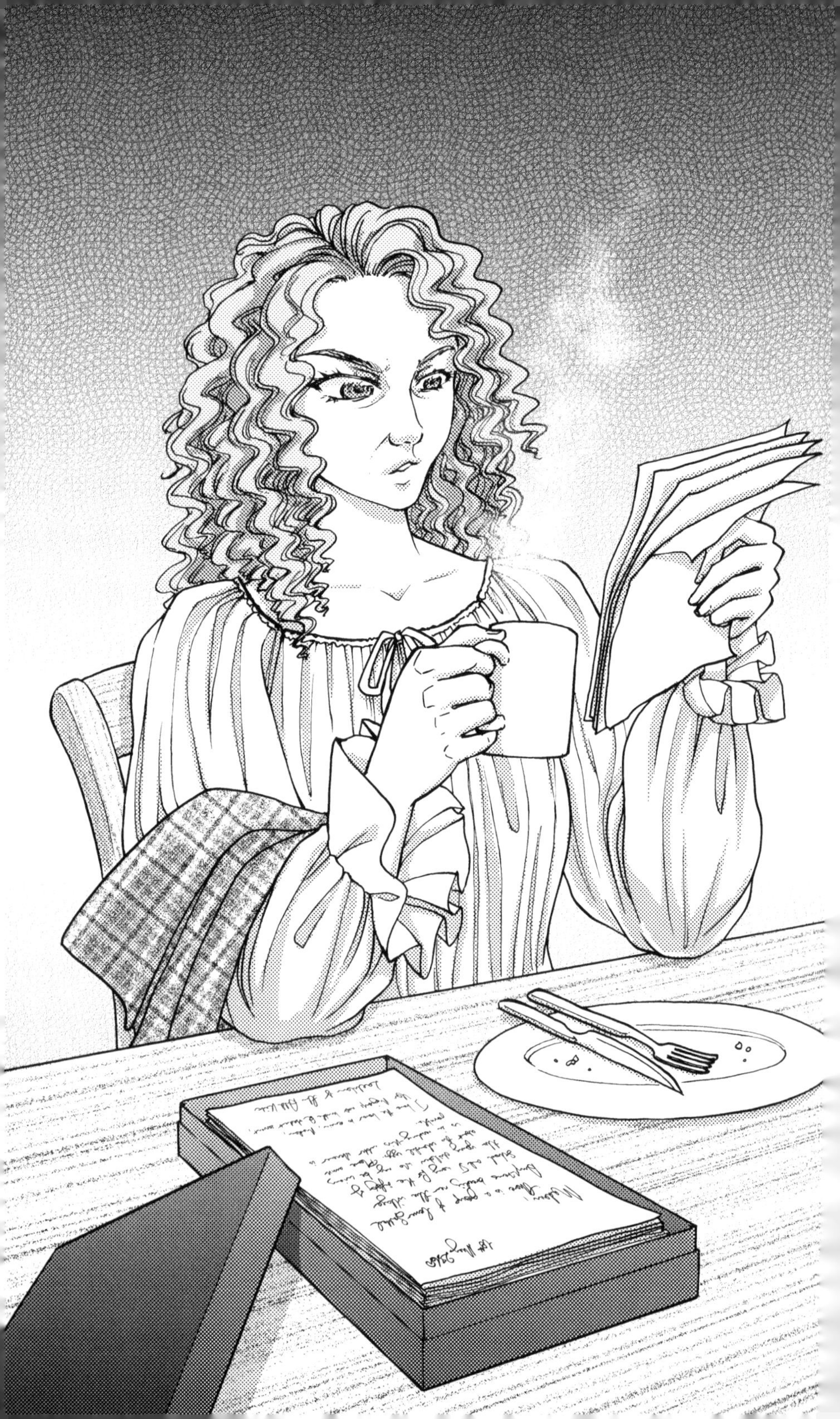

She passed another one of her papers to Rua, still munching on a piece of sausage.

'Rua, can you and Silas come with us today? There's a nest of Spotted Amphiteres that needs dealing with. Normally, those ones wouldn't need more than myself and Owyn, but the juveniles are fast maturing and they move quick.'

'Sure!' Rua said. 'Can I keep the feathers? I hear those fetch good coin!'

'Rua...' Silas warned. 'My inbox is still full...'

'Owyn,' Mum continued. 'Can you make sure the Dragoons bring enough nets? And whilst you're there, can you also tell them that the left wheels on the tower trap are squeaking? Oh, and can you send word to the local butchers to give us any leftover carcasses? We'll need as much bait as we can gather to get through all of these requests.'

Dad grunted and got up from his seat. As he walked past me, he ruffled my hair.

'You'll be fine.'

Niamh stood up as well.

'See you in the stables! Full kit, okay?' she called to me as she left.

I polished off my plate quickly and raced back to my room, where the head valet was waiting to help me into my new dragonhide armour. Once I was fully dressed, I walked into the courtyard. I felt my heart thumping faster again. The weight of my armour made today feel so much more real.

My first dragon. Would I be able to do it?

Buidhe, my dun cob, was saddled and waiting. My dragonbone sword, a birthday present from Mum, leant against the wall. It wasn't incredibly sharp, but it was large and near indestructible; perfect for breaking scales and chopping through tails.

Niamh drove up in her chariot, sunlight glinting off the metal framed scaffolding built around it. Her armour was bristling with wyvern claws and tail spikes. She even had two dragon horns on her shoulders.

I was jealous; I had no trophies to display on my plain armour. Yet.

'Ready?,' she asked. 'We've got about an hour's ride to the farmstead.'

I nodded and pulled Buidhe over to the mounting block to get on. We rode out with our small squad of Dragoon knights and a cart of supplies. We passed the time by having her quiz me on various aspects of dragonslaying. Normally I'd have found this a chore, but it settled the butterflies in my stomach.

"Dragon" was a catch-all term for large, fire-breathing lizards – though there were some varieties that didn't throw flames, the ones in Eira did, and could be categorised into four types: drakes, amphiteres, wyverns and true dragons.

A Lesser Wyvern was a type of dragon which had four limbs: two hind legs and two forearms that stretched into wings. As denoted by its name, this species was considerably smaller than the Greater Wyvern; those, like true dragons, could reach the size of a house. But it still wasn't going to be easy. There were many ways it could kill you. Its fiery breath was the first; though not as dangerous as the long-ranging fire balls that true dragons could spit, a wyvern's continuous stream of fire could reduce a tree to ashes in seconds. It was swift in flight and could run with considerable speed on land, Its tail spikes would be deadly if it caught you in a back swing.

The techniques for slaying a wyvern were similar to those for slaying a true dragon, as they presented similar obstacles. Prevent it flying away or attacking from above by damaging the wings or binding them with ropes or nets. Ensure you're armoured sufficiently for physical and fire damage; dodge whenever possible. Use large, heavy weapons to crack through its scales. Finally, its two most vulnerable points were the brain or the heart. The brain was usually too risky as its teeth and fire-breathing made timing a strike through the roof of the mouth nigh-impossible, but unlike a true six-limbed dragon, a wyvern's heart was easy to access from below; its forearms were its wings, high out of the way. Once the scales were removed, a well-aimed lance or royal claymore would do the trick, but it needed considerable force to penetrate deep enough. Hence we why needed tower traps and chariots with climbing frames to leap from.

We arrived at the farmstead where the shepherd, a weathered man in his seventies, warmly received us. As we fed and rested our horses, he told us where the sheep attacks had taken place; four had gone missing from one particular field of his, close to a stream that ran through his holding, near the base of a crag. Niamh confirmed the location on her map and we soon set off again.

The field was lush but empty; after the last attack, the shepherd had moved his sheep into his holding pens for fear of losing more to the wyvern. We combed the field for clues. One of the knights waved us over - she'd come across a dark patch with tufts of wool caught in the blades of grass.

Niamh narrowed her eyes.

'That's where it last feasted. Looks a few days old, as the shepherd said.'

She looked up towards the crag. It was like a giant claw, raking the sky.

'If I were a wyvern, I'd have found a nice place nearby... close to where tasty meat was, and easy to glide down from. And by now, I'd be getting hungry... but not hungry enough to bother roaming just yet. I'd be a bit lazy and hope the food comes back.'

I saw where this was going.

'Should I get that carcass out of the cart then?' I offered.

'I'll give you a hand. Dragoons, let's get a little fire going.'

We set up a fast burning spit roast, using the fire to warm and char the lamb's carcass we'd picked up from a local butcher. The smell of roast mutton soon filled the air. If that wyvern was around, it would only be a matter of time before it noticed.

Niamh began giving orders.

'Lili, you're the fastest, you stay turning the meat till it comes, then keep it down on the ground. Teagan, get back on Buidhe and go find some cover with Gordon, Iain and Caitlin. When it comes, you four focus on getting those wings wrapped. Daniel, you take cover on your own off that way so you can ambush or support as needed. Alasdair, you're with me, be prepared to drive the chariot when I tell you to.'

We all did as we were told. For a few minutes, I waited on horseback under the cover of trees in the corner of the field, running the ropes of my weighted net through my fingers. Lili, the knight left in the field, poked at the fire with a stick of willow. Suddenly, she threw it down and vaulted onto her horse, sending it into a gallop.

I heard it before I saw it. Unmistakably large pauses between wing flaps that only a very large flying creature could make. A hoarse, high-pitched, polyphonic sound between a shriek and a roar. We spurred our horses and broke out of our cover, whirling the nets the above our heads in readiness as it landed on the carcass.

The beast was as large as a stagecoach, no, larger still! From head to tail, it was longer than a canal boat, its wingspan nearly twice as wide. It hissed and rasped at Lili, who was menacing it with her lance.

As the others loosed their nets, I took aim with mine and threw. They hit their mark, falling over its back as it turned to face us. It tried to spread its wings, but couldn't – the weighted nets had tangled together.

Niamh cracked her reins and charged towards it, her knight riding close beside her. She pulled at one set of reins very slightly, then lashed them to her chariot.

'Alasdair! Keep 'em on the curve!'

The Dragoon leant forward in his saddle and grabbed the side reins of the nearest chariot horse. Niamh took her claymore, held it out sideways and crouched, bracing herself against the climbing frame. The horses veered towards the wyvern's front and she thrust the point of her claymore out, raking its tip along the lizards chest. The combined forces scraped an entire line of scales off, leaving a shallow cut in its flesh.

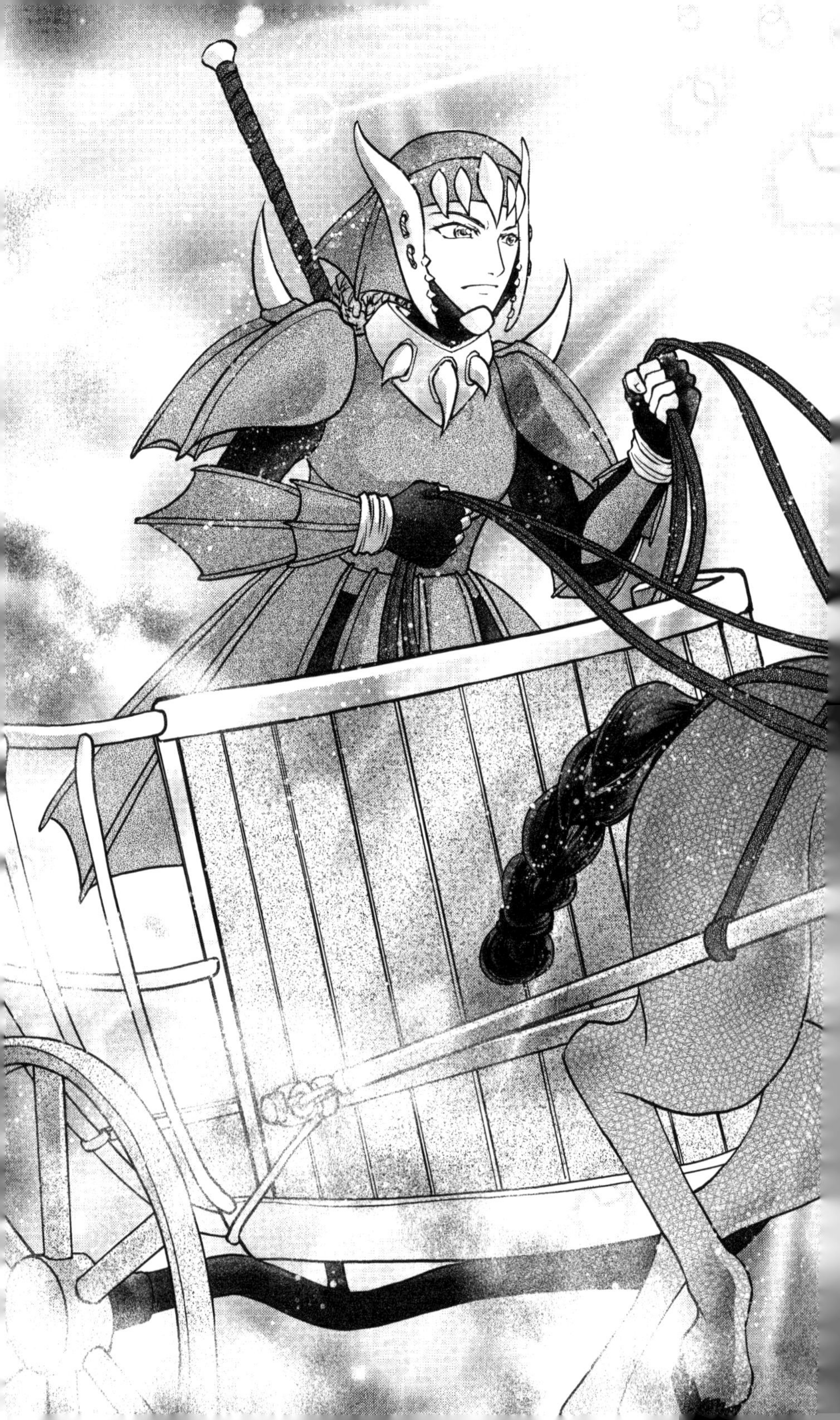

She immediately jumped and rolled under the wyvern as it roared in rage and pain, glaring at the moving frame. It unleashed a spray of fire at the back of the empty chariot as it raced away.

As soon as it ran out of breath, Niamh continued her assault on its chest scales, rolling out from its blind spot beneath its wings to take a few swings at a time, ducking as it spun, swinging its massive, spiked tail over her head.

'Sir, time your attacks carefully!' Iain called, as he tipped his lance to lead another charge. 'Aim to arrive just as its fire runs out and when it needs to breath in! Weaken its chest as much as you can!'

I gritted my teeth and urged my cob onwards, on the tail of Iain's destrier. I wound my reins around my saddle horn and braced my sword in both hands, guiding Buidhe with my knees.

It breathed another stream of fire as we got closer and closer. I prayed to Ciel that it would stop by the time we reached it. Just as we were close enough to see the slitted pupils in its eyes, the flames wobbled and died down. Iain knocked off a few scales with his lance. I rode behind him and swung hard with my sword as I swept past, knocking a entire patch of scales off. It shrieked again.

Niamh took this opportunity to dash away and jump back on her chariot.

'Chest is done, fall back to me! Everyone else, circle!' she ordered.

We retreated safely to her side, the wyvern breaking off its pursuit of us as the rest of Dragoons swept in, running rings around it.

'Lines!' Niamh shouted as she wheeled her chariot around.

As one, the circling knights reached for their saddles and picked up their pre-loaded crossbows, loosing barbed bolts with long ropes tied to their ends. They landed in its scales and in the nets. They continued to circle, winding the ropes around it, their chargers pulling the lines taut until the beast was thrown off-balance, collapsing onto its side. Niamh grinned.

'Iain, drive. Straight approach, left exit. Watch this, Teag.'

I took hold of his charger as he dismounted. Niamh handed him her reins and picked up her claymore, climbing into the metal frame on the back of her chariot.

'Go! As fast as you can!'

With a crack of the reins, their chariot leapt forward, racing towards the wyvern. It belched out puffs of flame as it struggled to get back on its feet. Niamh crouched on the bars like a coiled spring, facing out sideways, gripping her claymore under one arm.

As the chariot was about to crash into the wyvern, it swerved violently to the left. It was then that Niamh pushed off the frame, using her momentum to launch herself off the chariot. Her weight and velocity thrust the claymore deep into the wyvern's chest.

The beast shook, breathing in one last time, angling its head down towards her.

'Niamh! Watch out!' I shouted, spurring my horse towards her.

The flames burst forth, obscuring her from view. My heart was in my throat for a few seconds, but as they died down, I was relieved to see her stand up, a few feet away, unharmed. Her dragonhide armour was smoking ever so slightly.

'I forgot they did that sometimes,' she grumbled.

She gripped her claymore with both hands, and planting her foot on its chest, yanked out her sword. Then she used the tip to prise a talon out from its wing tips.

'Hey, Teag. Catch! You've earned it!'

I hurriedly dropped my sword to the floor and caught the talon. Still bloodied at the base, it gleamed blue-black in the afternoon sun.

My very first trophy.

III

The last week was a steep learning curve for me. We took on the most urgent requests first; where certain dragons had become notorious for frequently preying on livestock and were no longer shy of the peoples of Ciel. After our Lesser Wyvern and Mum's Spotted Amphiteres, Dad led a squad of Dragoons against an outbreak of Red-tailed Drakes in the suburbs of Dùn-Eidynne, the largest city in the Highlands. I experienced first-hand how quick Amphiteres were when Niamh took me with her to hunt a pair that had settled too close to a primary school.

I also gained a lot more respect for my sister. I'd sparred with her for practice but I never realised what she was capable of until I saw her in the field; commanding the Dragoons with confidence, facing down all manner of fire-breathing beasts and emerging from their flames to deliver finishing blows again and again. I didn't want to say it to her face, but she really was fit to be the next Queen.

In all of these encounters, however, I never struck that killing blow. Everyone assured me that I wasn't to do so until I'd had more practice getting the timings right. Given the things we went up against, I agreed.

But what if it was just a lone Common Drake? Those ones would be easy to handle; four-legged ground lizards, about the size of an ox, with a short-ranged flame. Yet whenever Mum looked through her request pile, she gave those to the Dragoons to handle, in favour of training me up on the larger ones with Niamh.

On my day off, I waited until everyone had left the dining room before rifling through Mum's latest papers. I found one that was perfect; a Common Drake that had taken up residence at the other end of Loch Dearg. This wouldn't normally present a problem but it had grown fond of raiding tourists' picnics, which affected the local inns badly. I fished it out of the pile and rearranged the papers back into place.

That evening, Mum and Dad were late for dinner. They'd been out all day, researching an Elder Dragon; the most fearsome beast in Ciel's Cradle. This species were dragon-killers, known for taking wyverns, even. But this request was of particular concern; locals had reported several missing persons of late. Chillingly, this coincided with sightings of it grasping things in its talons that were suspiciously Human-sized. And once a dragon got a taste for Humans, it had to be dealt with.

I excused myself as soon as I could. Before heading to my room, I stopped by the kitchens to ask for a picnic basket from Biddy, saying I was sneaking out to see a girl. She happily obliged in the name of young love, promising me she'd keep it a secret. I laced myself into my armour and crept to the stables, hiding my sword under my cloak. I told the same story to one of the stable lads. He laughed and helped me ready Buidhe.

I rode out into the night, along the shores of Loch Dearg. Its moonlit waters rippled from an icy breeze, funnelled between the crags. I wrapped my cloak around myself tighter and spurred Buidhe into a light canter. After a mile, we passed a couple of picnic benches. I turned back to look at Bàrrathair Castle, its lights glimmering in the distance. It seemed as good a spot as any.

I jumped off my horse and laid out the spread. I'd made sure I brought drake-friendly foods; a ham hock, some strong-smelling cheese and equally pungent paté. I spread the latter on some crackers to release its odour into the wind. Then I sat and waited. Twenty minutes passed as I tracked the stars across the sky. Another twenty minutes came and went. I heard some distant whinnying; probably some wild ponies.

As I was thinking about giving up for the night, I heard the crunch of claws on dried leaves and the rustle of scales slithering over pine needles. I ran to Buidhe just as the drake appeared from beneath the evergreens, its body rocking from side to side as it pulled its legs forward in circular motions to crawl.

I waited until it lowered its head to start eating before breaking into a full gallop, making a pass for its tail. I leant sideways out from the saddle, took aim and swung. It came clean off and the drake screeched in outrage, whirling around to face me.

I rode Buidhe hard, running around it in a tight circle. It hissed as it clumsily spun on the spot, trying to keep up. I pulled on the reins and my brave cob reared inwards, kicking his front hooves at the drake's eyes. It flung its head back, out of the way, its chest exposed. As Buidhe dropped back on all fours, I brought my sword down and tore through its scales, leaving a deep gash all the way down its neck and chest. The beast roared and drew in a deep breath. I shouted and my steed turned to kick out with his back legs before jumping out of the way of its flames. I wheeled Buidhe around and observed from a distance, timing how long it could sustain its fire; about five seconds.

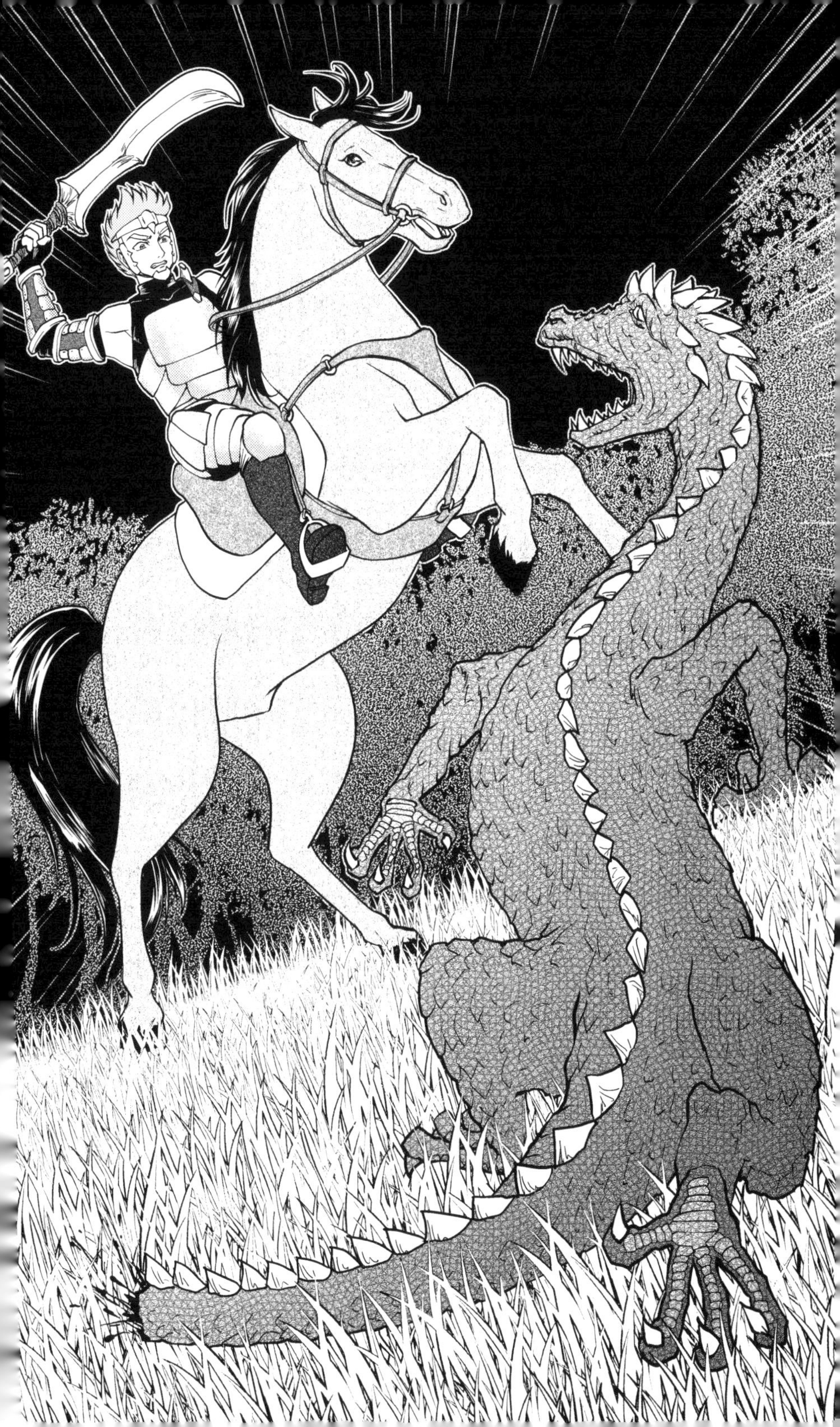

It advanced on us, its head low as it streaked over the ground. I held my nerve and kept my reins tight, waiting until the last moment before shouting again. Buidhe leapt sideways and I swung low as we flew past. My dragonbone blade raked all the way down its back, knocking off several back spikes and leaving a long, trailing wound. Now badly injured, it shrieked and rasped, its movements stilted. I rode in close, trying to tempt it into using up its breath on a shot of flame. It did, belching out fire as we dashed away in a circle. I counted the seconds, taking my feet out of my stirrups. The flames ended and I vaulted off my horse, hauling my sword through the air to slam it down, right between the beast's eyes. I felt the impact crack its skull and the blade sunk in, slicing into its brain. It collapsed. I yanked my sword back out and stumbled back, panting for breath. It didn't move.

It was over. I did it.

'Buidhe! Come 'ere boy!' I crowed to my horse, pumping my fists into the air.

He started to walk towards me, then shied and bolted off.

I heard giant wing beats; as if a storm was stopping and starting. Then crystal shards shot down from the sky, piercing the ground like deadly hailstones. The night breeze became a howling gale and the moon was obscured by an enormous shadow.

'Teagan! Get out of there, now!'

I blinked and suddenly Rua was there with Silas beneath the evergreens.

I ran as fast as my legs could carry me.

'What're you doing here?!' I exclaimed.

'Your Mum sent us to check on you. She thought you'd try something like this when she noticed the request was missing. You did good. But this; this is not good...'

My indignation at discovering I was being babysat all along was quelled by the worried look in her eyes as she looked behind me. I followed her gaze.

Its huge wings, like the main sails of a ship, blacked out the sky. All four of its legs, tipped with talons larger than my head, were stretched out to land. It bristled with fearsome crystalline growths from its nose to its tail. It was enormous; twice as large as the wyvern I fought last week. The ground quivered as it landed on the drake, tearing it apart as easily as I might carve a roasted chicken.

'Is... is that what I think it is?' asked Silas.

'Elder Dragon,' I breathed. 'I've never seen one before.'

'Oh, HELL no, we need to get out of here, RIGHT NOW!' cried Rua. 'Quick, whilst it's still eating!'

I took her words to heart and ran with them. Our respite was brief; we only managed fifty or so yards when those wing beats sounded again, uncomfortably close.

'Roll!' Rua shouted.

I did as I was told, but it wasn't enough. Those crystal shards came slicing through the air again. One glanced my shoulder but another landed in the back of my calf, slipping through the lacing. I cried out in pain and fell heavily, dropping my sword. The shard had embedded deep in my flesh; it was as large as a kitchen knife.

The dragon landed in front of us, folding its wings in neatly, taking its time. It knew I was wounded. It began to breathe in deeply.

'Silas!' Rua called.

'On it,' he acknowledged.

He placed himself squarely between us and the dragon, his eyes glowing green. He whispered as wisps of Air trailed behind his fingers, rapidly spinning into a spiral.

Then a continuous stream of fire shot from the dragon's mouth, lighting up the night. I flinched, curling up as I'd been taught to get the most protection out of my dragonhide armour, but I felt no flames heating up the steel near my skin. I looked up to see Silas, his arms outstretched, bracing against an angled shield made of wind. It cut through the flames like the bow of a ship, directing them harmlessly past us.

'May I?' Rua asked, as she picked up my dragonbone sword.

I nodded.

Silhouetted against the still-raging fire, she walked up behind Silas and patted him on the shoulder as he continued to hold the shield fast.

'Well, then. Ready to take it on, love?' she said in a matter-of-fact tone.

'Ready,' he confirmed.

'Are you guys mad?!' I yelled. 'Even if Mum and Dad had an entire platoon of Dragoon knights, they'd still have trouble with an Elder Dragon!'

'You cannot run and we cannot leave you,' Silas stated, his voice surprisingly calm. 'The course of action is simple. We fight.'

His quiet confidence left me speechless. This attitude from Rua wouldn't have surprised me, but Silas wasn't a highly experienced, centuries-old warrior; he was barely older than me. He hardly knew me, yet he was ready to defend me from one of the most dangerous beasts in the world. He was braver than I'd thought.

'Once its fire's out, I'll distract it for a bit so you can make Teagan a Spirit Fabric,' Rua said. 'Get ready and... go!'

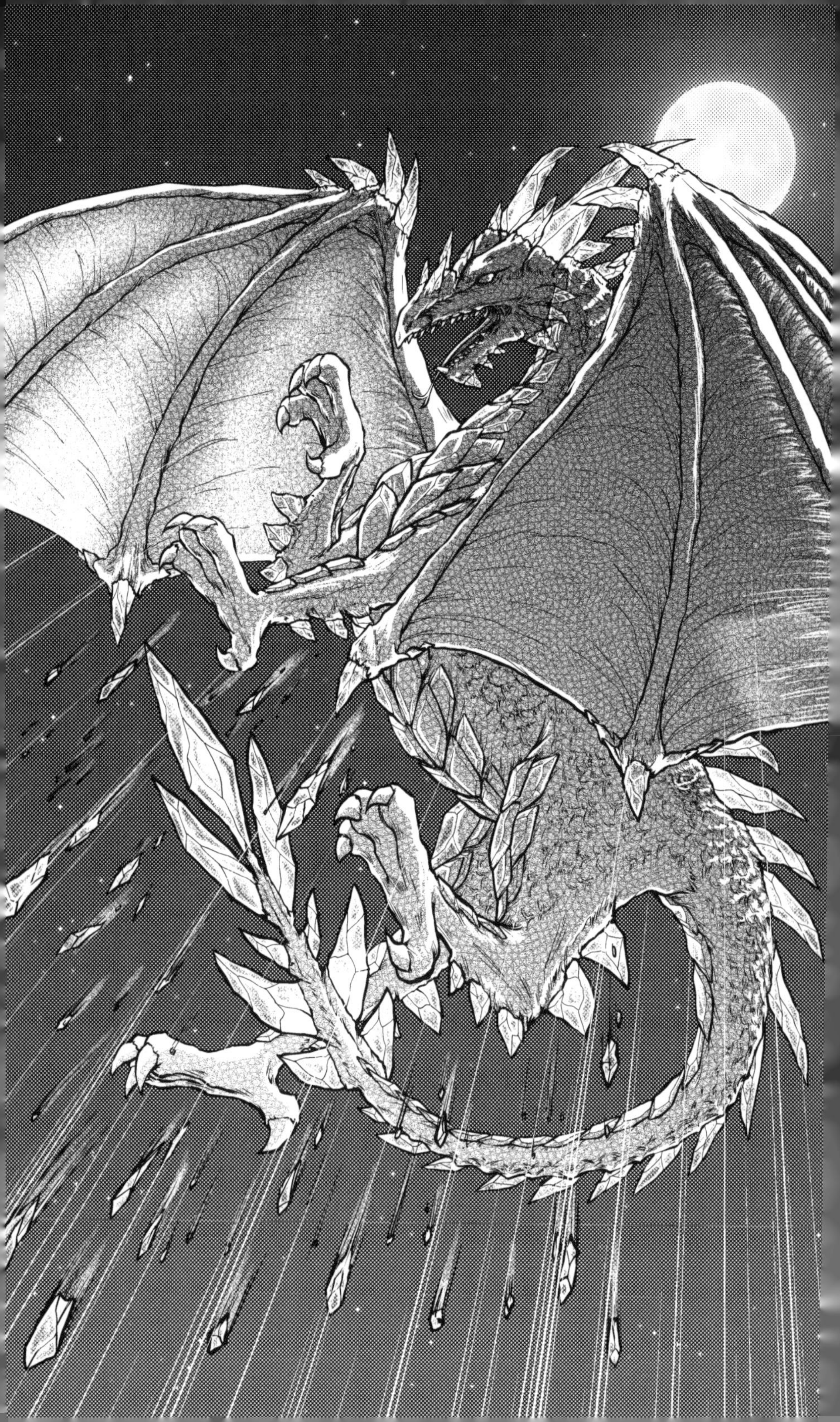

The dragon ran out of breath and Silas shook his hands, dismissing the shield. His eyes flashed white and he began to trace an intricate pattern with blistering speed; it almost looked like the weave of a traditional Eiran knitted jumper.

Rua bounded over his shoulder, then ran fast and low to the ground, gripping my sword behind her. She went straight for its head, rolling under its jaws as it snapped at her. She slashed at its belly, aiming for the edges of its crystal plates to prise them off. It crashed about, trying to trample her without success.

Silas finished drawing and he plucked the shimmering knit from the air. It vanished, but he held his hands in place, as if he were miming hanging a sheet on a washing line.

'Please take this,' he said. 'Throw it over yourself and retreat. You will be invisible.'

I felt silly as I grabbed at what looked like thin air, but was shocked when I touched the threads; they felt like spiderwebs. I threw it on and limped away, marvelling at how I could no longer see parts of myself.

Oh, the pranks I could get up to...

'Rua, what do you need?' Silas called.

'This blade is too short to reach its heart,' she replied as she stabbed its armpit, making it rear up in pain. 'So I've got to get it through the roof of its mouth and into its brain! But there's still too much fire for me to get close, whoa—'

The dragon had backed up to release another burst of flame at her. She leapt above the stream and retreated, circling around to its tail to make it harder for it hold its aim.

'Some water to put out its fire would be useful?'

'Yes, please!'

His eyes now glowed a brilliant blue as he looked towards the waters of the Loch. He reached out a hand and a swirling stream of water rose out of it like a snake poised to strike. He swept his arm towards the dragon and the water obeyed, darting through the air. It splashed down the dragon's throat just as it was taking another breath. Clouds of steam came from its mouth as it clambered back, coughing and choking.

Rua ran towards it with my sword at the ready, but it beat its wings furiously, launching itself into the sky with its powerful legs. The sudden downdraught knocked her back and caught me off-guard; I felt the silken threads slip from my fingers.

The Spirit Fabric had blown off.

I looked up into the sky to see the hovering dragon looking straight at me. It roared hoarsely and swooped, talons outstretched. I jumped and rolled as it landed inches from where I was hiding. Then it made a grab at me with its forearm. I tried to dodge again, but stumbled as the crystal shard in my calf tore deeper. I was yanked back; its claws had managed to hook around the plates of my armour. It started to beat its wings.

'Silas! Bind it, before it takes off!' Rua yelled, running towards me.

'*Catena ventus!*' Silas shouted, just seconds after.

I felt a blade of wind rush past me and the dragon shuddered, its legs and wings shaking with exertion as it strained against his spell.

Rua hopped onto the side of its forearm and began cutting me out of my armour.

But even magic couldn't restrain an Elder Dragon for long; its wings ripped through the wind and it pushed off the ground. The speed of our ascent was dizzying.

'Teagan, grab onto me! I've almost got you out!'

I held onto her leg as Rua sawed off the last strap, then she hoisted me up. We clung to the dragon's arm.

'Rua! Fifteen seconds! Then jump!' Silas called.

'Got it!' Rua shouted back. 'Fifteen... fourteen... thirteen...'

'Wait, WHAT?! WHAT DOES HE MEAN?' I cried.

'Shush, just keep counting! Ten... nine... eight... seven...'

We were high in the air, higher even than the towers of Liadan's Leap. Silas looked so small and insignificant, far below. Then the hairs on my arm start to rise. There was a prickle of static in the air and the clouds looked dark and ominous.

I could have sworn the sky was clear only moments ago.

'Three... two... one... Jump, NOW!'

We took our leap of faith. As we fell, I turned back to see the dragon, already banking sharply to pursue us. It felt as if I was looking death in the face.

Then all at once, the boiling clouds rippled and a blinding sheet of lightning blazed overhead with an ear-deafening clap of thunder. It coursed through the dragon, catching it in a net of crackling sparks. The dragon shrieked and fell out of the sky.

As we plummeted ever closer to the earth, I felt the rushing wind change into a gentle breeze and our rapid descent slowed. His hands mimicking our movements, Silas carefully lowered us down. His eyes were glowing a myriad of colours.

As my feet touched the ground, I fell to my knees; my bones were like jelly.

Rua hopped over to him and kissed him on the cheek.

'Thanks, love. I'll just go make sure it's fully dead.'

'Do you need anything else?' he asked.

'Nah, I'm sorted.'

She scampered to the charred beast, its scales still smoking, and thrust my sword into the back of its throat. It twitched.

Silas knelt by my side and drew a small Spirit portal, retrieving a roll of bandages. I winced when he pulled the crystal shard out of my calf. He started wrapping my leg, his eyes returning to their normal grey.

'It will need to be seen by a specialist, but this will staunch the bleeding for now.'

He stood up, offering me a hand.

I shook my head. I didn't want to take it, just yet. I was still trying to come to terms with what I'd just witnessed. I hadn't realised what the Weaver was truly capable of.

'Did you... was that... all your doing? You... commanded the lightning?!'

He flinched slightly and dropped his hand. He nodded, his ears dipping.

'It is not something I do very often,' he said, sadly.

I realised too late that I'd hurt his feelings. I raised my hand and mustered my best smile, even if my insides were still churning from it all.

His ears perked up and he pulled me to my feet.

I leant heavily on him as we began the long walk back to the castle. I tried to think of something to say.

'Thanks. And... sorry. It's all just been a bit of a shock.'

IV

I spun and cut the training dummy in two with a backhand slash. Satisfied, I planted the tip of my dragonbone sword in the ground and stood in the courtyard, panting for a moment to catch my breath. I didn't think I'd get tired that quick.

I'd spent the last five days resting, as the local healers instructed, but I was sure the cleric's blessing had sped up the process; the stitches on my calf looked ready to come out as the cut was healing so nicely. It barely stung when I walked. I was actually quite proud of it; I'd have the most impressive scar and a hell of a tale to go with it.

And if anyone dared to doubt me, I had the trophy to prove it. Rua and Silas were entitled to the spoils of course, but they made sure I got to keep the crystal shard that was in my leg. Elder Dragons were the only ones who had such growths, so no one could argue where it came from. It would look great in the middle of my torque.

Buidhe tossed his head and neighed over his stable door.

I waved my sword at him.

'Oh, shush, you! It took us three days to catch you, you reprobate! After all that running around, you can wait and all.'

I heard a familiar peal of laughter as Rua stepped out from behind a pillar.

'Look who's talking, Teagan. He's just as restless as you. Y'know, when the healers said to give it five days, it was a minimum recommendation...'

'I'm fine! It's not such a big deal—'

'Hey. It was a big deal. You could've died out there.'

I tried not to sulk. I didn't want to hear all of this from Rua, I'd had enough of it from Mum. She was furious, of course. She didn't have to be. She knew I was going after that drake, so why didn't she call me out on it instead of sending Rua and Silas after me? She must've thought that I could handle it.

To be fair, she didn't anticipate the Elder Dragon joining in. Maybe it wasn't me she was mad at. Maybe she was more angry with herself, for letting me go out at all.

'I know. But I didn't, okay? And it wasn't really my fault.'

'Nobody said it was.'

'Then can I just get back in the field, already? I'm not one to shirk my duties.'

She eyed me for a few moments, then nodded.

'Alright. Pass me that training sword. You grab one too.'

I went to the weapons rack and stowed my dragonbone sword, swapping it for one with a blunted edge. I pulled out another one and threw it to her.

She caught it, whirling it around her wrist.

'You last two minutes with me, I'll deem you fit to fight. Deal?'

'Deal.'

We squared off against each other, circling with swords in hand. I waited until she made a move, lunging towards my chest. I parried and side-stepped, running my blade up hers to slash at her head. She ducked and swung low; I jumped back, out of range. She stood up and cocked her head.

'Y'know, I didn't get much of chance to tell you at the time, but you fought really well against that drake on your own.'

I smiled at her compliment.

'Thanks! I was making an effort to be careful; I needed to learn how it moved.'

Now I tried to attack, feinting right, then left, before coming in with a low slash. She tracked my movements, her blade flicking from side to side before she leapt over my sword and behind me. I guessed she would jump high, so I kept up my momentum, spinning until I faced the other way. I kicked off the ground to hurtle into her path with a backhand strike. She angled her blade low to block her legs. My blade hit hers with full force before she reached the ground, sweeping her sideways. She landed on her feet, but had to steady herself by touching her hilt to the ground.

She grinned.

'Very good. You're a quick learner. I knew I didn't have anything to worry about. Silas, on the other hand, was like a mother hen. Kept on telling me to jump in.'

I rushed at her with a lunge to her torso. She parried and countered low; I parried that and countered high. She blocked my downward strike and held fast, locking her hilt into mine as I continued to bear down on her with my weight.

'What did he have to worry about?' I asked through gritted teeth. 'He could've taken out that drake with a single lightning bolt, if he so chose?'

Her eyes narrowed.

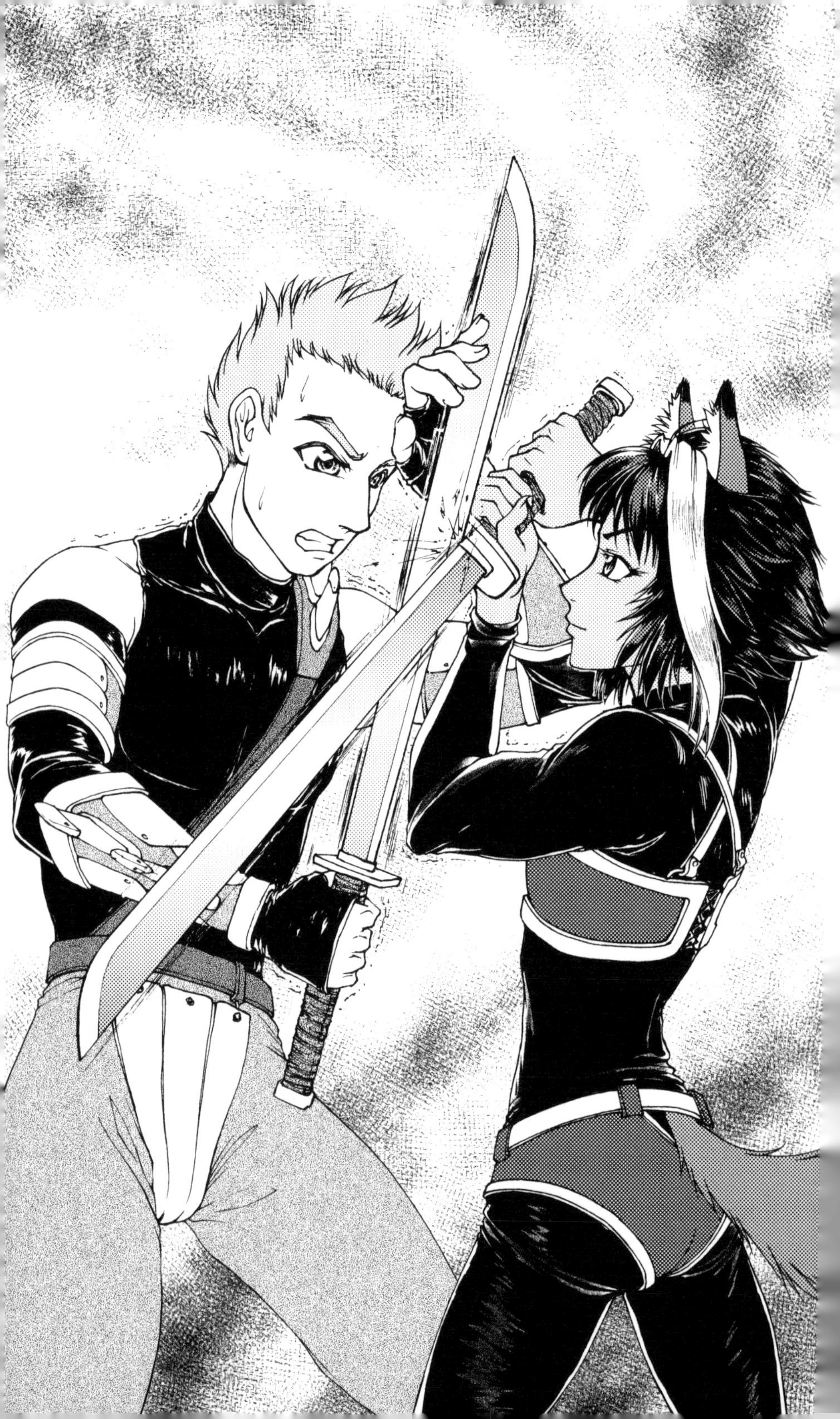

'Silas would never use lightning in front of others unless he had absolutely no choice. Or have you forgotten how you felt after you saw him use it for the first time?'

She surged upwards, flinging me back. Then she leapt towards me, her blade flashing. I could barely keep up with her assault; I was reduced to blocking to the left, then to the right, desperately trying to sneak in a slash here and there. Even when I retreated, she was right there, pushing me to the limit. Then I dropped down and swiped at her feet. She somersaulted back and I swiped low again, trying to time it with her landing so she couldn't avoid it. She surprised me by landing on my blade with her own, pulling me down to the floor with her weight. Continuing to flip backwards, she stood on our swords, pinning them to the floor and aimed her foot at my chest, kicking me back across the courtyard.

I tried to scrabble to my feet but froze when she appeared in front of me, both blades aimed at my throat.

'Two minutes and ten seconds. You pass.'

I breathed a sigh of relief.

She tucked the swords under one arm and helped me up from the floor.

'Besides,' she said, carrying on her earlier thread. 'It's a helluva spell to set up. There was no way he could cast it uninterrupted whilst the dragon was in close range. He would've been vulnerable the whole time. Actually, I'd've been angry if he'd tried; even I can't guarantee his safety against an Elder Dragon for that long.'

'Even if he did it to save you?'

'Especially if he did it to save me. Others, I'd understand, but me – I don't need saving. I think he's seen that now, however hard it is for him to bear it.'

She thrust the training swords into the weapons rack and walked with me along the path down to the Loch.

The pair were having the day off and because it was warm, Silas suggested a picnic by the shore, seeing as the hamper-hungry drake was no more.

'I waited so long for Ciel to deliver him to me,' she mused. 'Now that I finally have him, I'm... terrified of losing him. At times, I don't want to let him out of my sight.'

I stayed quiet. It was rare for her to show fear. Rarer still for her to admit it.

'And yet...' she continued. 'Coddling him would be selfish. He's the Weaver. He's faced the Dark Goddess herself, twice, and escaped with barely a scratch. If he can't help me save the world, who can?'

The waters of the Loch sparkled in the afternoon sun. A little distance away on the grassy hillside, a gingham blanket was spread with plates already laid out, wrapped parcels of food on top of the picnic basket.

Silas appeared to be napping; he was flat on his back, hands behind his head as a cushion, with a book spread open over his face to shade his eyes.

Rua pointed at him, barely keeping her face straight.

'Behold, Teagan, the most powerful mage in existence!'

We broke down in hoots of laughter.

He stirred then, pulling his book from his face to look at us. He nodded at me before rolling onto his side and propping himself up on his elbow. Now smiling at Rua, he beckoned her over with his hand.

She giggled. I'd never seen her act so giddy before.

'You really love him, don't you?' I thought out loud.

She pricked her ears at me and grinned.

'Yes, I do.'

As she bounded over to him I realised she didn't need another warrior or battle mage. She needed someone who was both like her, and unlike her. Someone who understood what it was like to be terrifyingly powerful. Most importantly, someone who would comfort her, no matter what she put him through. That was one hell of a lifelong mission, but he was definitely the right man for the job.

I shook my head, remembering what I said in the carriage on the way up here. I had to admit I was wrong about him after all.

Ciel's sake, Niamh managed to win this argument without even being around.

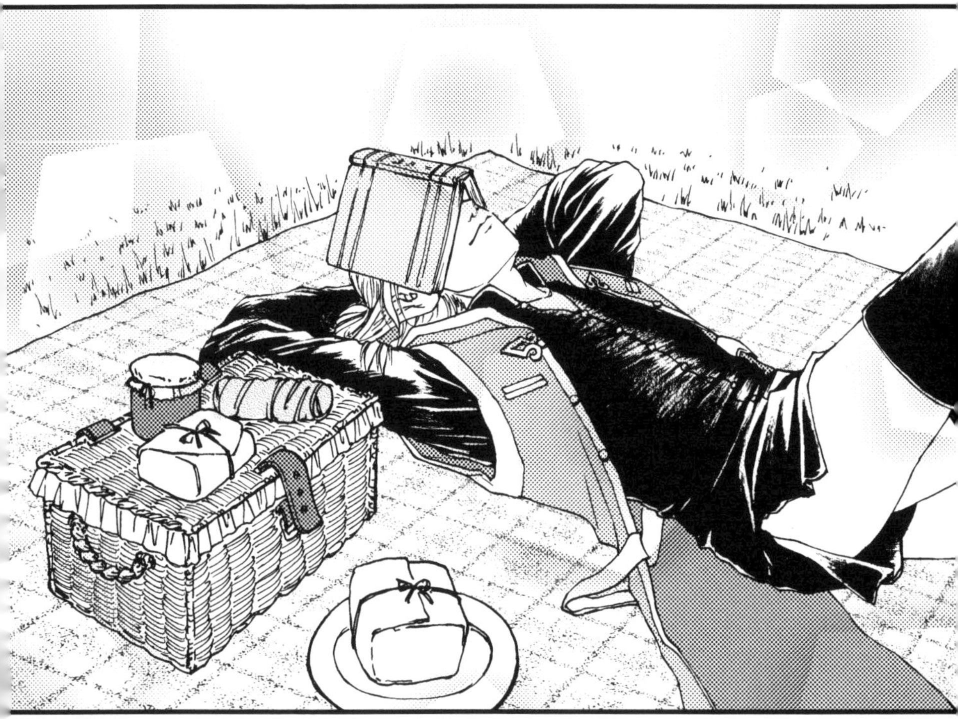

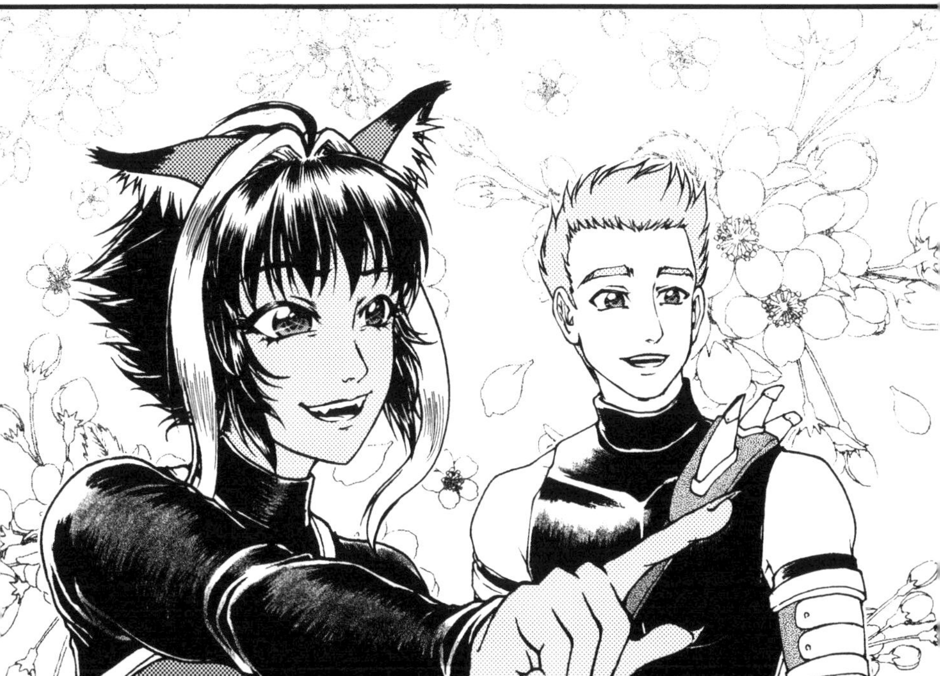

~Part Two~

Dagger Diplomacy

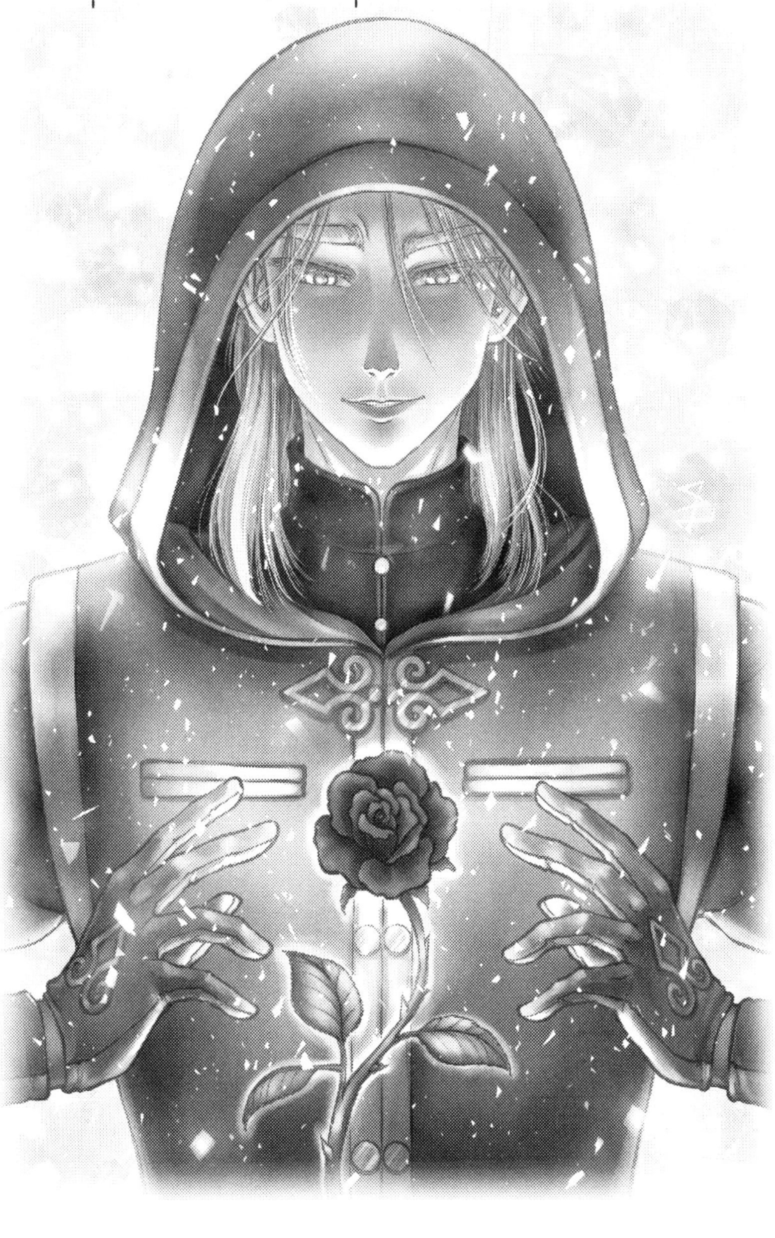

I

'Och, laddie, I was nae but a wee bairn when I las' saw this spell wi me ane een!'

Silas couldn't help raising his eyebrows, but otherwise tried not to show his utter lack of comprehension on his face.

Rua leant over to whisper into his ear.

'She was very young when she last saw this spell cast with her own eyes.'

'Oh, were you, madam?' he said, loudly. 'Fascinating!'

As the old crone nodded happily and carried on searching through her drawers, his voice dropped to a whisper.

'How can you even tell what she saying?' he confided to Rua. 'It is almost like an entirely different language!'

'It pretty much is, and it changes loads from island to island; I'm struggling myself!'

The cottage shuddered slightly as the icy cold wind blew over the thatched roof. He shivered in response, even though the flames danced merrily in the nearby stove. He had not travelled to such a remote place before; although he was no stranger to cold winters, he was finding it a little difficult adjusting to the savage sea storms that buffeted the tiny villages dotted in and about The Claws; the northernmost islands off the main isle of Eira.

After spending a few weeks at the Eiran royal family's holiday home in the Highlands, Silas was keen to pick up his PhD research; looking for rare and ancient magic spells to add to his grimoire and to the library of the Lyceum Arcanus in Fleurys. Based on what the gamekeepers of Bàrrathair Castle told them, they decided to take a short trip north to The Claws by rowing boat. The islands were sparsely inhabited, but its locals were very friendly and welcoming; they loved visitors of any kind, particularly if they had come on the royal family's recommendation. Queen Éilís was from the line of Fiag'Arachs, a Duchy of the Highlands, so there was fierce loyalty in these parts.

Their latest host was Magus Mairi, a little old lady who had long since retired from working on the ferries and passenger ships along the east coast.

'I didnae ken it wis thare!' the old woman exclaimed, as she pulled a scroll from the back of a cupboard and dropped it in Silas's lap.

'Thank you,' he said, smiling at her, as he unrolled it carefully.

His heart fluttered with excitement; this was definitely a spell pattern he had never seen before. In fact, it was in a totally unique form of notation. It almost looked like one laid over another, with some sections integrated like two pieces of a jigsaw puzzle that joined together. He traced over the curling florets of the Earth pattern in yellow ink with his fingers, then did the same for the swirling arrows of Water tucked into the gaps in blue. It was a spell that needed both Earth and Water threads to be simultaneously cast and woven together to make plants grow.

He could barely contain himself; he was already finding an excuse to head outside where no one could see him so that he could try it out. Of course, he didn't want anyone here to know that he could use more than one element at once.

Picking up his grimoire, he spread it open, flicking through it until he found a blank page. He spread the scroll out on the dining table, weighing the edges down with some paperweights. Then he brought out his quill and ink bottle and started copying the patterns into his grimoire.

The old crone sighed.

'Och ay, if anely ye war an Earth Master, we could've had a go!'

Silas caught one bit of that; he suspected this could lead somewhere.

'Um, could you elaborate, madam?'

'A'm a Watter Mistress. An the fek o' mages in The Claws're Watter or Air. Earth mages're seendle seen hereaboots.'

He threw a desperate look at Rua.

She rolled her eyes at him.

'So Mairi, is that why it's been so long since you last saw this spell being used?' she asked the old woman. 'You're a Water Mistress, but you so seldom come across Earth mages here, you've not been able to cast the spell? Well–'

'It just so happens that I am an Earth Master!' Silas interjected.

Well, technically he was. As the Weaver, he was a Master of all the elements, but to keep up the appearance of a normal mage when dealing with strangers, he would just pick one and stick to it.

Mairi's eyes lit up and she clapped her hands.

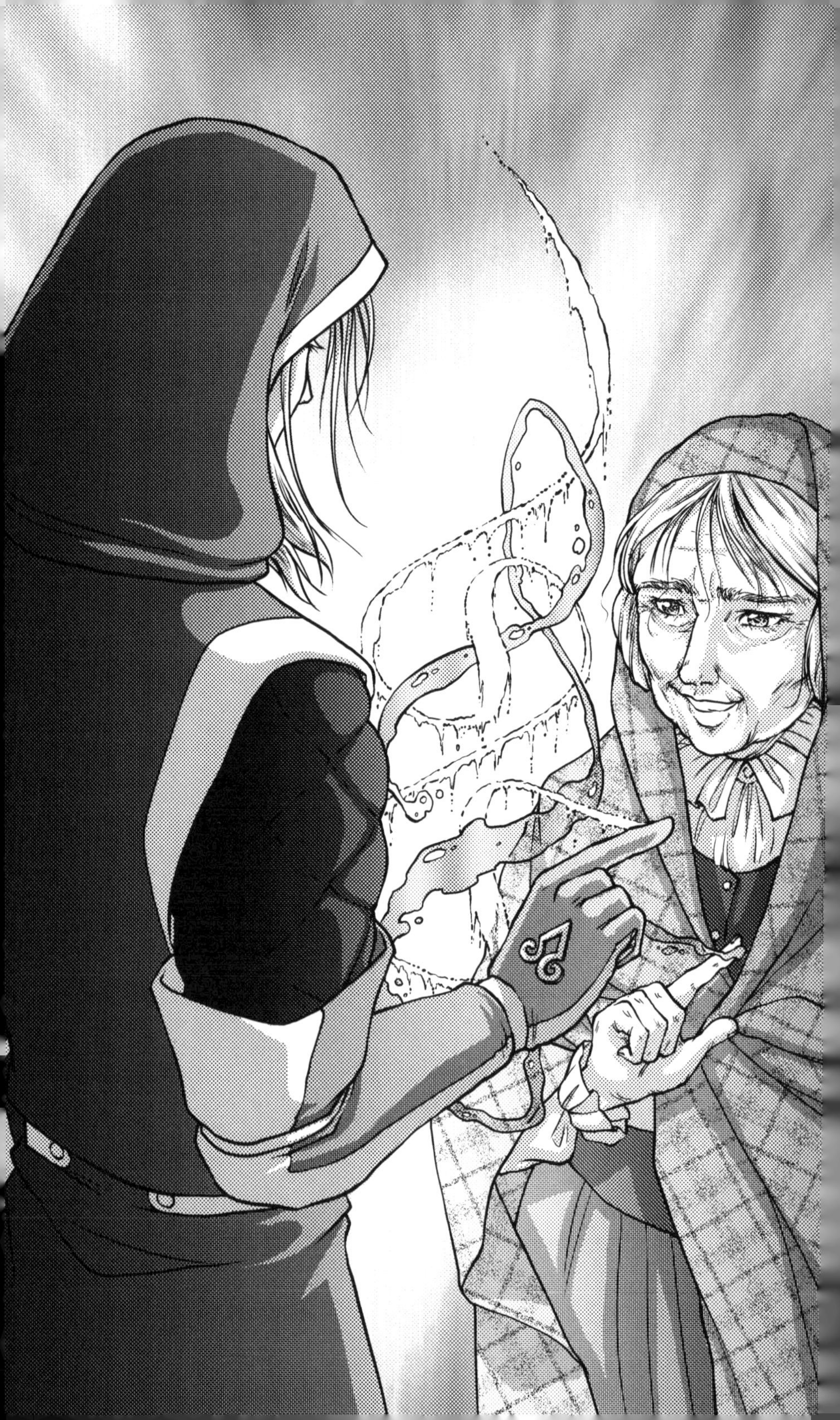

'Och, ye cannie lad! Come awa wi me; A'v a buckie-breer ootby.'

She got up to wrap a heavy shawl around her shoulders and Rua got up as well, grabbing her hooded cloak.

Silas blinked, still unsure about what was going on.

Rua patted him on the shoulder.

'Come on, you clever boy. We're following her; there's a briar rose outside.'

He hurriedly got up and pulled on his extra long gloves over the padded sleeves of his winter doublet. As they opened the door and a few snowflakes blew in, he flinched and hurriedly belted up his robe, pulling his hood up over his ears.

They trudged through the snow. The ice crystals, dusted on top on each snowdrift by the winds, were sparkling softly in the hazy mid-morning sunlight. They walked around to the back of the cottage where he could see various shrubs covered in clumps of snow.

'Thare!' Mairi said, pointing to one of the bushes.

She brushed the snow off it. Its bare branches were dark against the white ground. She looked at him, her eyes now glowing with a bright blue light.

'A'm redd as ye! G'on!'

Silas hoped that meant that she wanted him to start.

He concentrated for a moment, switching his eyes into the Earth spectrum. Plenty of yellow threads around for him to weave with. He extended a hand and directed the threads into his index finger. Then he started drawing in the air, the yellow threads transforming into grains of sand trailing his finger as he recreated the pattern he had seen on the scroll. He spoke softly.

'*Terra et solum...*'

Earth and soil...

Mairi drew her half of the pattern in floating rivulets of water, timing it just a few seconds after he started so that she could overlap some of his lines with hers. She spoke in the Ancient tongue as well.

'*Aqua...*'

Water...

She looked at him for timing; he nodded.

They both spoke in unison and pointed to the bare rose bush.

'*Enutri!*'

Nourish!

The interlocked pattern in yellow and blue shot towards the shrub, disappearing in a dusty splash as it hit the branches. Silas, with only his Earth spectrum in place, could see the yellow threads building beneath the rose bush in puffs and waves, shaped similarly to the curly florets he drew. He wished he could also layer his Water spectrum on top in order to see the actions of the blue threads, but he didn't want to do so in front of Mairi and risk frightening her.

As the trio watched in awe, the branches shivered as elemental energy pulsed through them from root to tip. They started growing new leaves, soon unfurling in rows of dark green. Then flower buds sprung up, getting larger and larger until they, too, unwrapped themselves and burst into scarlet red roses.

Rua clapped her hands, laughing joyfully at the red roses blooming in the snow.

Silas smiled; he loved nothing more than making her happy.

'I think that bush has had enough now, yes?' he suggested to Mairi.

The old woman nodded; they dismissed their threads and sight spectra. Beaming with delight, she went over to her newly-bloomed roses.

'Ye'v made an auld-dame verra contentit. Thank ye! Here, hae't.'

She picked a bloom out of the bush and handed it to him. He didn't understand the words, but he understood the gesture and gratefully accepted.

She rubbed at her shoulders and shivered.

'Och, it's a wee bit cauld oot! Haste ye back, eh?'

She started making her way back to the door of the cottage, leaving Silas and Rua behind. The wind had died down completely and the sea mist was burning off as the sun reached its zenith. The bright sunlight now shone down, making the entire landscape look as if it was showered with diamonds.

Standing in the glittering snow, Rua looked adorable; her wide, golden eyes matching the rich, brassy tones of the blonde streaks in her garnet red hair falling across her cheeky face. The hood of her short, woollen cape had fallen back just enough to reveal the black tips of her ears, pricked forward. Her irresistible russet tail was fluffed up to fullest for warmth.

He walked up to her and bowed, presenting her with the rose.

'A red rose for my red-haired love.'

Her eyes went wide and she blushed. She smiled shyly and took it, pushing it through a buttonhole in her cloak. She threw her arms around his neck and he bent down to give her a kiss. Her nose felt cold against his cheek, but her lips were warm.

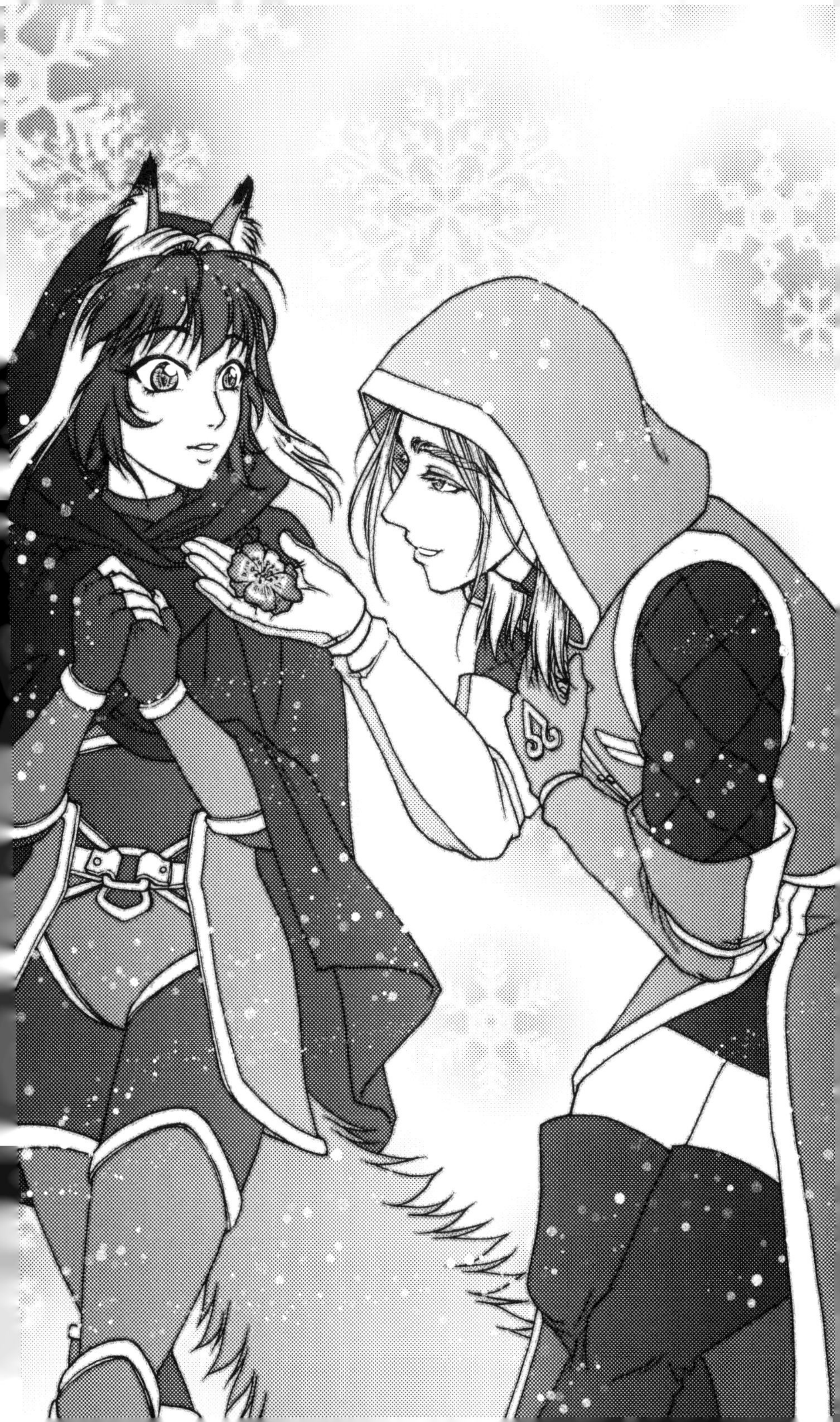

When she pulled back, he noticed her frown out to sea. He followed her gaze.

There was a boat approaching; the small craft bobbed above the choppy waves, three men rowing it to shore as the fourth, a Queen's Guard, collapsed the square sail.

'What's a soldier doing on that yoal boat?' Rua puzzled.

She scampered across the snow, treading lightly over the drifts to make her way down to the shore. The snow gave way to the tide line and she dashed onto the beach, waving. The soldier hailed them back.

'Champion! Magus!' he called, jumping off the boat and saluting. 'Her Majesty has sent me to retrieve you at once! You are to return to Dúnragnhildt Palace at your nearest convenience. Prince Owyn will escort you from Bàrrathair Castle.'

Rua nodded at him.

'Understood, soldier. We'll be ready in an hour. Please, have yourself and your oarsmen come to the cottage; I'm sure Magus Mairi will be happy to offer some tea.'

He saluted and turned to help pull the boat up onto the shore.

Rua started walking back to the cottage and Silas fell in line with her.

'What do you suppose this is all about?' he asked her in a low voice.

'It's not a casual request. Éilís wouldn't do this to me unless it was a matter of national importance. I can only hope it's not another terrorist threat... but the soldier would've said something if that was the case. We'll have to wait and see.'

They gathered their belongings and bid a protracted farewell to the old lady after accepting a tin of shortbread fingers. They soon rowed out of the bay with speed; the oarsmen refreshed by mugs of Mairi's strong tea. After an hour, they could see the main isle. As they got closer, the tall, imposing figure of Prince Owyn was standing on the jetty with several Dragoon knights behind him.

The oarsmen threw the securing lines onto the jetty, bringing the yoal in close. They motioned at Silas for him to disembark first. Owyn came to the side, bending down and offering his hand. With him pulling up and Rua boosting from below, Silas sighed with relief when he was finally on solid ground.

'Owyn, what's going on?' Rua asked, as she hopped onto the jetty.

The Prince Consort was a man of few words; his answer was straight to the point.

'The Emperor of the Palatinate died two days ago. His funeral and the coronation of House Aristarchus's Crown Princess Arafel will take place in ten days' time.'

II

As the soldiers bustled around him, readying their horses to leave, all Silas could think about was Arafel. His childhood friend had been dreading this moment all of her life. For it to come so soon was totally unexpected. The shock on his face must have been apparent as Rua touched his arm with a look of concern.

'I am fine,' he reassured her. 'But I must write to Arafel—'

'Of course, love. You do that; it'll be a few more minutes anyway.'

He hurriedly drew a Spirit portal to his magus inbox and retrieved his letter set. Kneeling on the wooden boards of the jetty, he scribbled a note.

My dearest Arafel, I have just heard the news. Are you alright? Yours always ~S

He folded it up, touched his fingertip, threaded with Spirit, to his lips.

'Arafel,' he whispered.

Now imbued with intent, his finger traced the folded edge of the letter and sealed it with Spirit. He picked up another Spirit thread and concentrated as he Harmonised it to match Arafel's Spirit Protocol. The thread shimmered and the glow around its edges altered very slightly; its ripples and pulses now different to his own natural signature. He drew another Spirit portal with this altered thread and accessed Arafel's inbox, dropping his letter inside.

The horses were ready by the time he had finished. As carriages were useless in the mountainous terrain they rode on horseback, picking their way carefully through the snow and rocks. Silas felt insignificantly small amongst the snow-dusted black crags rising high above acres of pine forest, all mirrored in the sparkling waters of the Lochs in the valleys below. But he found it difficult to enjoy the view; if he wasn't worrying over Arafel, he was trying to quell his panic whenever his horse veered close to the steep drops at the edge of the path.

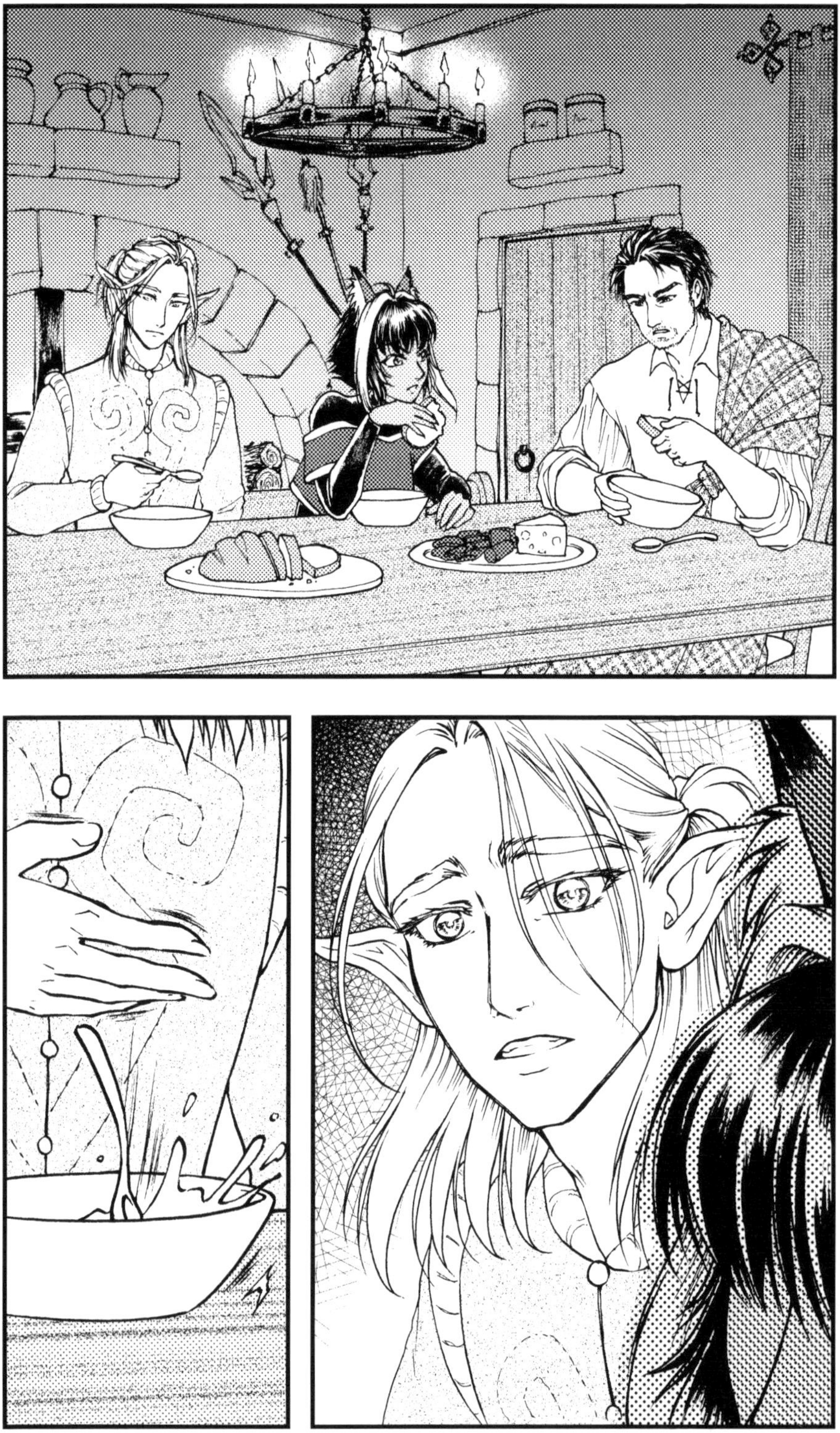

Nightfall came quickly in the Highlands during the winter, just a few hours into the afternoon. They were only a few degrees north of Vertcielle, but Silas was still surprised by how much difference it made to the length of a day. Thankfully, they made it safely down off the steep crags and into the gentle slopes of the muirs. The lights of Bàrrathair Castle beckoned in the distance.

Finally, they rode into the stables. As the grooms took their horses, Silas and Rua followed Owyn into the front hall.

'Go, wash up. We will talk at dinner,' the prince said, in his usual dour way.

He gave them a curt bow and walked up the staircase, disappearing from sight.

Silas looked to Rua for guidance.

She harrumphed and went up the stairs, heading into the guest wing. She stopped a passing housemaid and shyly asked for some hot water for their room. She squirmed when the maid curtseyed profusely and ran off. He tried hard not to chuckle.

It was such a strange and cute quirk of hers. She had no trouble at all commanding and disciplining entire armies, even barking orders at members of royalty, but she struggled when dealing with servants or civilians who made a fuss over her.

A quick splash and scrub and they were soon back downstairs at the dining table, waiting for Owyn. As soon as he sat down, the servants brought through some cold cuts, bread and soup.

Rua did her best to coax some answers out of Owyn whilst they ate.

'So Teagan and Niamh have already gone back to Albanon with Éilís?'

'Mmm.'

'I suppose she'll need all hands on deck to deal with looking after the country whilst you both are away.'

'Mmm.'

'Am I supposed to help look after affairs in Albanon too?'

'No. You are coming with us.'

Silas dropped his spoon. She was going to Drachenheim? Whatever for?

Rua frowned.

'I've never accompanied a queen to a Palatinate coronation before. Why now?'

'Éilís has received intelligence that your presence may be necessary.'

Silas's heart thumped harder in his chest. If Rua was needed, then–

'Is the Queen in danger? What... what about Arafel?!' he exclaimed.

'Possibly.'

Rua scrunched up her forehead again and took a large bite of ham, chewing for a minute before swallowing. She kept her voice level.

'Logistics, Owyn. Tell me the plan.'

'We will travel to Albanon, whereupon we will sail to Vertcielle. Éilís has received an invitation from King Xavier IV to use the Great Gates of Fleurys to transfer through to Drachenheim to speed up travel. We will be in Drachenheim within a week.'

Silas tried not to choke on his soup. The last time he had been through the Great Gates was when he and his family fled Drachenheim after his abilities were discovered. He would follow Rua to the depths of Hell if she needed him, but he wasn't expecting to return and face his own demons so soon.

They finished their meal promptly; appetites vanished. After informing them of their early start in the morning, Owyn bid them goodnight and strode off, leaving them to return to their room in silence.

As they readied themselves for bed, Silas checked his magus inbox. Arafel had replied. He pulled out her letter, unfolding it as soon as the Spirit seal dissipated.

I'm scared. I know it's hard for you, but please, will you come?

His heart lurched. For her to admit her fear so readily; she must have been in a state. And she, of all people, knew how much he wanted to avoid returning to Drachenheim. But of course, he would.

He looked at Rua, her face grave with concern.

There was more than one person who needed him there.

***

In the morning, breakfast was without ceremony; their appetites still muted by anxiety. The servants loaded their carriage with the bare minimum of supplies; they had to get to Albanon as soon as possible, changing horses at every stop.

Rua couldn't prise anything further out of Owyn. He remained silent throughout much of the journey. She used the time to sleep and suggested that Silas do the same.

He couldn't. He stayed in constant contact with Arafel, firing off notes to her, checking his magus inbox every time they changed horses. The knot in his chest got tighter with every reply he received.

Silas
n scared. I know it's
ard for you but please.
Will you come?

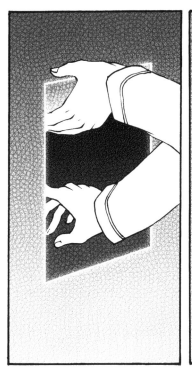

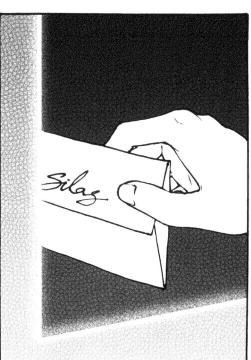

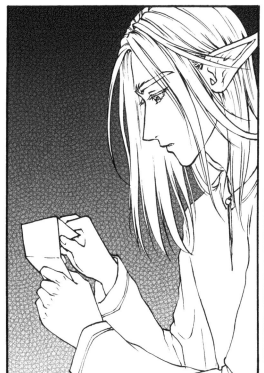

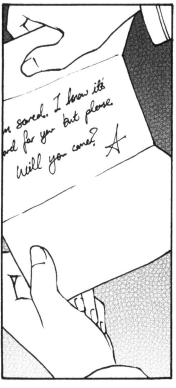

Arafel had been in her usual lessons at the Lyceum Arcanus, when she was hastily brought to Maestra Véronique's office to be told the news of her grandfather's passing. Within hours, she was packed up and escorted by Imperial Knights of the Palatinate through the Great Gates to Drachenheim. It was a lonely and frightening upheaval for the Crown Princess. She had little family left in Drachenheim; most of them were assassinated ten years ago.

The barrage of notes made him feel so helpless; he was already travelling as fast as he could. All he could do was to keep writing back to her.

Overnight, the coachmen took it in turns to catch up with sleep in shifts as they went through each stage at a blistering pace and by mid-afternoon on the following day, the countryside gradually gave way to the familiar sights and sounds of the Eiran capital. They drove past Liadán's Leap as the sun set early over the river Tamesis, bathing the bustling city in a rosy twilight glow. Everyone was still going about their daily business, seemingly unaware of the impending coronation and its ramifications.

The clatter of their horses' hooves echoed violently as they drove through the gatehouse tunnel of Dúnragnhildt Palace. When they pulled up at the entrance steps, Owyn jumped out of the carriage and waved for them to follow, striding off without a second glance. They wound their way through the corridors and into Éilís's private sitting room.

The Eiran Queen placed down her mug of tea and stood up to greet them.

'Well met, Rua, Silas,' she said, clasping their forearms in turn.

She sat back down and gestured to the settee. They took their seats as Owyn went to stand by her side, touching her shoulder briefly before settling his hands behind his back. She gave them a conciliatory smile.

'Sorry for hurrying you two down here. State funerals are always a rush job, but when the Palatinate is involved, it takes on a whole new level of urgency, especially given the circumstances.'

Rua shrugged.

'I understand the urgency of the funeral; as all of us in Ciel's Cradle know, the volcano beneath Drachenheim must recognise its new master within a fortnight, lest it rampages out of control. But why involve us? I haven't had to accompany any past queens to this coronation before.'

'Even I can't explain very much at this point. King Xavier IV forwarded several reports from his top advisor. From her spies in the Palatinate, Chancellor Tempête suspects foul play around the Emperor's death. And as part of the Eiran-Vertciellen military exchange program, we've agreed to share all intelligence whenever each other's countries may be affected. As we are all attending the coronation, this is most certainly the case.'

Silas's ears twitched.

'The King's advisor?' he asked. 'You mean, Maestra Véronique?'

Éilís raised an eyebrow.

'Your PhD supervisor is one helluva woman, Silas. I'm glad she's on our side.'

She picked up her mug and drained her tea in one go.

'Now, I have to head to the entrance to keep an eye out for my entourage – a fair few nobles and officers squabbled over who could come on this trip, and some have come a long way. None of them are to know about our suspicions, so keep your smiles on and pretend you're just as eager to attend the coronation. I'm not gonna force you to have dinner with them, but we'll all be sharing the clipper to Port Profond before dawn.'

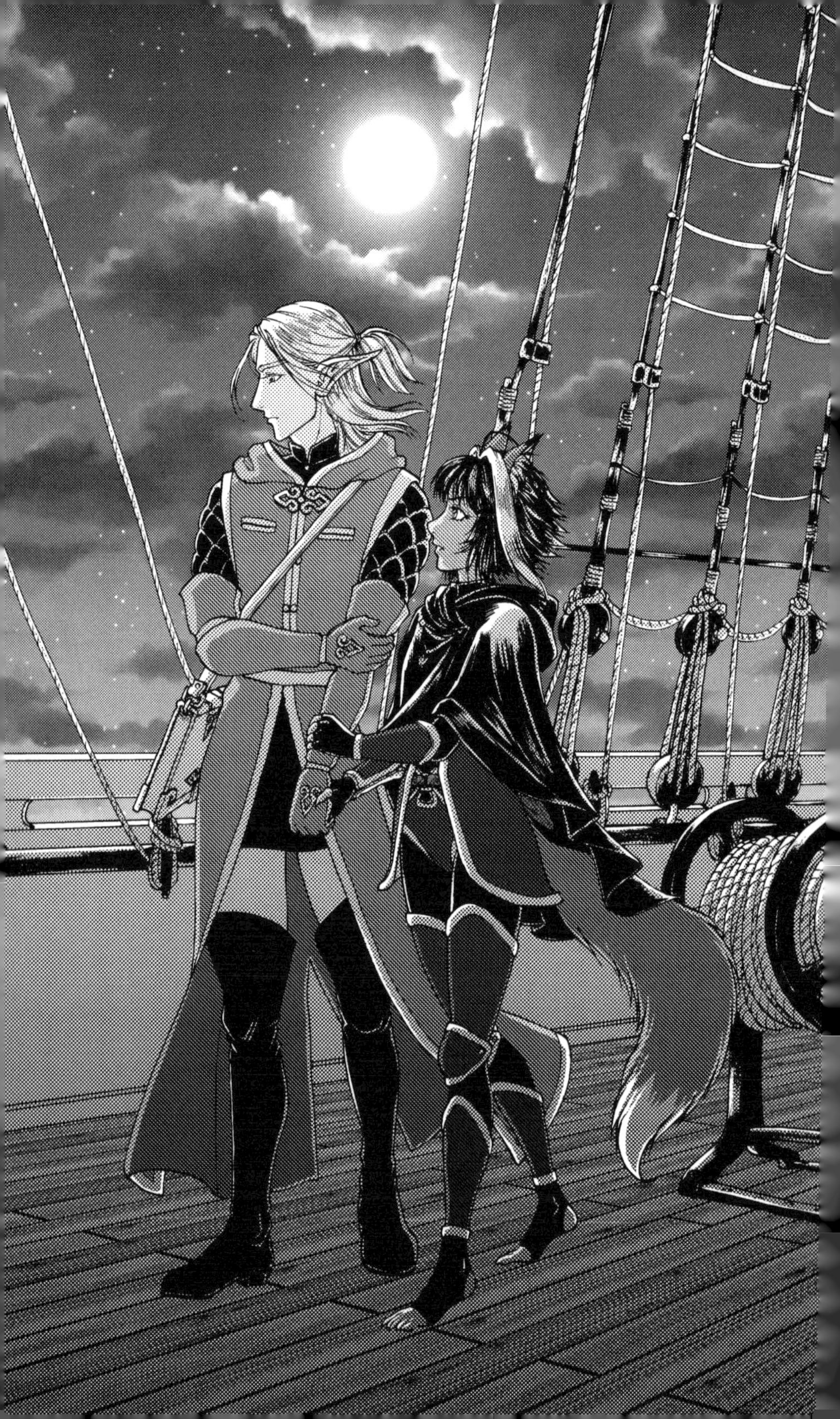

III

It had been three days since Silas left The Claws on a tiny boat. But despite the need to hurry, it still felt too soon for him to be on the waters again. He shivered as he stood at the stern of their clipper ship as it was tugged out of the Southbank Docks, keeping his eyes occupied on the skies, still dark with stars. The Tamesis was much calmer than The Pinch was likely to be, but he wasn't going to take any chances.

He felt Rua's hand over his.

'How're ya feelin', love?' she asked.

'Not nauseous... yet. And you?'

She kept smiling, but she twiddled her ears as she looked at the lightening clouds.

'Cagey. Something's up. Something big. I... just know.'

He swallowed, trying to quell his unease.

'Me too. Like Ciel's Cradle is on the edge of a precipice and we might fall.'

'Hey. Even if it did, we'd pick it up and set it right. You and I... Ciel made us for times like this.'

She squeezed his hand.

She was right, of course. Rua would always succeed, no matter the cost to her. He couldn't begin to imagine the countless times she had been pivotal to the course of history. He hoped that he was strong enough to do the same.

The sky began to turn pink, then orange as they watched the impressive buildings on the banks of the river gradually give way to frost-covered fields dotted with sheep, round from their winter coats. The Tamesis branched south from the capital, bypassing the forests of Saint Leona and cutting a valley through the Dess Downs. The tugboats, powered by Water mages, kept up a surprisingly brisk pace; their early start added a few knots to their speed as the tide helped to carry them out. The Queen had commissioned several commercial tugs along the river to ensure consistent progress. They aimed to reach The Pinch before nightfall.

Silas passed the time by trying to eat little and often; Rua had thoughtfully provided him with some ginger biscuits and encouraged him to snack well before they reached the estuary.

He also set himself the task of memorising the various faces and names of those on board. As Rua went below deck to grab a hot toddy for herself, he leant back on the ship's rail and observed the Queen's retinue. Some, he had already met during the Silver Jubilee celebrations, but there were a few he had only been introduced to that morning.

The Queen conversed with the willowy Duchess of Camboricum, a well-loved philanthropist, over various charities to help children from poorer homes. The swarthy Duke of Blestium was enthusiastically recounting war stories to the politely-nodding Duke of Dubrae, whilst the elderly Duchess of Valentia, wrapped in furs, barely concealed her boredom. The Prince Consort was playing chess against Brigadier Sorcha, who was biting her lip with indecision as her king was checked. Colonel Lyr, General Aoife and Field Marshal Driskell were spectating and jovially offering strategic advice.

They all seem pleasant enough, he thought. *I hope they remain as such.*

By the late afternoon, the Tamesis began to broaden out. The tugs released the ship to return to the capital. There was a flurry of activity as the crew took up their positions; ropes hissed as they were pulled through rings; all above him the sails unfurled at such speed that they sounded like whip cracks.

'You might be in luck,' Rua said, bounding over. 'The Captain says we'll be very nearly running with the wind, so it's full sails ahead, less time and less heeling.'

'Ciel be praised...' Silas sighed. 'That gives me a fighting chance, no?'

The crossing was far less choppy than he remembered; having the wind on their side made a huge difference to his comfort. Now that it was winter, any sea spray would have felt much worse. The sleek clipper was also far swifter than the ferry they had used from Vertcielle to Eira and barely two hours passed before they could see the shimmering lights of Port Profond.

They pulled into the harbour, furling sails to slow down. Eiran sailors threw their mooring lines, expertly caught and tied down by Vertciellen dockhands. As the passengers all lined up to disembark, Silas peered down the gangplank.

He was surprised to see his mentor, Véronique Tempête, waiting for them. She stood eerily still in the lamplight, her long, blonde hair and emerald robes rippling slowly; far slower than everyone else's clothes being buffeted by the winds. Her eyes were faintly glowing green; she was controlling the air around her for comfort, as usual.

She curtsied as Éilís approached her.

'Your Majesty,' she said, adjusting her glasses as she rose. 'We are most honoured to receive you. I am Chancellor Véronique Tempête. His Majesty King Xavier IV has requested that I personally escort you and your courtiers to the Palais des Étoiles.'

She gestured to the three ornate carriages behind her.

'They may be small, but they are swift. May I suggest that your Majesty, his Royal Highness the Prince Consort and the Weaver join me in the first one? And perhaps the Dagger may wish to ride alongside on horseback? That would provide maximum comfort for the Dukes, Duchesses and officers.'

That was awfully forward of her, Silas thought, frowning.

But Éilís smiled and nodded without missing a beat.

'Thank you, Chancellor, that sounds splendid. Come!' she called, waving to the others. 'Please, you four take this one and you four can get in that one. Rua, you don't mind, do you?'

The vixen stretched and grinned, making her way over to the saddled horse.

'Nah, I'd have preferred it anyway.'

Éilís climbed into the carriage and paused, throwing a look over her shoulder.

'Hurry up, Silas!'

He jumped and jogged over, trying not to falter under Véronique's disparaging gaze as she held the door open for him to clamber inside.

The Chancellor stepped in and closed the door, then rapped her knuckles on the underside of the roof. The carriage set off at a fast trot and Rua matched their speed on her horse.

'Good move, Véronique,' Éilís said softly. 'Now we can talk in private without offending my duchies. An Air Barrier would have been too obvious in a larger coach. And Rua, can you hear us fine?'

'Perfectly well,' she replied through the window. 'No need to raise your voices.'

Silas was humbled; Véronique had planned their seating arrangements meticulously. The Chancellor was always several steps ahead.

'Ma'am, I trust you have read my reports?' Véronique asked. 'I could not disclose all the details in writing for security reasons, but I will tell you what I know. The Emperor's death was truly unexpected. He was hale and hearty. He hosted a dinner party for Bashkendian merchant leaders at Schloss Drachen only last week; apparently delivered one of the finest speeches in living memory on trade and the world economy. Yet the official line is that the Emperor had died of old age, in his sleep. After all, there were no marks on his body, no obvious substances or smells, no disturbances or cries for help. But there are plenty of ways to kill someone quickly and silently without leaving a trace.'

The cool delivery of her last sentence was slightly unnerving.

She tucked a strand of hair behind her pointed ear and continued.

'The truth is that one of his valets has disappeared. The Imperial Knights are searching for him, but they cannot do this too publicly for fear of scandal. What particularly concerns me is that this valet had been in his employ for many years and was trusted by everyone. So... this was all part of a very long waiting game.'

'Arafel,' Silas found himself saying.

She glanced at him and nodded.

'What has always puzzled me over the last nine years is why there have been no further assassination attempts on the Crown Princess or on her two cousins. If this was simply a succession coup, surely dispatching the current heirs would achieve such aims and put them next in line? No, it is unlikely that the other Palatinate Houses are wanting to take over. So what has changed now?'

They sat in silence for a few moments. Then Owyn finally spoke.

'Time,' he grunted. 'They needed time.'

Véronique steepled her fingers against her lips.

'Yes... Arafel has just turned twenty one this year. This means she has the full right to ascend to the Imperial Throne as Empress. Again, if this was an issue about control, they would have attempted to force the succession sooner. A child Empress is mostly powerless, as all decisions would be signed off by her Regent. As it is now, the Emperor's death means there must be an immediate formal coronation...'

Rua ducked her head down to the window.

'Wait a sec, so if the Emperor had died, say, five years ago, the Palatinate would have appointed a Regent and there would have been a less formal handover of power; y'know, private rituals, rather than a full coronation ceremony?'

'Yes. She would have had to complete the ancient rites of succession with the volcano, but as a child, they would have been performed quietly with only close friends or family in attendance. Likewise, the appointment of a Regent would have been muted as well, certainly not an event that would be attended by rulers from around the world.'

'That's it, then,' Rua growled.

'The coronation itself must be significant,' Véronique agreed.

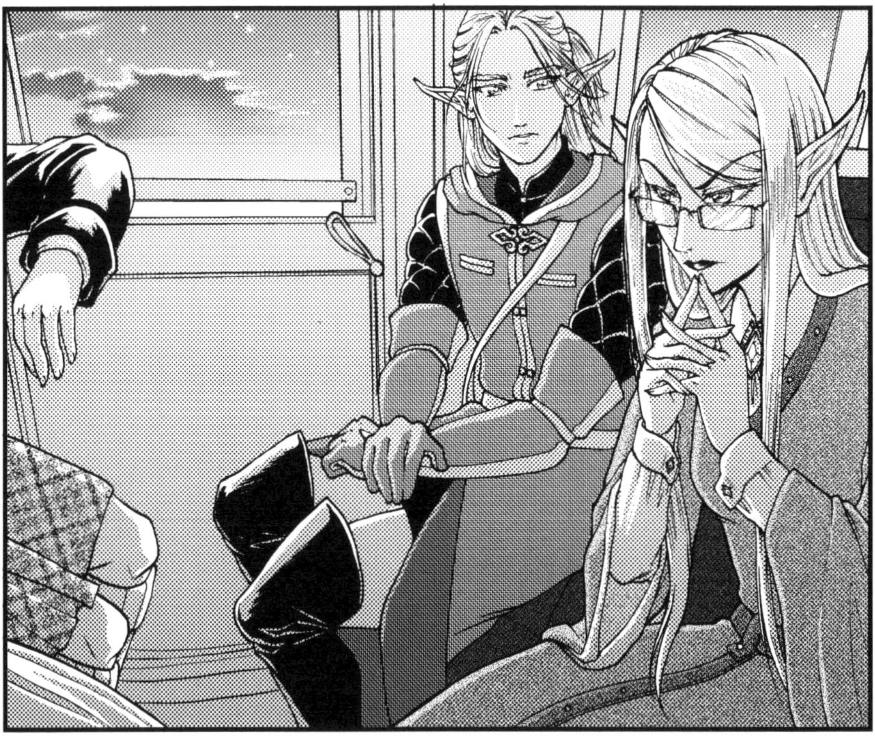
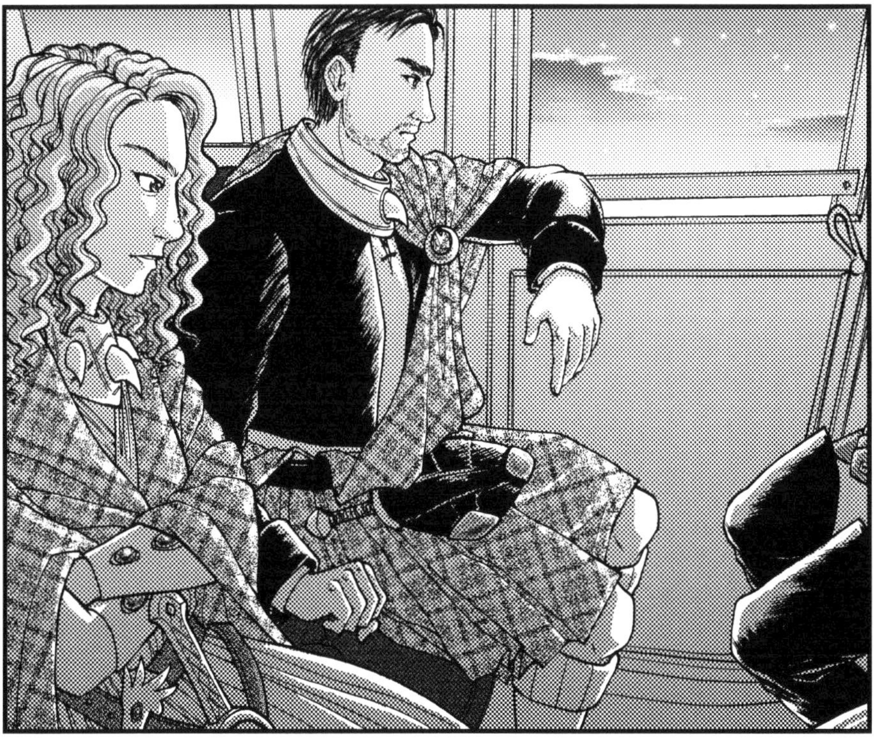

Éilís clenched her fist, enraged.

'My Silver Jubilee procession was very nearly the excuse for a bloodbath because of the way everyone had gathered to celebrate... Will these cowards ever think about the innocent lives they'll ruin just for politics?!'

Owyn placed his hand over her fist, trying to calm her down.

Véronique patiently regarded the Eiran Queen.

'Ma'am, I doubt the general public will be in danger, thankfully, as I believe relatively few civilians are invited to the actual events. If anyone was going to get killed, they would specifically be amongst the guests attending the ceremony. In other words; it may be one of us.'

IV

They stayed at the villas of various nobles en route to Fleurys, who were delighted to have the honour of hosting the Queen of Eira. Éilís played up to it; charming them with tales of dragon slaying, told in her strong Highland accent. Silas found that some of them treated him with fear; sadly, he couldn't avoid all the gossip that went around the Houses about the Weaver. But far worse was when a Lady – and on another night, a Lord – cornered him after dinner with more than talk in mind. He was always grateful when Rua conveniently appeared with some request from the Queen.

Three days in, they broke through the northern stretches of the forest of Châtaignon and skirted the west side of Fleurys. They drove down the wide avenues of the left bank of the Sancesse, the bare-branched trees reflected in the icy waters below. As the sunlight faded, the gilding on the street lamps gave way to the burning lamp lights. Silas knew this road well; it led right past his family home. Soon, all around them were beautifully manicured gardens behind ornate gold rails, embellished with sprays of stars. The winter snow made the box hedge mazes look like immaculate plasterwork with perfectly smooth tops and sides. The immense golden gates to the Palais des Étoiles opened, flanked by Chevaliers standing to attention. They circled around the enormous fountain, topped with pale carvings of beautiful maidens in flowing robes.

Their carriage came to a stop on the decorative tiles in front of the double doors of the palace, gold vine leaves trailing up the graceful columns on each side. Footmen sprang to attention, helping them out of the carriages and bowing as they backed away.

Véronique led them through the wide corridors, lavishly decorated in gilded mirrors, oil paintings and marble statues. Whilst he was no stranger to luxurious Vertciellen interiors, this was on a whole new level. Silas had only been in these ostentatious halls once before, as a young child, during an informal reception. Upon reflection, he preferred Dúnragnhildt Palace; its rustic furnishings felt more tangible and real.

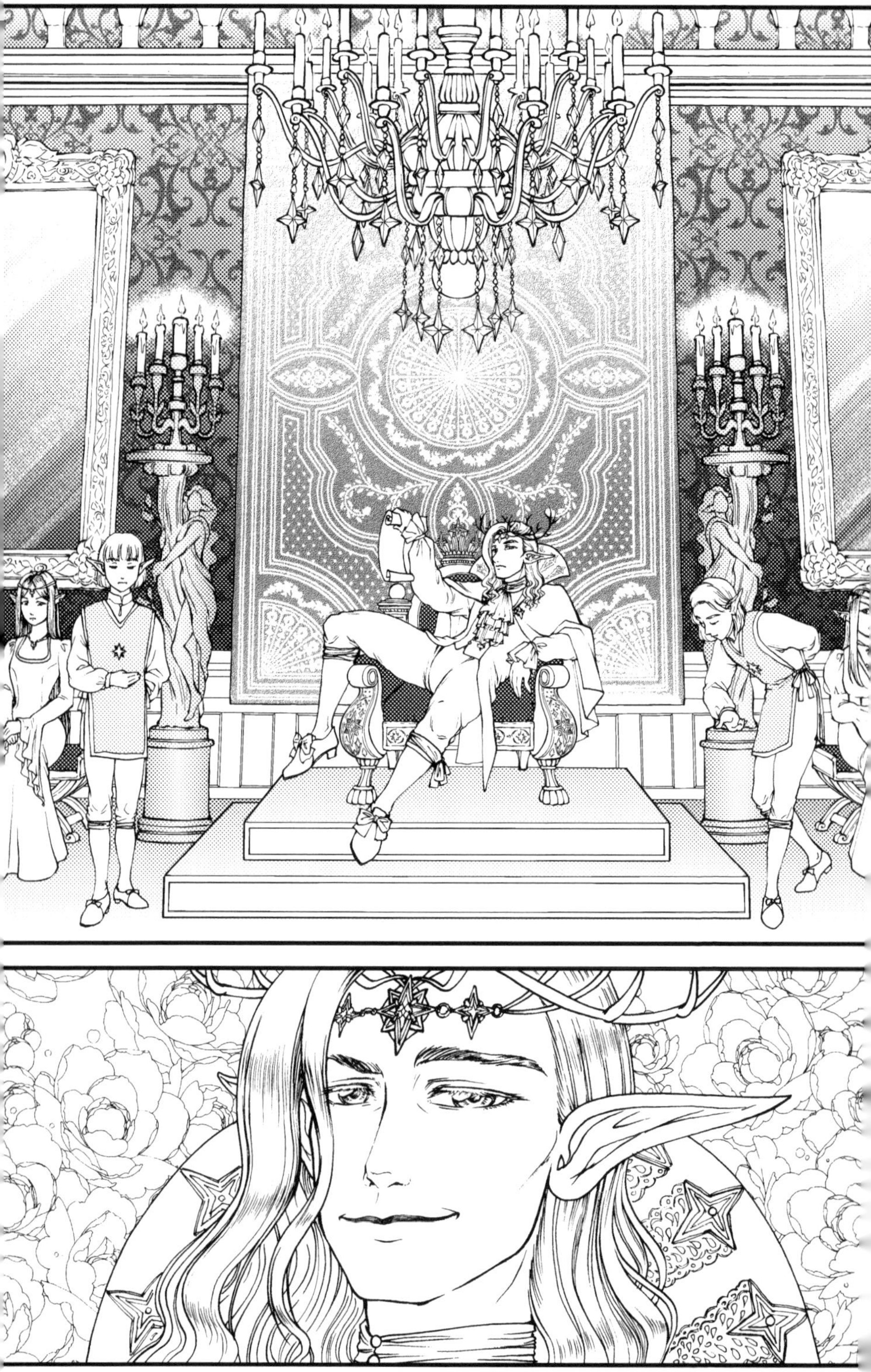

They came to another set of double doors, covered in gold leaf. The Chevaliers clicked their heels and held them open. Three enormous chandeliers, dripping with precious stones, hung from the painted ceiling, awash with brilliant stars. Embedded crystals mapped out the constellations with beasts outlined in gold. This twinkling night sky was framed by gilded columns, interspersed with mirrors on red damask walls, their floral patterns giving off a lustrous sheen as floor-standing candelabras added even more light to the extravagant room.

Lounging on the red velvet cushions of his golden throne, encrusted with rubies and emeralds, was the most beautiful man Silas had ever seen.

In his early hundreds, he was an Elf in his prime, his perfectly chiselled features rivalling the most celebrated sculptures in Vertcielle. His silvery-blond hair fell in waves over his broad shoulders, casually swept over parts of his crown; slivers of gold rising up like antlers from a trio of stars on his forehead, set with sparkling diamonds. His large, gold-embroidered collar framed him in a halo of lace comets.

L'Elfe Roi-Étoiles. The Elven Star King; Xavier IV.

His turquoise eyes lazily dragged themselves away from the scroll he was reading to fall upon his newly arrived audience and his full lips shaped into an equally lazy smile.

'Ah, Véronique, *mon ange,* what would I do without you?' he drawled.

He tossed the scroll to a page and rose, sweeping his silk cape behind him. He spread his arms wide as he descended from the raised dais.

'*Bienvenue,* welcome, one and all! Éilís, *ma chère,* it is always wonderful to see you.'

The Eiran Queen bowed her head and offered her hand to his lips.

'Likewise, Xavier. Thanks for giving us transport through the Great Gates; it bought me enough time to bring these two along. I don't believe you've met?'

Despite the King's insouciant smile as he regarded him through half-lidded eyes, Silas still felt like a nervous mageling under inspection from a head tutor.

'Ah, yes... Lord L'Heritier's boy. What a fine young man you have turned out to be. And Ruaidhrí'ogan, is it? Marvellous to have you with us.'

Before either of them could say anything, he waved one of his pages over.

'Now, I know you both are here on protection detail, but the Palais des Étoiles is perfectly secure. You are dismissed until dinner. Do follow Hugo to your quarters.'

The pair were briskly ushered out of the throne room as the King began heaping compliments on the Eiran Dukes and Duchesses.

Silas opened his mouth to speak, but Rua shot him a look that made him hesitate.

They walked along the corridors in silence until the page halted and opened a door.

'Your room, mi'lord, mi'lady. His Majesty has left a note on your dressing table detailing tonight's events. Please pull the servants' cord if you require any assistance.'

Silas watched him slip away, then closed the door.

'The King does not appear overly concerned about the situation,' he began.

Rua ripped open the sealed letter and started reading.

'Oh, he's just very good at appearing that way. We've been summoned to his private chambers after dinner, and we're to be discreet about it. He's even included a map. And dinner will be in two hours in the Hall of a Hundred Suns... sounds posh, but aha, no written request for formal wear, thank Ciel.'

'Is Eiran formal dress really that bad?'

She sighed in exasperation.

'Y'know how much we prize our warriors, yeah? Well, the way we show off our strength is to be as unarmoured and unarmed as possible; to prove we can fight without. That's why a Queen's Guard only wears a light cuirass and dagger. Even the Queen, an accomplished dragonslayer, wears a single, long bolt of cloth. Can you imagine what that means for me, the best warrior in Eira?'

He started imagining. He liked what he imagined.

She puffed up her cheeks and punched him in the arm.

'You can stop that, right now!'

***

Silas was all too happy to follow Rua through the opulent corridors, as she had committed the map to memory. Down a grand staircase and through an archway, Vertcielle's nobility and militaire had gathered with the Eiran guests in the anteroom, drinking aperitifs. The steward bowed and announced them.

'The Weaver of Ciel, Silas L'Heritier and the Dagger of Ciel, Ruaidhri'ogan!'

There were audible gasps and murmurs from the Vertciellens. Rua bristled slightly and Silas's heart jumped into his throat; he wasn't expecting both of them to be introduced so bluntly when they were accustomed to hiding their true abilities.

'Ah, *mon doudou, ma louloutte!*'

Lady L'Heritier descended on them, covering their cheeks in kisses. His father soon worked his way out of the throng, grinning as he offered them glasses of sherry.

'Well, that's a hell of an entrance, you two. The King must really want you to make an impression.'

'Let's hope it's the right one,' Rua grumbled. 'It took me decades to fade into obscurity in these parts.'

Véronique came over, closely followed by Owyn.

'Do not doubt the King,' she warned. 'Everything he does is down to reason.'

The steward rang the dinner gong.

'Please be seated!'

Everyone filed into the hall, searching for their place names before taking their seats. The two gilded chairs at the head of the table were conspicuously empty. After a few minutes, the gong rang again.

'His Majesty, King Xavier IV and her Majesty, Queen Éilís the Enlightened!'

Everyone rose as the Elven Star King appeared, the Eiran Queen holding his arm. They processed slowly through the doors and sat down in their chairs. Xavier waved his hand and the guests took their seats once more.

'It is with great pleasure that I invite all of you here for dinner,' he intoned. 'Our two nations share a long and varied history, but I am keen to forge new friendships. Now, I won't take up any more of your time; this is just a friendly, casual affair...'

He winked amidst polite laughter.

'So please enjoy yourselves. Music! Service!'

He clapped his hands and the court musicians began to play as delectable trays of food were brought to the table. Fresh oysters sprinkled with shallots and vinegar, delicate vol-au-vents filled with cream and ham. A crystal clear beef consommé, then perfectly sautéed fillets of plaice drizzled with lemon butter followed by roasted squab with tarragon velouté.

Silas found himself next to General Aoife, refereeing her conversation with Lord Durant, Duc de Valmarais, who disagreed with the Eiran practice of women serving in the military. Thankfully, they kept it civil, if awkward.

Suddenly, there were raised voices from the other end of the table.

The Duke of Blestium jabbed a finger into Maréchal Lefèvre's chest.

'I dare you to say that again!'

'Fine, I will! Vertcielle suffers the effects of the Great Wars, even now! How many of our sons were butchered in cold blood by your barbarians?! Our kind cannot simply replace the fallen like yours; you Humans can breed like rats!'

'And whose fault was it that the Great Wars happened in the first place?! You Elves got greedy; remember, you invaded us, not the other way around! What did you expect, that we'd go easy on you weaklings?'

By the grace of Ciel, this cannot be happening, Silas thought, going white.

A spinning blur went flying past his head. The Eiran dagger landed in the chair between the two men, who backed away from each other in shock. The room was now silent. Rua leapt onto the table, stalking down its length without disturbing a single piece of crockery. She fixed them with her eyes and spoke, her voice dark.

'You have no idea what it was like during the Great Wars. I WAS THERE. I saw all the stupid decisions that led to it; the stubbornness of mortals with too much ambition and too little compassion. All for what?! A fancy bit of jewellery? The authority to say some bit of grass was theirs? Taking revenge on an entire nation just because one idiot killed another?'

She pulled her dagger out from the chair and sheathed it, glowering down at them.

'It took me almost a hundred years to unravel that tangled web of instigators, traitors and power hungry rulers. In that time, so many people were ordered to their deaths. So much blood was shed. Ciel wept for her children. Her bitter, squabbling children, who were constantly finding reasons to kill each other. And she asked me to stop it. D'you know, it was one of the hardest things she had to do; picking a side. Can you imagine: a mother, choosing one child over another, for the greater good? So... I did as she asked. And I killed thousands of her children.'

Close to tears, she addressed the whole room.

'I am more sorry than you will ever know, Vertcielle. You just happened to be on the wrong side, that time. But the truth is... we all lost. And I fear we will never learn.'

No one spoke as she hopped off the table and made back towards her seat.

After a few moments, Lord L'Heritier began to sing in Old Eiran.

'*Sé mo laoch mo ghile mear, sé mo chaesar, ghile mear...*'

Silas did not recognise the song, but Rua froze and pricked her ears in surprise. She went to his father and took his hand, adding her voice to his.

'*Suan ná séan ni bhfuaireas féin, Ó chuaigh i gcéin mo ghile mear...*'

Slowly, one by one, the Eirans joined in as they began remembering the words.

'*Bímse buan ar buaidhirt gach ló, ag caoi go cruaidh 's ag tuar na ndeór.*

Mar scaoileadh uaim an buachaill beó, 'S ná ríomhtar tuairisc uaidh, mo bhrón.'

Éilís smiled warmly and sang the chorus once more.

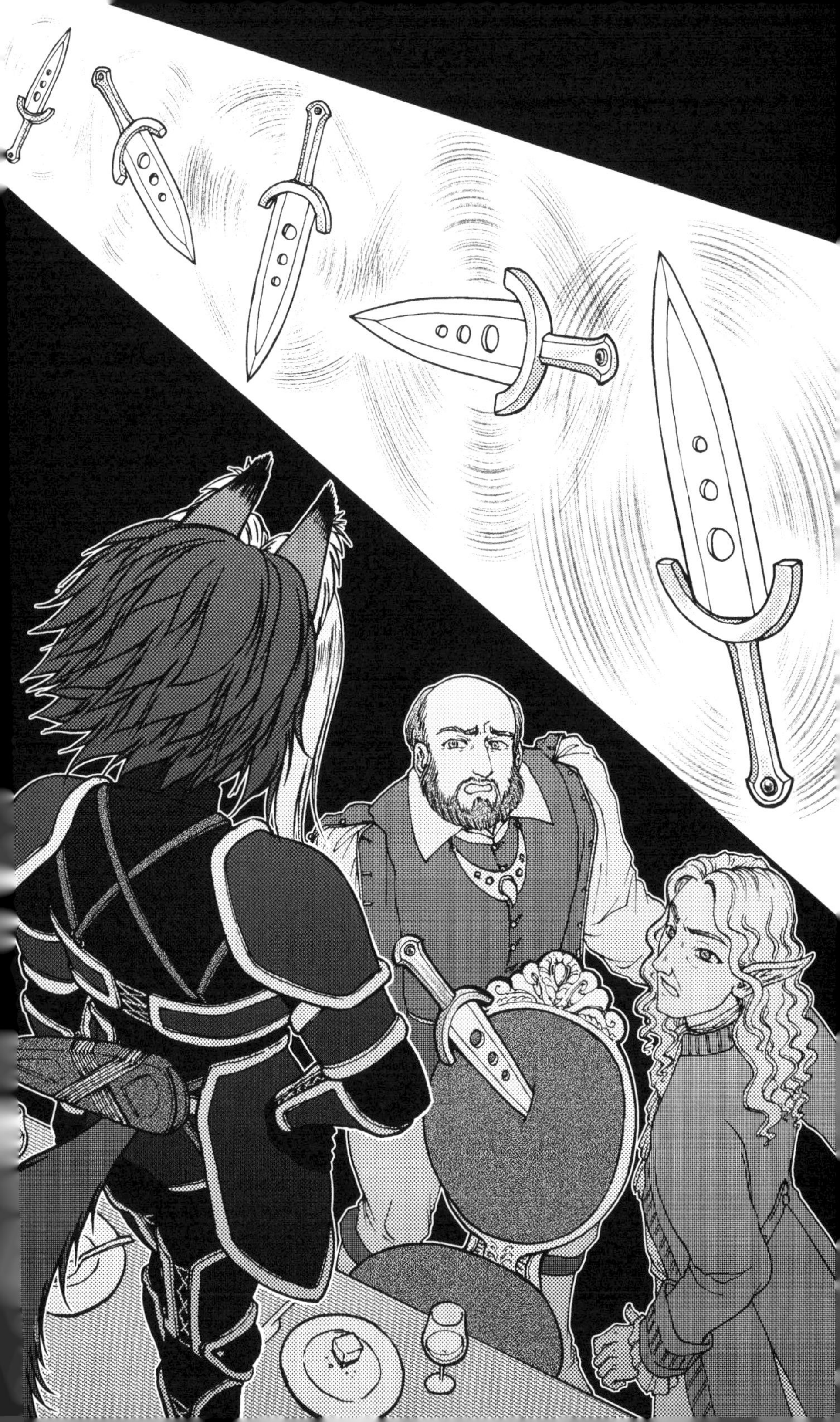

'Sé mo laoch mo ghile mear, sé mo chaesar, ghile mear,

Suan ná séan ni bhfuaireas féin, Ó chuaigh i gcéin mo ghile mear.'

Rua threw her arms around Lord L'Heritier.

'Thank you,' she mumbled into his chest.

'You're welcome,' he replied, patting her head fondly.

Silas had never felt so proud of his father than at that moment.

The Eiran Queen rose from her seat, clapping.

'Lord L'Heritier, I was not expecting anyone from Vertcielle to know that song. Even most Eirans have trouble recalling the lyrics.'

'What use is a Foreign Secretary who knows not of other cultures? My eldest, Gildas, taught it to me. He said, amongst your soldiers, it was a lament of great significance.'

'It is. The spirit of Eira mourning the loss of her gallant soldiers.'

'And Vertcielle mourns together with Eira. We are all Ciel's children.'

Silas watched as Éilís walked over to his father to clasp his forearm and quietly chat about Gildas's exploits. The tension in the air was gone and the comforting hum of conversation between Eirans and Vertciellens soon returned. He breathed a sigh of relief and glanced at the King.

Xavier had that same lazy smile as always, but his eyes were unusually sharp.

V

'Silas, leave my tail alone.'

'Sorry...'

He reluctantly released it and took Rua's hand instead. She needed to be close for his Spirit Fabric to cover them both. No need for Air spells to cushion their feet; the plush carpets muffled their footsteps as they crept around the corridors. Eventually they arrived at an unassuming door halfway down one of the quiet side passages.

Rua knocked three times and waited for a few seconds.

They heard a single knock in reply.

'It's us,' Rua whispered.

The latch went and Véronique held the door open, holding a finger to her lips. The pair slipped in and Silas dismissed his Fabric. It appeared to be a cosy drawing room.

The Chancellor locked the door and went to a bookcase. She pulled out a large volume of financial records and reached into the space behind it. There was a soft clicking noise. She replaced the tome, then went to the floor length mirror opposite. She pushed it to one side to reveal a secret passage. Creating a small Spirit ball in her palm, she stepped into the darkness without looking back. They followed swiftly, the mirror sliding back into place behind them. After twenty yards, they stopped in front of a wooden panel. She knocked on it three times and there was a knock in return.

'We're here,' Véronique stated.

The panel pulled back and they emerged into an exquisite antechamber; the gilded woodwork and cornicing shimmering from the flickering flames in the marble fireplace.

Silas looked back to see his father pushing a life-sized oil painting of King Xavier IV astride a magnificent white stallion back into position, concealing the secret passage.

Xavier himself sat on an armchair beside an intricately embroidered fire screen, opposite Éilís and Owyn on a settee. He gestured to the empty chairs remaining.

'Please, sit. Véronique?'

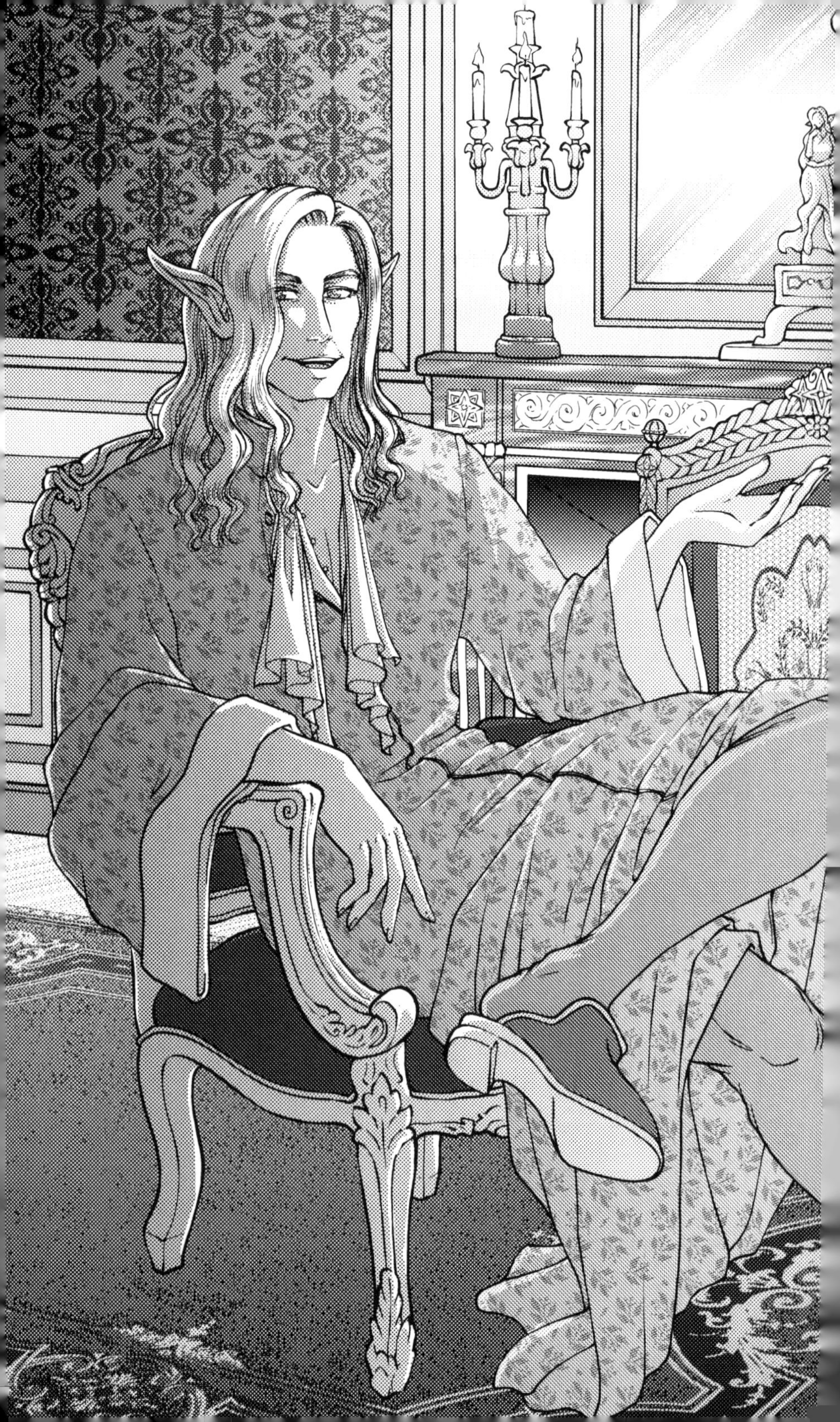

Silas recognised the simple cube she drew out of Air threads: an Air Barrier. She stretched it apart at the corners until it disappeared.

'Done, your Majesty. It is safe to speak.'

'Thank you.'

Xavier looked at his assembled guests pointedly.

'Please understand the precautions I have taken to ensure our meeting remains secret; we wouldn't want any of our nobles suspecting anything. You are all here because you are the only people I trust. Éilís and I have worked closely together over the past forty years to ensure peace and stability between our nations. But the recent partnership of Vertcielle's Weaver and Eira's Dagger is divine proof that it is Ciel's wish for us to be a force of good for the Cradle, perhaps even for the rest of the world.'

He frowned.

'I am convinced that the full coronation of a new Empress of the Palatinate has been orchestrated to achieve some evil intention. What makes this event significant is the hurried gathering of rulers from across the Cradle and beyond to witness the volcanic ritual. Any one of them could be a target. And if this is the culmination of a long waiting game, there may be sleeper agents within their courts. Including ours. Now, betrayal by my own *noblesse* wouldn't surprise me; I don't trust any of them anyway. Éilís; I hope you can keep yourself safe from yours. As for the rest of them...'

The King turned to Silas's father.

'L'Heritier, tomorrow we're stepping into the lion's den. How many lions?'

Lord L'Heritier bowed.

'All the usual suspects of course; rulers from Sturmgaard, Orbos, Petrovka, Bashkendir, Sharaafdi, Alekhandros, Pontiazza and Hesperia. And beyond the Cradle: Amliga is sending a chieftain from their east coast, then there are two Ifriq queens from the south and a large Tianxian delegation coming from Shuntien.'

'Tianxia haven't attended before. Any more details on that?'

'I believe the Empress Dowager Wei Xianwen and her grandson Prince Wei Xianrong will be visiting.'

'Very interesting. He's of a marriageable age, for a Human. Will he try for the biggest prize? Now, give me some leverage over those lions. What are they up to?'

'Little has changed over the past week. Due to increased consumer confidence, overland trade and travel has doubled in the Arberge region as crime has fallen dramatically over the past six months. The Iskarian States have been attracting a lot of investment lately due to Orbos striking a new seam in the mines, but their fishing fleet is still getting into trouble with the Tsithians, despite multiple warnings. The Bashkendien navy has offered to patrol and escort in the Tarshan Sea; I'm tempted to hand it over, but I fear the possibility of vested interests. On the other hand, Hesperia is in a bit of slump; I've heard rumours that one of the Princes has been gambling, so parts of Puerto Benigno are in need of urgent repair.'

'I'd bet it was Lorencio,' Xavier muttered. 'That boy was always getting in over his head. I wonder who he owes... it would be ironic if it was Pontiazza; their own flood defences are crumbling. Never build a city on top of a marsh unless you're willing to throw never-ending money at it.'

Lord L'Heritier scratched his chin.

'The Principe of Pontiazza has been hosting a lot of foreign trade delegations lately, from Amliga and Ifriqikah... he's definitely courting investment from outside the Cradle. And Prince Lorencio has been seen during the Carnevales at the same time. I think you've done it again, your Majesty. Do you even need a Foreign Secretary?'

'Having you around to stroke my ego never hurts, L'Heritier.'

Silas watched this exchange with quiet fascination. Rua was right; the King was indeed, very good at acting. All that nonchalant, languid indifference was gone. The man was arrogant, but he was also shrewd, calculating and quick.

Xavier drummed his fingers on his chair.

'All of these grievances are potential reasons for a stab in the back. The question is, which one? Perhaps even several people at once? And who would send the assassin? Is it the work of one country alone, or some form of evil alliance? This is all still speculation... *non*, nothing is concrete!'

He clenched his fingers into a fist.

'We cannot prevent an assassination until we know who the target is; only then can we identify the would-be assassin. I fear we will get no closer to uncovering this plot until we are in Drachenheim. Then, in the days before the ceremony, we can tempt them into the open. Lull them into a false sense of security. Catch them red-handed.'

He fixed Silas with his turquoise stare.

'I want Véronique and Silas near me at all times in Drachenheim. Only then is my safety guaranteed. You both will stay in my quarters.'

Éilís folded her arms and looked at Rua, her expression grim.

'And Rua, I don't call in favours lightly. You must stick with me in my rooms. If anyone tries to kill me, I'm sure either you or Owyn will stop them.'

Silas's heart sank. He was anxious enough about returning to Drachenheim, but to be separated from Rua as well?

They both began to protest at once.

'I-I cannot leave Rua's side! We work much better together–'

'It's a snake pit out there! I can't protect him–'

Xavier held up his hand for silence, but Silas persisted.

'What about Arafel? Perhaps we ought to be assigned to her as a pair?'

The King shook his head.

'It would look highly suspicious if a Verticiellen and an Eiran were with the Crown Princess instead of protecting their own royals. Besides, no one's tried to kill her for the last nine years; I doubt they are going to start now.'

'But–' Rua began.

'Stand down,' Éilís ordered.

Rua bit her lip and glared at the floor, her ears pinned back sullenly.

Xavier raised an eyebrow at Lord L'Heritier, who looked apologetic in response.

'I don't envy you, L'Heritier. Having these two home for the holidays must be quite the handful.'

He rose, prompting everyone else to get to their feet as well.

'Put on your best dress and smiles,' he advised. 'Charm them all and learn as much as you can, but stay on guard. We go through the Great Gates tomorrow at noon. Silas, Rua, I'm afraid you have to go out the back way. The rest of you can leave through the Guard Room at your leisure.'

Véronique waved her hand to dismiss the Air Barrier then ushered them out through the secret passage and drawing room, where she left them. As the mirror pulled itself back into place, Silas could see Rua's face in its reflection.

He couldn't tell if she was sad, angry or both.

He cast a Spirit Fabric once more, threw it over the both of them and took her hand. They walked in silence through the corridors, still busy with staff preparing for the journey tomorrow. Once in front of their room, he waited until it was quiet before dismissing the Fabric. He held the door open for her, then closed it behind them.

She went and sat on the far side of the bed, fiddling with the straps on her armour.

He stood for a minute, gauging her mood. Then he walked around the foot of the bed and sat next to her.

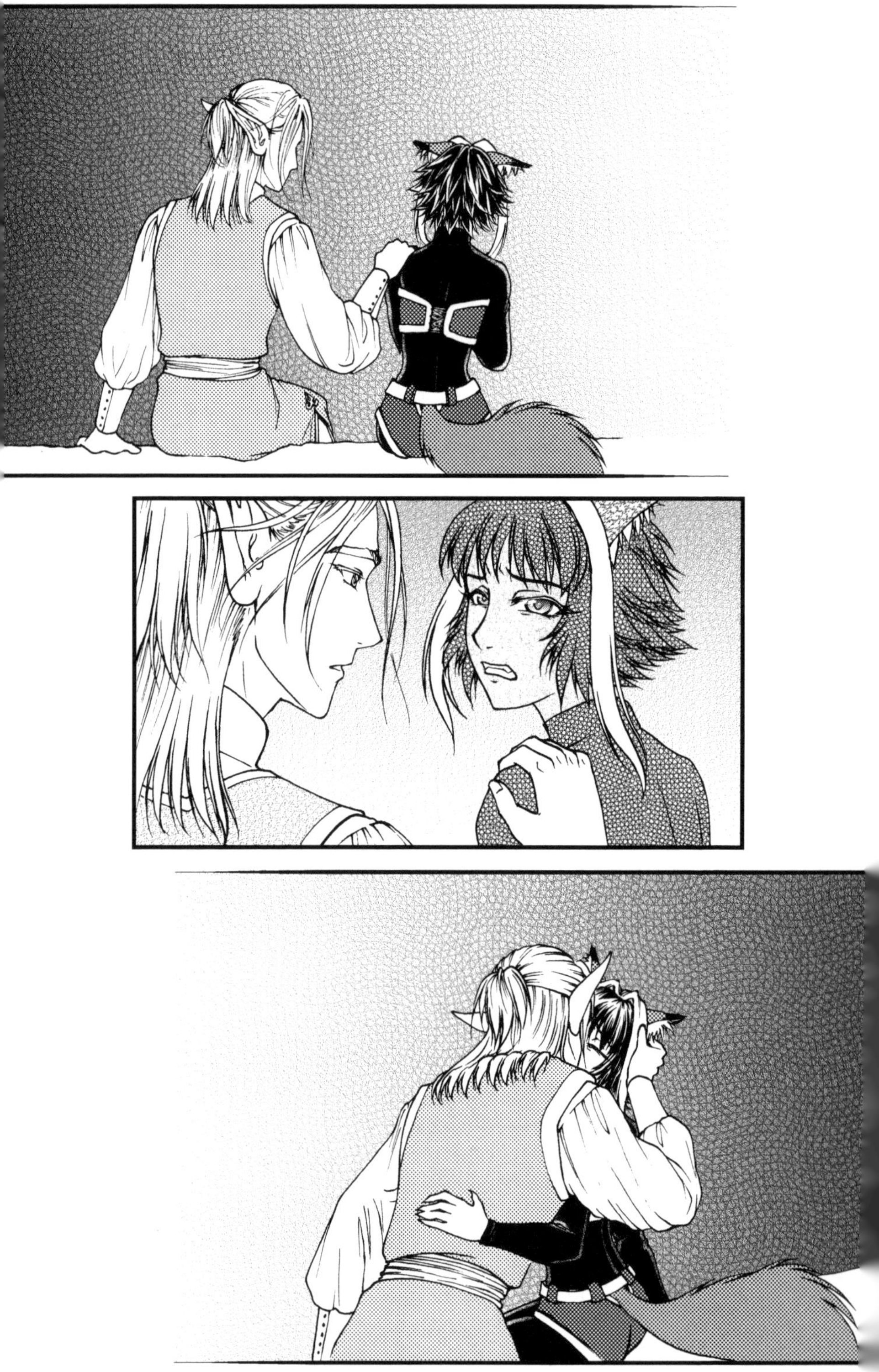

'Please, let me help you with that,' he offered.

She gave him a curt nod before turning away again to work on her arm bracers. He unclipped her dagger from her lower back and placed it on the dressing table. He started pulling the straps out of her hip plates.

'I am not looking forward to tomorrow,' he began, stacking the armour on the floor.

She stayed silent.

Silas continued to speak, now loosening her shoulder pauldrons.

'Returning to Drachenheim is bad enough, but what makes it worse...'

He lifted off the pauldrons and stacked them on top of the hip plates. He gave her shoulders a squeeze.

'...Is that we have to be apart.'

Rua twisted around to face him now. Her expression was brittle; like she could shatter at any moment.

'Oh, Silas, I've been selfish. I wasn't even thinking about how it was going to be like for you to go back, I was just... I... now that I have you, I don't ever want to leave you. Not even for a single night.'

His heart lurched. Whilst it was reassuring that she felt the same way, it pained him to see her like this.

He leant forward and kissed her delicately before looking into her panicked eyes.

'Then let me love you tonight.'

Her eyes gradually calmed and she sat there for a few moments, solemnly. Then she reached behind her back, undid her breastplate and dropped it on the floor. She took hold of his hands and placed them on her chest. He could feel her heartbeat under his palms. Slowly, he ran his hands down her knitted top, then slipped them underneath to clutch at the small swells of her breasts before lifting the jumper up and over her head. She fell back on the bed, bare-chested and breathless.

He forced himself to breathe measuredly as he quickly undressed and slid under the covers alongside her. Kissing her again, he trailed his fingers along her belly and gripped the waistband of her hose, pulling it down until it ruched around her knees. She tugged her tail out of it, then kicked it off her ankles. She arched into him and raked her claws down his back, wordlessly asking for more. Before she could get her claws into anything else, he grabbed her wrists and held them back above her head.

She growled, baring her fangs.

'No,' he asserted. 'Let *me* love you.'

Her honey-gold eyes grew wide, then softened.

She relaxed, offering no resistance. His pulse quickened at the sight of her surrender. He started exploring her body with his mouth and free hand, and aside from her cries and tremors of pleasure, she remained completely receptive. Even when he eventually took her, over and over, throughout the night. This was the first time he had taken charge of their lovemaking.

He hoped that it wouldn't be their last.

VI

Right in the heart of the city, the Place d'Étoiles was one of the few open squares that were large enough to accommodate the Great Gates of Fleurys. The roads were cordoned off for the day in anticipation of the crowds, but it was still a tight squeeze as spectators overflowed off the pavements, into the roads, and onto the steps of the buildings opposite. It was as if the whole of Fleurys had turned out to see the King and his royal visitors from Eira.

Silas wished he was in the throngs below; perhaps the winter wind wouldn't be quite so biting. He pulled his gloves further up his arms before glancing surreptitiously around him, then hiked up his thigh boots beneath his robes. Standing on the raised walkway leading to the Great Gates, he felt rather self-conscious, despite being surrounded by members of the *noblesse* in much fancier outfits. He recognised some from the previous night's dinner; the Duc de Valmarais, the Comte de Maçoncourt, the Marquis de la Fontaine and from Vertcielle's *militaire*, Général Hugolin, Commandant Desrosiers and the inflammatory Maréchal Lefèvre.

However plain Silas looked in comparison, having to stay right next to the King as his bodyguard didn't help matters. Xavier was resplendent in a dark blue cloak, embroidered with silver stars and garnets. He had chosen his outfit carefully, in homage to the Imperial colours of the Palatinate.

Lord L'Heritier looked towards the clock tower, then bowed to the King.

'It's almost time. I will return to the Palais to hold the fort. May Ciel watch over your Majesty and your servants in Drachenheim.'

He shared a look with Silas.

'Son, I know this will be difficult, but... you can do this. You must.'

Silas gulped, his heart thumping loudly in his chest. He had been dreading this moment since Owyn first revealed their travelling plans a week ago. It had been nine years since he last used a Great Gate. Nine years since that day he found Arafel's mother beheaded in the halls of Schloss Drachen, and he discovered his gift in the process of trying to protect her daughter. Nine years since the night he and his family were escorted through the gates by Chevaliers to the icy glares of Drachenheim's nobles and officials; angry chants of "the Weaver child" and frightened whispers of "Terra's lightning caster" ringing in his ears.

He glanced behind him for reassurance, searching for the Eiran delegation. He wanted Rua's presence more than anything.

There she was, her golden streaks shining in the sunlight, like a beacon. Their eyes met and she smiled breezily, giving him a wink and a thumbs up gesture.

He nodded at her hesitantly and turned back to face ahead.

The Great Gates were impressive to any traveller, even to those who had used them before. The raised walkway led through two enormous circles cast in bronze, one placed in front of the other. The first was enchanted for sending travellers to other Gates located around the world, the second was for receiving them. The Gates of Fleurys were one of the oldest, made to link with Drachenheim several thousand years ago.

The bells of the clock tower opposite started to toll. Five Spirit mages stepped up to the walkway, the emblems on their robes marking them out as Gate operators. Their eyes glowed white and in unison, they traced out a complex pattern of flourishes before directing the mass of Spirit threads into the sending Gate. The whole circle lit up and the air inside the Gate shimmered as the giant Spirit portal opened. Like a mist clearing, the view through the portal came into sharp focus. It was like looking at a giant painting of Drachenheim within the bronze frame, but parts of the picture were moving; the trails of smoke twisting in the sky, the colourful clothes flapping in the wind.

One of the Spirit mages turned to the King and nodded, his eyes still glowing white as he concentrated on maintaining the spell. There was little ceremony at this point as all travellers, whether they were kings or commoners, had to pass through the portal as quickly as possible whilst the operators were able to keep the Gate open.

Xavier waved his hand and leading the procession, they began walking briskly in threes and fours; the Vertciellens first, followed by the Eirans.

Silas held his breath and closed his eyes as he stepped through the portal. He stumbled slightly as his foot came down onto a carpeted walkway that was a couple of inches lower than the one he had left. Véronique grabbed at his arm, forcing his pace so as not to hold up the travellers behind them. Only when he felt her hand leave did he slow down and look back at the Gates as they closed, the Place d'Étoiles shimmering and fading out of sight. Fleurys was far away and Drachenheim was all that remained.

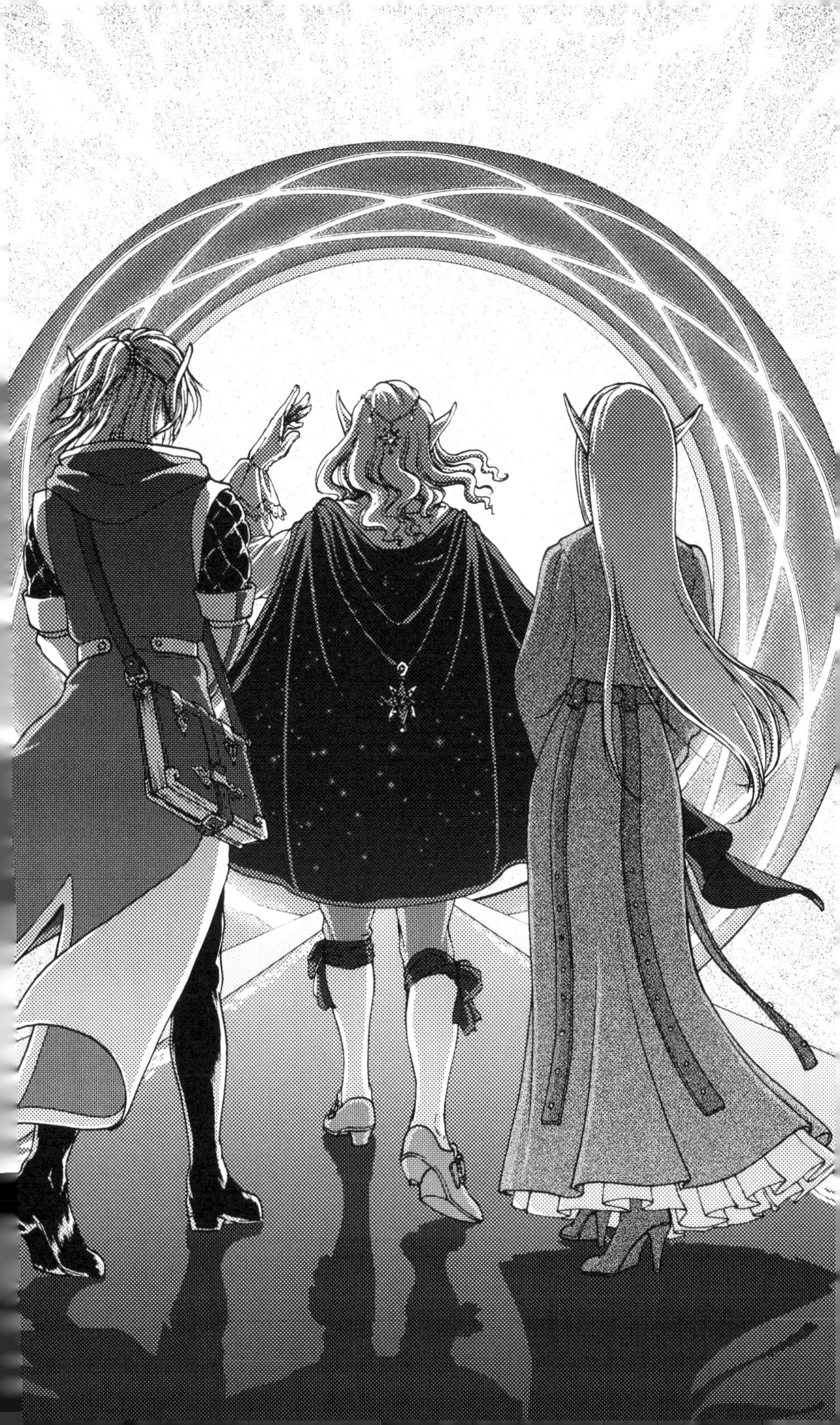

He finally took a breath and it was as if he had never left.

There was a distinct smell of smoke and metal in the air from the advanced ore refineries that smelted the precious metals of Ciel's Cradle, imported to the continent's leading industrial heartland. The air was cold, but the humidity was strikingly familiar.

Drachenheim was built on Himmelsleiter, one of the tallest inhabited mountains in the world, rising out of the White Lake, formed from the many streams running off Heaven's Ring, the surrounding circular mountain range. Locals called the immense moat the Nebelsee, as the smoke from the refineries merged with the mists that constantly enshrouded them from the mainland.

All of the feelings of isolation, fear and hatred he had experienced as a child after the events of his tenth birthday came flooding back and he felt like he was trapped in one of his own nightmares. A little boy in a city who had cast him out. Except he couldn't just wake up. Because now it was real; now he was actually here.

He wobbled and clutched at his chest. His heart was racing and he was gasping for breath. His anxiety was spiralling out of control and he didn't know how to stop it.

Then he felt her hands rubbing the small of his back.

'Hey, are you okay?' Rua asked, softly. 'Come on, you can lean on me.'

'You... should be with... your Queen–' he said weakly.

'I'll go wherever I damn well please!'

She looked at Xavier, who was watching them with his usual mask of indifference.

'We have a few minutes,' he said, shrugging.

She put his arm across her shoulders and walked him out to one of the stone benches by the side of the Platz. She sat him down in front of her and she hugged him, laying his head on her chest, stroking his cheek, whispering reassurances in his ear.

That was then, this was now. He was a grown man. He had proven himself as a force for good, time and time again. He was needed. He was wanted. He was loved.

His breathing steadied as he calmed down. He looked into Rua's determined eyes.

'Thank you.'

'It's alright, love.'

She gave him a quick kiss and with one last pat on the cheek, skipped back to take her place with Éilís, who rolled her eyes in exasperation at her errant Champion.

He stood up gingerly and tried not to trip over anything whilst getting back to his place. As he reached Xavier's side, the King murmured.

'Well, well – it seems someone else was watching your little episode.'

Silas looked ahead to the Palatinate welcoming party. There was Arafel, flanked by two young girls with a familial resemblance; her cousins, he presumed. The Empress Incumbent was encased in silver jewellery; dressed magnificently in purple silk robes lined in bright blues and pinks. The Imperial dragon sceptre shook slightly in her hands as he caught a glimpse of her stormy eyes, dark as umber. His heart sank like a stone. For a fleeting moment, she looked as if she had been betrayed.

***

Silas took a deep breath in front of the mirror before attempting the straps on his corset again. He had seen the court's battle mages wear these formal waist shapers before, but he had little idea how he was supposed to get it on. Both ornamental and defensive, it hugged the wearer's body, protecting vital organs and providing clips for a mage's grimoire to be hung from the hip. He regretted his initial delight of finding some time alone after the past two days; he could have used Véronique's help right then.

From the moment they left the Great Gates at Platz der Pfalz, there were social events late into the evening with Drachenheim's nobles. It was tortuous seeing how they reacted when they realised who he was; torn between shunning him, or buttering him up due to his apparent closeness to the Elven Star King. Xavier would casually touch his shoulder to whisper to him, or bring him into conversations; making it obvious that Silas was one of his favourites. That went a long way in high society.

Then they had an early start the next morning, spending the whole day meeting with expatriate Elves in and around his former home, the Vertciellen Ambassade. This was more pleasant as the new Ambassador and his family were well acquainted with Lord L'Heritier, treating Silas warmly.

Now they were back in Schloss Drachen. He was already exhausted but tonight was the ball as the last of the foreign dignitaries had arrived today. Xavier had gone early to a light dinner service with Véronique so Silas had less than an hour to himself in the King's apartments, twenty minutes of which he had wasted on getting dressed.

There was a knock on the door.

He frowned; it wasn't Xavier or Véronique, they would have come straight in. Had a guard come to fetch him for something? Was there an emergency?

He threw open the door, his corset dangling around his hips. No one was there.

'Silas, it's me,' Arafel whispered.

'Wh- what are you doing here?!' he whispered, unsure where to look.

'Just hurry up and let me in, before anyone notices you talking to thin air!'

He stepped back and felt her brush past him before closing the door. She suddenly appeared, her eyes glowing white as she dismissed her Spirit Fabric before fading into their usual dark brown. She was barefooted, dressed in only a long, white chemise.

'Before you ask, I told them I was taking a long bath before the ball, okay?' she sighed. 'It was the only way I could sneak out without them noticing.'

She looked at him, scrunching her forehead when her eyes lingered on the corset.

'Oh, Si, you've made a total mess of it. Get over to that mirror; I'll help you.'

He meekly walked back to the mirror and watched her reflection fix his clothes.

'You have to lace it halfway before closing the front busk straps, then tighten the lacing afterwards,' she fussed. 'And you tie them in the middle, at your waist, not at the top or bottom. You watching? You'll need to learn to do this by yourself, you know.'

'I am watching! Slow down, I cannot see– OOF!'

'Sorry, was that a bit tight? I think these mage's corsets are supposed to fully close.'

'No, I am fine, it was just... unexpected. Thank you.'

Silas studied her as she deftly wove the laces through the eyelets. She looked as she always did during their lessons together; her long, black hair falling over her face, tilted down as she frowned, deep in concentration. It all seemed so long ago, now.

'Arafel... are you alright? I apologise that I have not had a chance to send you any letters of late. I cannot imagine how stressful all of this must be for you.'

She smiled at him in the mirror and continued to neaten up the lacing.

'I'm mostly okay now. Well, I think I am. I've known I would be Empress for a long time; after all, I've been preparing for this for nine years. And Maestra Véronique has been very helpful since the summer. I'm really sorry if I worried you, it was just such a shock at first; no one expected *Opa* to... I can only hope he died swiftly.'

'May Ciel bless his soul. We will find out who is behind all of this. I assure you, King Xavier and Queen Éilís are committed to supporting you, the Palatinate and Ciel's Cradle. That is why we are here. Rua and I, especially, will do everything we can to protect you.'

She went silent as she finished tying his laces in a bow.

Then her pale wrists came around his waist and she clung tightly to his back.

I am sorry, he thought. *I am so sorry.*

She started to sob.

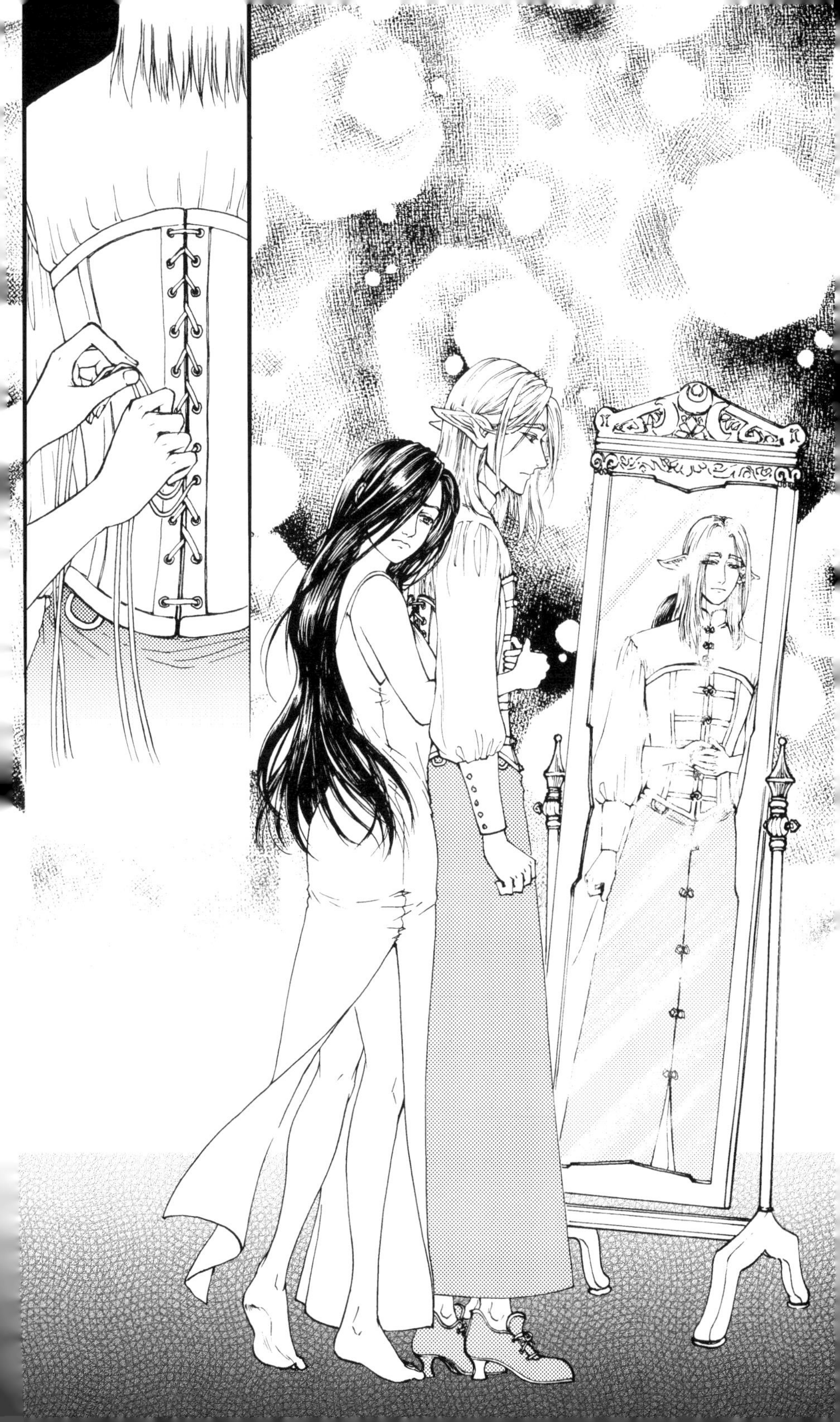

'I knew. I knew it the moment I met her. The way you looked at her.'

'Arafel, I...'

'No, no. Don't. It's okay. You were always my best friend and... we could never have been more, anyway. I told myself that a long time ago. I mean, I'm going to be Empress, right? And you're an Elf, the Weaver, no less. There's no way you and I...'

He stayed silent, letting her cry it out.

After a while, she took a deep breath and sighed.

'It still hurts, though,' she mumbled.

He patted the back of her hands.

'I do not doubt it.'

He turned around to face her.

'I will always love you, Arafel. You know the real me. And when you become Empress, I will still know the real you.'

She gave him a watery smile.

'And I'll be forever grateful for that.'

She rose up on her toes to kiss him on the cheek. Then she hugged him warmly.

'I'm not going to fight Ciel's choice for you. Frankly, if it had to be anyone, I'm glad it's her! I just hope Ciel has someone in mind for me.'

He gave her a squeeze and leant back with a wry smile.

'I am sure she does. She gave me the distinct impression that she knew what she was doing when we last spoke.'

'You *Dummkopf!* Don't talk about the Goddess like that, it's rude.'

VII

'His Majesty, King Xavier IV of Vertcielle, with the Chancellor of the Lyceum Arcanus, Maestra Véronique Tempête, and the Weaver of Ciel, Magus Silas L'Heritier!'

Silas tried to ignore the murmurs from the assembled nobles of Drachenheim as he followed Xavier. In his dazzling cream and gold robes, the Elven Star King drew everyone's attention as he sauntered into the grand ballroom of Schloss Drachen, flashing his lazy smile to the fluttering ladies and audaciously winking at several blushing gentlemen.

'Come on, Silas,' Xavier murmured. 'Relax. After all I did for you on Wednesday, none of them will dare criticise you in my presence.'

'If you cannot relax, at the very least, maintain your composure,' Véronique whispered. 'You are supposed to be a show of strength, not weakness.'

Silas couldn't smile, so he settled on frowning whilst trying to keep his hair out of his eyes. He had left it loose as was the custom amongst Elves for formal occasions. He had to shorten his stride as his skirt was more closely cut than his other outfits. His court shoes also needed breaking in. Even his brocade corset was tighter than anything he'd ever worn before. All in all, he had a lot of reasons to be uncomfortable.

They made their way to their seats as the rest of Vertcielle's *noblesse* were introduced in turn. Once seated, they observed the foreign dignitaries as they entered.

First up were the Ocean King Santiago and Queen Dolores of Hesperia with their sons. These Elves were accomplished seafarers with sun-kissed complexions. Xavier elbowed Silas as Prince Lorencio passed; a sleepy-eyed youth.

Principe Marco and Principessa Angela of Pontiazza were next, a stout Human couple, followed by nobles from the other Southern city-states. The men kept their dark beards and their hair short; the women had their hair coiled into extravagant headpieces.

The swarthy Dwarven rulers of Sturmgaard, Jarl Thyge and Jarl-kona Liesel came in, their intricately braided beards clinking with beads. They were escorted by their shieldmaiden Gunnælf, her silvery hair and taupe skin typical of cave-dwelling Elves. Also from Iskar was Jarl Rikvald of Orbos and his sister, shieldmaiden Sigrid. Like their Dwarven neighbours, these pale Humans also dressed their blond hair in braids.

Tsar Vadim and Tsaritsa Liliya of Tsithia were the most ostentatious yet, their crowns and fur-edged robes sparkling with gemstones. Their eldest son Kazimir was equally fancy, his friend Baron Zharykhin less so.

Then the High Priestess of Alekhandros paraded in, her long train held up by her Hierophants. The spiritual leader of Ciel's Cradle, Silas was taken aback by her resemblance to the Goddess herself with her wavy, red hair and flowing robes.

Hailing from across the Great Western Ocean was the Amligan Chieftain Yuma accompanied by five of his warriors; eagle feathers woven into the bright, geometric beadwork ornamenting their hair and suede jackets.

From the Desert Corridor, Bey Kaspar and Begum Fairuzah of Bashkendir were similarly dressed to Sultan Saif and Sultana Ashraqat of Sharaafdi; wearing long robes belted with jewelled chains, their hair covered with veils and held in place by diadems.

Further still was the continent of Ifriqikah. In walked Queen Nakato of the southern coast of Umzania and Queen Aminatu of the Nzaidiran heartlands, wrapped in colourful sashes and festooned with bracelets, anklets and necklaces. Silas was fascinated by the Queen of Nzaidira; he had never seen an Elf from this part of the world before. Her deep, black skin looked almost blue in the lamplight.

The statuesque Aminatu, noticing his scrutiny, glanced at him. Then her eyes drifted right and she winked at Véronique as she took her seat opposite.

The Chancellor quickly looked down at the floor, her ears ever so slightly pink.

Silas tried to hide a smile; he had never seen his mentor flustered by anyone before.

'Her Majesty, Queen Éilís of Eira and His Royal Highness, Prince Consort Owyn, with the Queen's Champion, Ruaidhri'ogan, the Dagger of Ciel!'

Silas's heart thumped in anticipation. He had not seen Rua for the past two days.

Éilís came in, striding confidently. The warrior queen had a single piece of white cloth draped over one shoulder to her ankles and a tartan stole across the other, held in place with a gold, dragon-headed belt. She still looked fearsome with her crown of carved dragon teeth and her gold neck torque bristling with claws.

Owyn was even more scantily dressed; his tartan folded into a short kilt, leaving his legs and one half of his tattooed chest bare. He was equally fierce in appearance; war paint over his face, his silver arm and shin bracers barbed with dragon teeth.

Rua prowled in behind them and Silas stopped breathing.

Like her queen, Rua wore a single piece of cloth but it was far shorter, only just covering the tops of her thighs. The white linen hung from the back of her neck and flowed down her front, fastened at her waist with her gold belt. The sides of her body were completely exposed as was most of her back, save for a tiny skirt fluttering over her tail. With gold bracers on her arms and legs, she looked like a maiden dressed to perform rituals for Ciel; the dagger on her hip being the only reminder that she wasn't.

She had a sullen look on her face; no doubt from being forced to wear her formal attire. She continued to pout all the way through the ballroom until she noticed Silas.

Her eyes widened as she took in his outfit. She bit her lip coyly.

He looked her up and down, slowly and deliberately. He raised his eyebrows.

She blushed and hurried to her place.

'Her Imperial Majesty, Empress Dowager Wei Xianwen of Tianxia and his Imperial Highness Prince Wei Xianrong, with Premier Yuan Shenwu!'

A petite, elderly woman appeared. Her greying hair was pulled into an elaborate headdress, tinkling with bells and tassels, and her colourful silk robes trailed behind her, the layers forming a rainbow. A young man in red and gold robes supported her arm as she walked. He looked to be in his early twenties, for a Human; with long, jet black hair swept back from his face by the straps of his gold cap. Behind them, a gentleman in black and red with a long, thin beard and moustache.

'All rise, for their Imperial Highnesses of the Palatinate, Crown Princess Arafel Crescentia Eltares von und zu Aristarchus, Princess Serefah Crescentia Lupiz von und zu Aristarchus, and Princess Mayim Crescentia Belaska von und zu Aristarchus!'

The sound of a hundred skirts rustling filled the air as everyone stood.

Arafel walked through the doors, flanked by her two cousins. She was majestic in a velvet gown in deep purple with pearls running along her neckline and down the length of her sleeves. The twin crescent moons of her House were a recurring motif; from the jewels sewn onto her bodice to the crescent-shaped charms on her forehead. Even her hair, wound around a large headpiece, created a glossy black crescent above her head. Her cousins were similarly attired, though marginally less embellished, in navy and fuchsia velvet dresses.

Her face was composed and calm as she processed through the room, her dragon sceptre in hand. Climbing the short steps to the dais, she took her seat. As everyone else took theirs, she waited for the room to quieten again before speaking.

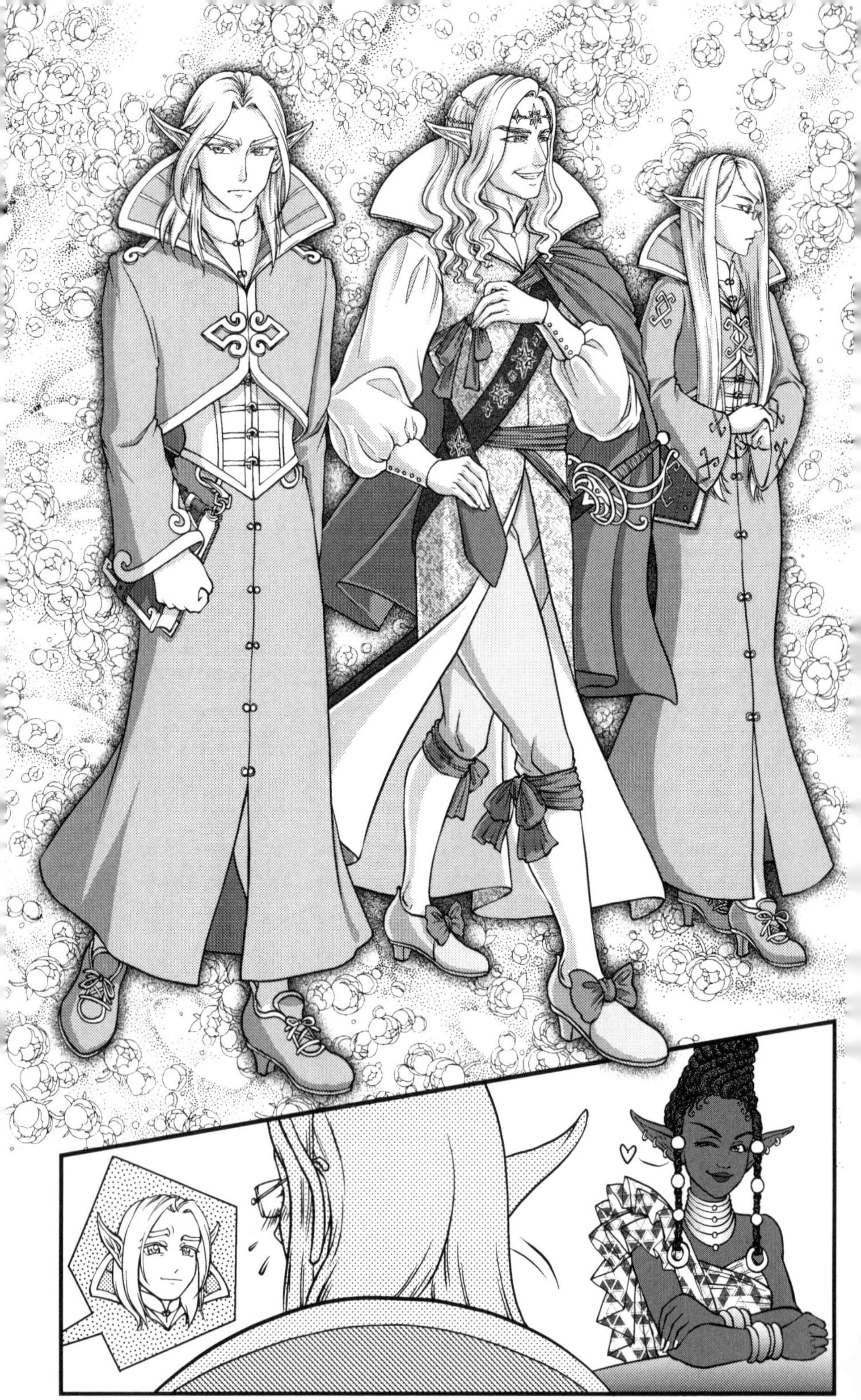

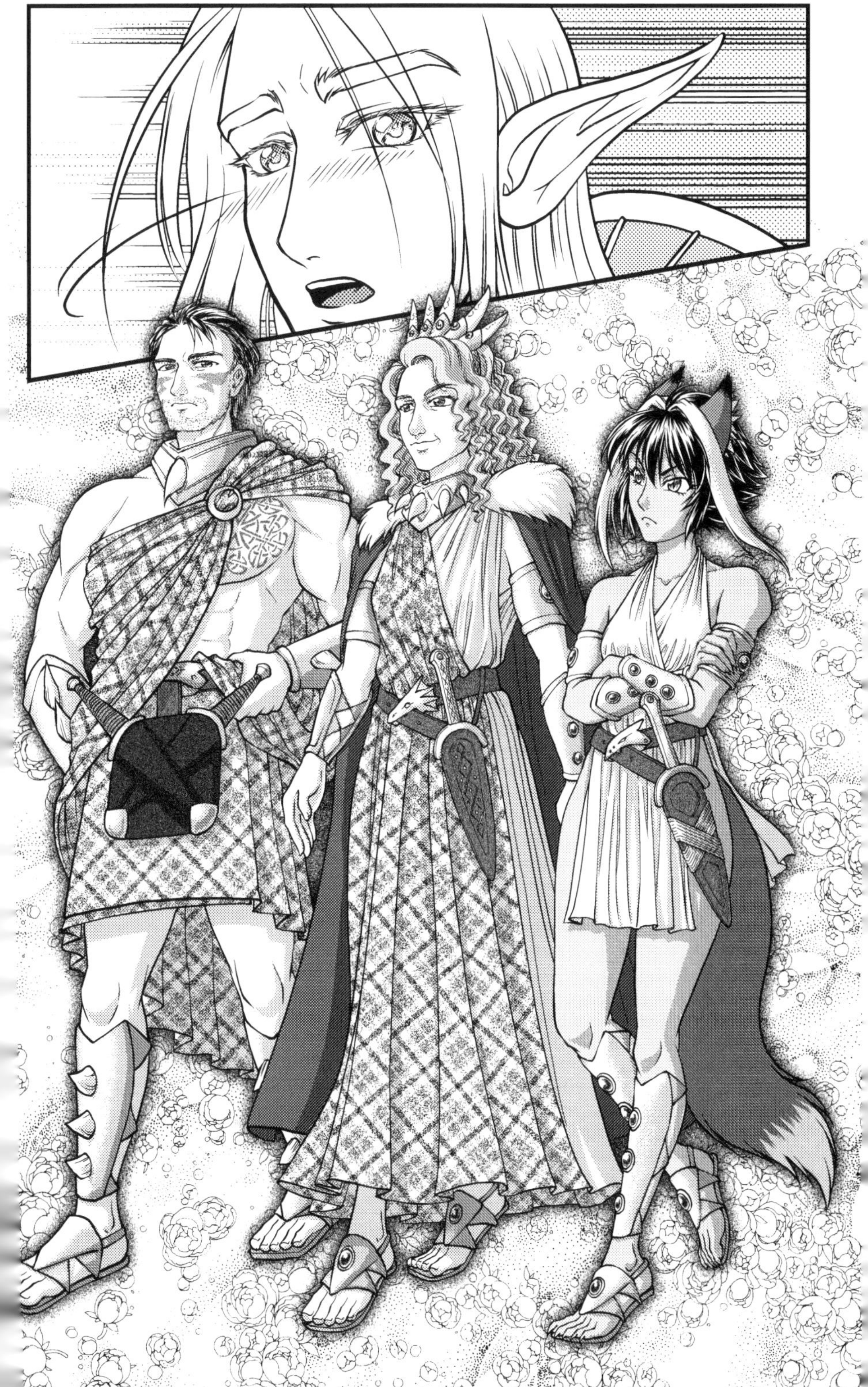

'Good evening everyone and welcome to Drachenheim. Allow me to express my deepest gratitude for your efforts in coming here on such short notice. It is ever thus, and has been since time immemorial, that when the bearer of the burning heart of Ciel's Cradle passes, another must take their place swiftly, lest its fires consume us all. During the ceremony itself, we will mourn the man to whom this solemn duty was given, and from whom it was taken away too soon. However, tonight is a celebration of his life and of us, the children of Ciel, coming together. I would be most delighted to hear any stories you have of my grandfather throughout the evening. But first, I would like to open the festivities with a personal project of mine. '

She nodded to the musicians, who began to strum their lutes in low notes, drums accenting the off-beats. She rose from her seat, holding her dragon sceptre high.

Her dark eyes flashed into the white of the Spirit spectrum.

Silas was surprised by the gasps and murmurs in the room. Those from further afield might not have known, but it was common knowledge in Ciel's Cradle that the Crown Princess was a student at the Lyceum Arcanus. Maybe they thought it was a prestige placement, or that she was on a non-magical course. Perhaps she wanted to remind them all that she was a Spirit Mistress – and a force to be reckoned with.

The silver dragon atop her sceptre began to glow brightly and in a flash of light, it transformed into a large Spirit dragon, its wing tips nearly touching the ceiling. The tambourines shook and the flutes played a sinuous melody. The glowing dragon shimmered and came to life; twisting, turning and flapping its wings in time to the music. It danced through the air above its amazed audience, circling around the chandeliers and jumping off the walls of the ballroom.

Silas was very impressed. To build an illusion of that scale and have it interact so naturally with the environment took great skill in arranging Spirit threads to track the parts visible to the naked eye and separate them from those visible only to the mage. He resisted the urge to tune into the Spirit spectrum himself to see those inner workings.

As a final flourish, the dancing dragon flew back to Arafel, curling itself around her protectively before breathing out a shimmering stream of iridescent fire. It vanished in tendrils of Spirit smoke, along with the glow in Arafel's eyes.

She bowed her head and the room erupted with applause.

'Thank you so much. Now, please – eat, drink, dance and be merry!'

The musicians started up another tune and conversation began to flow as serving staff streamed into the room with assorted trays of food and drink.

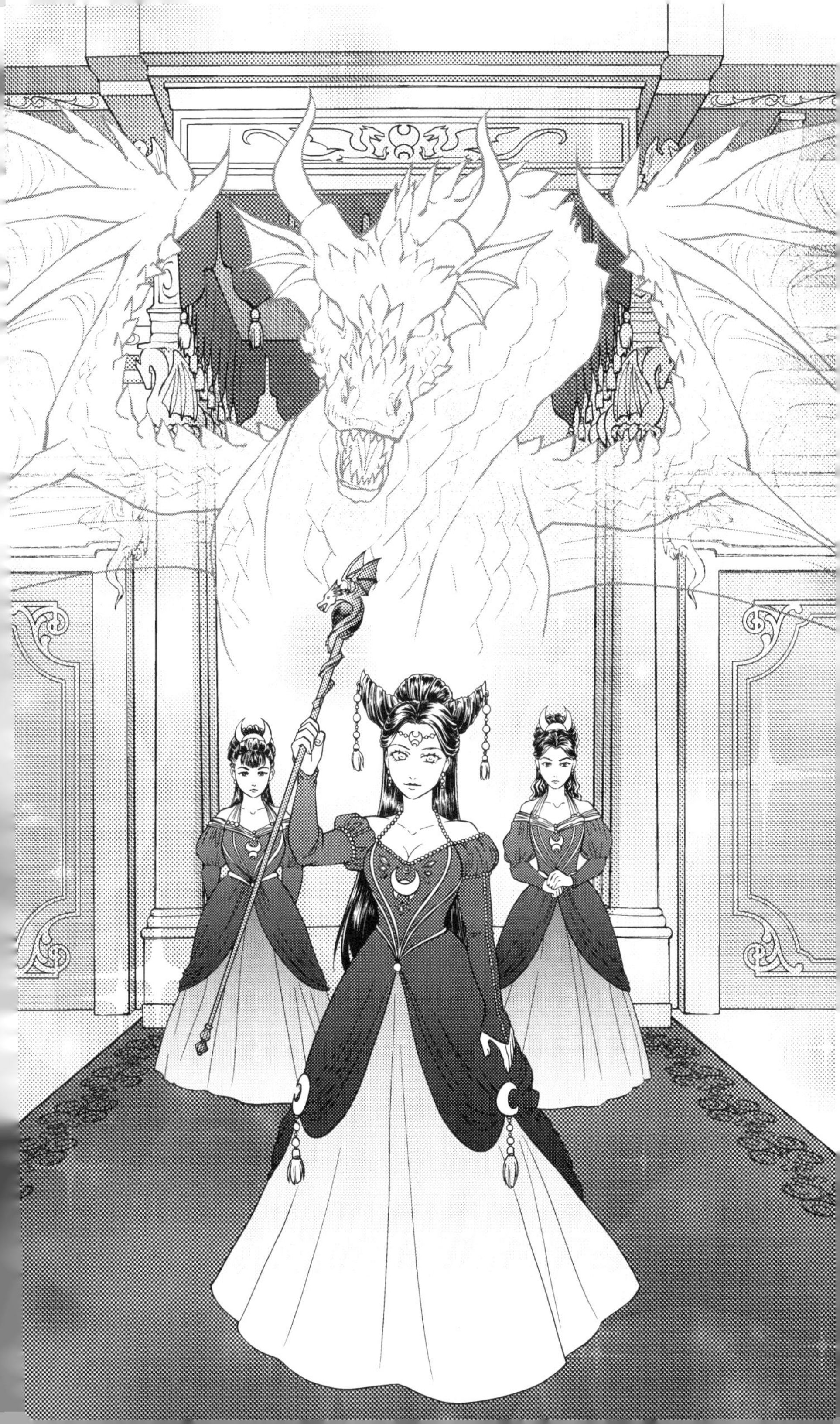

Xavier kept his face bored, but his voice low.

'Véronique, work the crowds. Discover what you can. Oh, and *mon ange?* Try not to scare them off. Perhaps you should stick to the ladies... I daresay Queen Aminatu finds you... most becoming.'

The usually composed Chancellor hurriedly adjusted her glasses and walked away.

From across the room, Eílís looked in their direction.

Xavier nodded at her and bent his head towards Silas.

'We need to have an audience with Arafel. Without others listening too closely.'

The King accepted a tall glass of sparkling wine from a passing tray and twisted around, raising it to his entourage. As they took their glasses, he quickly drained his and placed it on the side table as he rose, gesturing to his *noblesse* to stay seated.

'No need, *mes amis*, take time to enjoy your drinks. I am simply eager to pay my respects to the Empress Incumbent before anyone else! Silas, with me.'

Silas followed his king to the front of the emerging line of dignitaries who were hoping to do the same. Eílís had mirrored their movements, with Rua close behind.

The Vertciellen King smiled and bowed extravagantly, offering his arm.

The Eiran Queen curtsied and took it.

Arafel's face lit up when she saw her closest friend and allies approach.

'Your Majesties, Champion, Magus,' she said, bowing her head at each of them in turn. 'You honour me. Please, all of you, come closer, to save my voice this evening.'

She set her sceptre in her lap and held out her hands for Xavier and Eílís to take.

'Silas has informed me of your support and concerns,' she said, soft enough for only the four of them to hear. 'I am forever grateful for your kindness.'

Xavier allowed his mask to slip, his face gravely serious as he reassured her.

'Your Highness, never have I been more convinced that your right to rule has been divinely sanctioned than after the events of this summer, which Véronique relayed to me. When Ciel herself speaks, one listens. We must all work together to maintain peace.'

Eílís patted Arafel's hand warmly.

'Myself and my Champion are mere servants of Ciel, Mother to all. We may not be fanciful, but we are fiercely loyal and we know a good egg when we see it. You'll make a good Empress, girl. Whenever you need our help, you've but to ask.'

Arafel's eyes went bright and she blinked, trying to hide her emotions.

'Thank you,' she whispered. 'I will organise another time when we can speak at length, in private.'

She pulled back from them, raising her head and her voice.

'I treasure your counsel. Please, enjoy the rest of the evening.'

They bowed to Arafel again, but before they could withdraw, Rua piped up.

'What about you? D'you want me to get you anything? Looks like you're gonna be stuck here for a while...'

She motioned to the long queue of nobles behind them and grimaced.

'A stiff drink or three oughta make it more bearable!'

Arafel tried to keep a straight face, but couldn't hold it in. She laughed out loud.

'Rua, that's a marvellous suggestion! Don't worry, I'll sort myself out. Now, go on. Have a dance for me; I think they're about to start the Allemande.'

Rua grinned at them.

'You heard the Princess, let's dance!'

She bounded off to find a space in the line of women gathering on the dance floor and Eílís shook her head with a sigh, joining her.

'Come on, Silas.' Xavier said, shrugging his shoulders. 'Put that pretty face of yours to good use. That is what I do with mine.'

The King walked to the head of the men's line and Silas unwillingly followed.

Silas was moderately terrified as he bowed to the Hesperian princess in the line facing him, who fluttered her eyelashes back in response and curtsied. He took her hand and the line of couples began to walk in time to the music; three steps quick, one step slow. Although it was a relatively easy dance to begin the evening with, he was incredibly grateful for his long skirts as they covered up his shaky footwork.

'Forgive me, Your Highness,' he said. 'It has been some time since I last danced.'

'I can see that, but I don't mind. Aren't you serving in the Star King's court?'

'I have only recently come into his employ. How should court life be?'

'Ha! I can't decide whether I want less scandals or more.'

Silas took Xavier's words to heart and gave the princess his best smile.

'Oh, pray tell...' he implored, looking into her eyes as they spun around each other.

She flushed to the tips of her pointed ears.

'Well! Usually all I hear about from Uncle Santiago is nothing but complaints about how Puerto Benigno never gets to see the benefit from his investments into our navy. That's because he's been too busy bailing out cousin Lorencio... that boy gets away with everything, never mind if he loses a royal heirloom on a card game! But...'

She paused as Silas spun her around again and continued in an excited whisper.

'...Uncle hasn't mentioned that at all lately. Like as if the problem had vanished! Yet I've seen... I mean, I've heard... that Lorencio and his cronies are still frequenting the casinos and they haven't crowed about winning any big games – so how has he paid off his debts? I think someone else is financing them...'

As she gossiped away, Silas gradually settled into the patterns of the dance and was able to observe the others on the floor.

Xavier was an amazing dancer, precise yet effortless, his fitted breeches and hose showing his footwork to full effect. He was partnered with the High Priestess of Alekhandros whose style was graceful and calm. She chatted with him amiably, amidst surreptitious glances from many other ladies.

Eílís was further down the line, paired with the Amligan Chieftain. It appeared that she was giving him instructions as he had a look of intense concentration on his face, his eyes trained on his feet. If this was his first Allemande, he was doing quite well.

Then Silas saw that familiar flash of russet red fur.

Rua was dancing with the Principe of Pontiazza. She rolled her hips with each step, flicking her tail to accentuate her movements, her bare back displaying every rippling muscle as she twisted and turned. She pouted, then laughed at whatever he was saying, giving him a wink before he twirled her around, her raised arms exposing her sides entirely, her skirt fluttering so high that they threatened to expose everything else.

Silas knew she was laying on the charm to gather information but that did little to stop his feelings of desire and jealousy.

The music stopped and he dragged his eyes away from her to bow to his dance partner. It was customary at this point for the women to take a few steps along the line so that new couples would be formed for the next dance.

He straightened up and was pleasantly surprised that he was face to face with Rua.

There was a clap from the dais; it was Arafel.

'La Volta!' she shouted. 'For my dear friends, the Weaver and the Dagger!'

They both stared at her in shock as the dance floor cleared.

She wiggled her fingers at them with a mischievous smile.

'She remembered,' Silas mumbled.

'That scheming... wait, what?' Rua backtracked. 'What d'you mean?'

'We used to dance this at parties in Drachenheim. It was one of the only dances I could get right. Hands were never a problem for me, it was always my feet. And because it uses the *galliard* five step as a constant base...'

He smiled winningly at Rua and stepped in close, raising his hand up.

'May I have this dance, mi'lady?'

Rua's eyes blazed as she pressed her palm to his.

'You, most certainly, may.'

He pushed at her hand hard, spinning her away to the far side of the dance floor.

The music began.

He raised his fingers to his mouth and blew her a kiss in a flamboyant salute.

She played at catching the kiss and curtsied low.

With flowing hand gestures accenting each five step sequence; his, small and neat under his long skirts; hers, bare-legged, exuberant and high; they came towards each other again in diagonal passes.

Meeting in the middle, palms now touching as they rounded on each other, her fingertips felt like fire against his skin as their eyes locked.

'I saw you the way you danced with the Principe,' he whispered.

'Did you like it?' she challenged him, hotly.

'...Yes, and no.'

'Good.'

She broke away, stepping back around him. She embellished her routine with an extra twirl and with her hand in his, they skipped together, side by side, in a large circle.

The tambourine shook. Rua put her hands on Silas's shoulders as he moved in closer to her, placing one hand in the small of her back and the other on her belt buckle. He was reminded about how little she was wearing when his fingers brushed against her bare skin.

As the musicians struck their bells, she hopped and he lifted her high, raising his thigh to push against the backs of hers to carry her around him in a spin. She made it halfway around before touching down for a split second before he lifted her up again.

She laughed, enjoying the brief ride. She released his shoulders and bounded away, tracing a claw against his cheek as she went.

'Again! Higher!' she requested, as she danced around him.

He chuckled, an idea forming.

'Yes, ma'am.'

His eyes glowed a soft white as he tuned into the Spirit spectrum. He pulled the white threads to concentrate below his feet.

The crowd gasped in awe as the Spirit threads manifested into a glowing spiral.

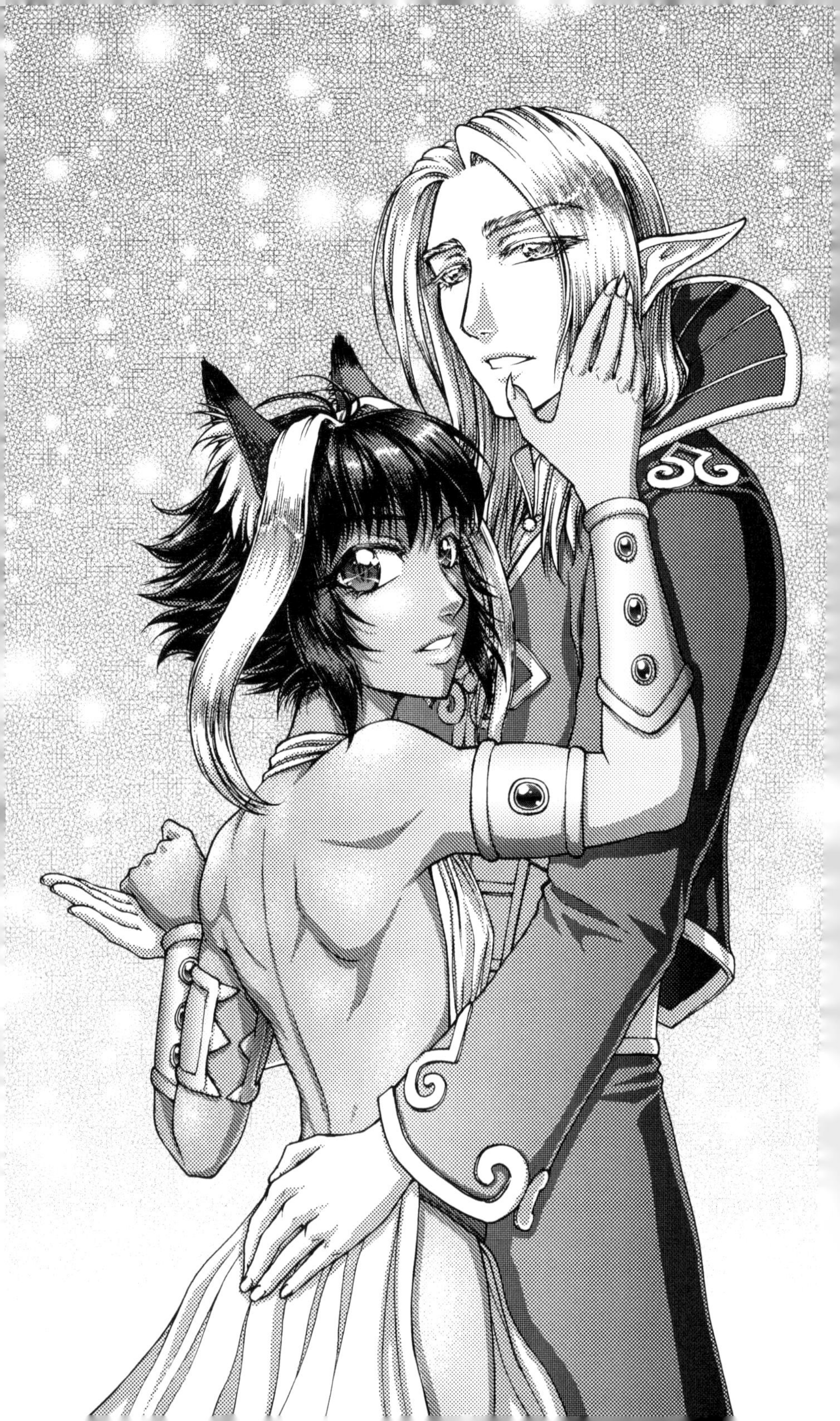

'Come!' he called to her.

She skipped towards him and leapt into his arms.

He caught her and matching the spiral to her momentum, he spun her above his head with just one hand, using Spirit threads to support her high in the air.

Silas had never seen anything quite as beautiful. With her golden eyes full of life, her dress fluttering as she flew through the air and the white halo of Spirit surrounding her, Rua truly looked like a divine agent of Ciel.

He gradually pulled her back in with Spirit, then dismissed the threads once he took hold of her waist. The spiral beneath them slowed and dispersed into glowing sparkles as he removed his Spirit spectrum and set her down on the ground.

For a moment, it was just the two of them, looking into each other's eyes, not needing to speak to know what the other wanted to say.

The music ended and the crowd erupted into applause.

The pair hastily turned to face Arafel, bowing and curtseying.

She was giving them a standing ovation. Her smiling face was full of pride.

Thank you, Silas mouthed to her.

You're welcome, she mouthed back.

They paid their respects to the rest of the room and Rua rejoined Éilís at her table.

Xavier and Véronique were waiting for him at the side of the dance floor.

'You really are a star student,' Xavier drawled, clapping his hands. 'You couldn't have made yourself look more dashing if you tried. I'd be tempted to keep you in my court permanently if Ciel hadn't already claimed you.'

Véronique inclined her head approvingly at Silas.

'Your performance was eye-catching enough to distract most of the people in the room. I was able to make several observations without notice. It was very helpful.'

Xavier raised an eyebrow at her.

'What she means to say is "Thank you." Now, dear boy, you should capitalise on your current fame; I'd venture few in this room would resist your charms. Get back out there. Véronique will look after me.'

He took Silas by the shoulders, turned him around and gave him a little push towards a group of ladies with lovestruck expressions on their faces.

As they giggled and gathered around him, Silas looked back at Xavier pleadingly.

The Elven Star King waved him off with a smile and walked away.

VIII

There was a soft knock on Silas's door, startling him awake. Sunlight glowed at the edges of his curtains; that meant he needed to hurry. He dressed quickly, stepping out of his bedroom and into the King's sitting room as he did up his last button.

Xavier was already lounging on the settee, reading a letter.

'Good morning, Silas. Ah, no need to apologise; you youngsters need your sleep, especially after such an exciting evening...'

Véronique obviously disagreed, glaring at Silas tight-lipped.

Caught between his King and his mentor, Silas did his best to look contrite.

Xavier folded up the letter and handed it to Véronique.

'Arafel has arranged for us to breakfast with her in the East Wing. Come.'

The three of them walked through the corridors of Schloss Drachen, escorted by an Imperial Knight. He guided them to the eastern dining room, where two more knights saluted and admitted them inside.

Silas was immediately comforted by the sight of Rua sitting at the table with Eílís and Owyn. Her plate was already piled high with bread rolls and cured meats.

'Morning, all!' she called to them, her mouth full of salami. 'The buffet's over there; the ham's good, but the liverwurst is amazing!'

'Rua...' Eílís began in an admonishing tone. 'You're doing us no favours with your table manners...'

Xavier laughed.

'On the contrary, Eílís! It is refreshing for me to see someone behave so freely. This liverwurst, you say? I will try it.'

Silas was no stranger to Palatine breakfasts but chose to forgo Rua's recommendation of the pungent spread in favour of thinly sliced cheese to top his bread rolls. He spotted the jams and hastily added dollops of them to his plate as well.

The Vertciellens finished filling their plates and sat opposite the Eirans. Before they could tuck in, the door opened and Arafel breezed into the room.

'Good morning everyone,' she said, cheerfully.

They greeted her back as she walked to the samovar to make a chrysanthemum tisane. Keeping her voice light as she stirred her drink, she looked at Silas.

'Si, could you go through all of your spectra, please?'

Silas frowned for a second, then realised she wanted him to scan the room for spells. She really wasn't taking any chances.

He obliged, his eyes flashing white as he tuned into the Spirit spectrum.

He stood up and spun around slowly, searching for any telltale signs of threads being woven into a Spirit Mesh or Fabric.

No, he couldn't see anything suspicious.

He switched over to the Fire spectrum and looked all over the room again, his eyes glowing red. Still, he detected nothing. He observed the green threads of Air next; they were dispersed throughout the room as normal. His eyes flicked into the brilliant blue of Water and once more, there were no spell signatures to be seen.

Then he engaged the Earth spectrum.

His heart jumped into his throat as he suddenly saw a concentrated twist of yellow tendrils beneath the floor of the dining table.

'Earth Bore!' he gasped.

He flung his arms out, grabbing a spare Earth thread and throwing it like a harpoon down into the Earth Bore to track the spell back to its caster, but it was too late; the tendrils rapidly dispersed. They must have realised he was onto them.

Everyone had leapt back from their plates in alarm, staring at him.

He sighed with frustration and shook his head at Véronique.

Now they all looked at her.

'Mages who resonate with Spirit and Air are most suited to espionage,' she explained. 'However, there are a few spells from the other elements which can be useful. An Earth Bore is one such spell. It works like an ear horn – an amplifier, if you will – by picking up the vibrations of the room, allowing the caster to eavesdrop from a considerable distance.'

She folded her arms and frowned.

'It wasn't obvious to me who was an Earth mage at the ball last night. Please, allow me to create an Air Barrier before we continue.'

She swiftly drew the cuboid pattern of Air threads before pinching its corners and pulling it apart. She nodded to indicate it was done.

They gingerly took their seats and began to talk in earnest over their breakfasts.

'So, what did we all hear about last night?' Xavier asked, slicing open a roll. 'I can make a start, if it helps? I became acquainted with the High Priestess during the opening dance. Parthenope was most relieved to talk to a man who didn't wish to argue with her, for a change – she seemed worn out from the Hierophants challenging all of her recent decisions. Perhaps one or more of them are looking to vote another priestess into her place. Silas, you definitely made an impression on the ladies last night. What did the Ocean King's niece tell you?'

Silas quickly swallowed his mouthful of bread.

'As Your Majesty suspected, Prince Lorencio has been gambling, but he is no longer draining his father's coffers. His debts have been cleared despite his continuing habit. It appears that someone else is financing him.'

'Oh, how delicious. Véronique, anything juicy to contribute?'

The Chancellor sipped at her coffee delicately.

'I overheard an argument between Tsar Vadim's eldest and the Jarl of Orbos. Tsesarevich Kazimir challenged Jarl Rikvald to a duel. The Tsarina was not impressed. Neither was the Jarl's sister. No blades were drawn.'

'The old 'Waikinger Horde' name-calling, I presume.'

'Correct, Your Majesty.'

'Is that all? I am curious to know what you thought of Queen Aminatu.'

Véronique kept her eyes firmly fixed on her coffee.

'The Ifriqs are... rather blunt with their opinions. Queen Aminatu was very... friendly towards me. Queen Nakato was not. She barely concealed her hostility.'

'Speaking of the Ifriqs,' Rua interjected. 'The Principe of Pontiazza has been getting a lot of attention from Ifriqikah and Amliga. He wants free trade. But he couldn't stop complaining about the Economic Commission for Ciel's Cradle. He's not happy with the ECCC's agreed tax rates for countries outside our bloc.'

Xavier drummed his fingers on the table.

'Of course. Much harder to butter them up if they can't get a good deal. And what about the edge of the Cradle? Any news from the Desert Corridor?'

Eílís shook her head.

'Kaspar and Saif are old friends of ours. They argued as they always do about who was better at what, nothing out of the ordinary there, was there, Owyn?'

The Prince Consort grunted in agreement.

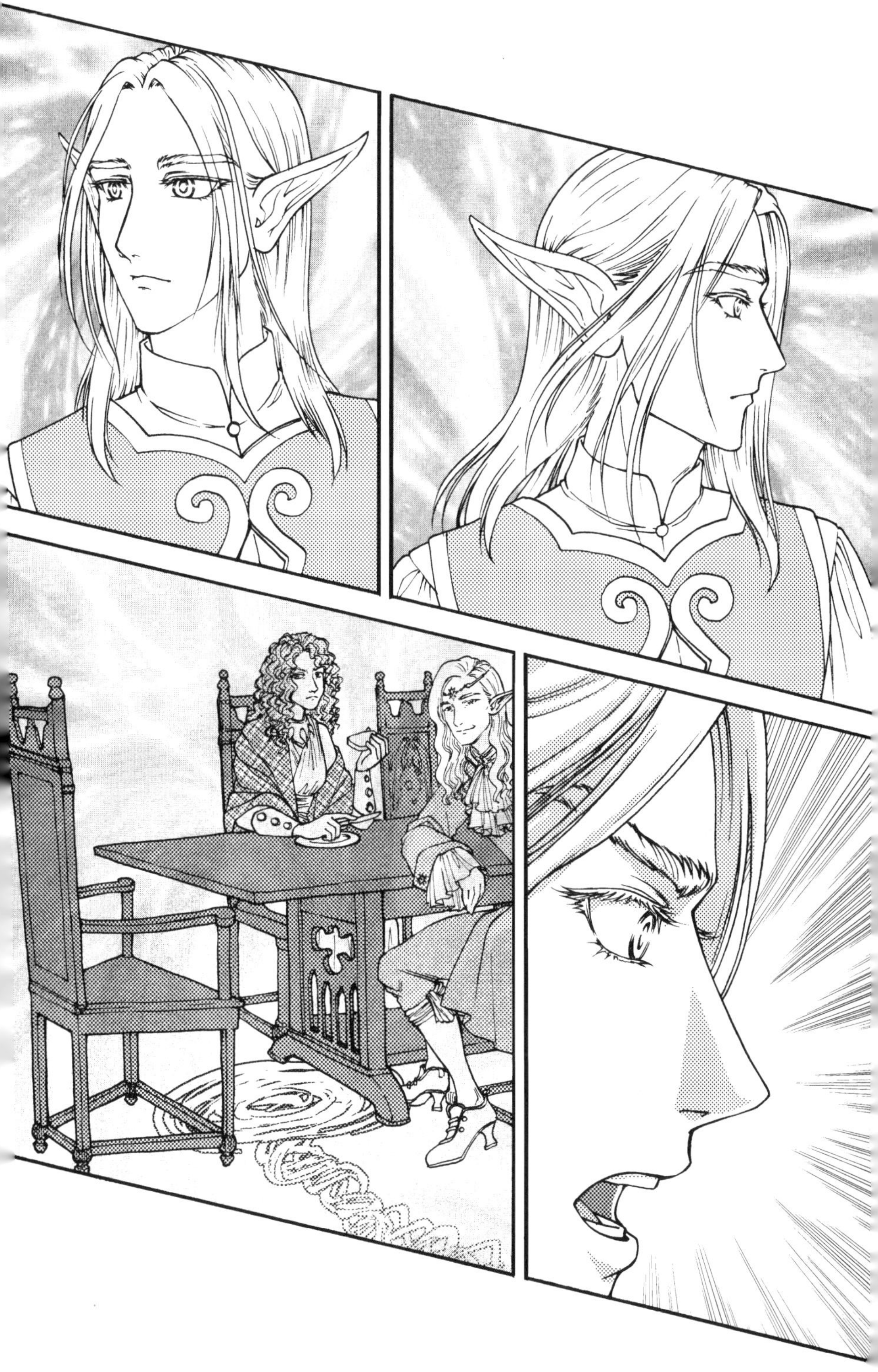

The Queen got up to make another cup of tea, musing as she went.

'No, after the work Rua did with them thirty years ago to dismantle that slave trading ring, Bashkendir has always had a healthy respect for Eira. If there's any wrongdoing in those parts, I'll bet the Bey himself isn't involved. It'll be others in his court. And that was what I was keeping an eye on; everyone's entourage. My own Duke of Blestium had a nice, long chat with that Elf from Sturmgaard.'

She looked at Xavier.

'And your Maréchal Lefèvre met up with Baron Zharykhin of Tsithia.'

The Star King narrowed his eyes.

'Interesting. Our two were the ones bickering back in Fleurys. It seems we have an awful lot of people to keep track of. Any other news?'

Arafel had been silent all this time, but cleared her throat to speak.

'I have an announcement to make. The Tianxian delegation has informally approached me on the subject of marriage. To Prince Wei Xianrong.'

Silas dropped his knife onto his plate and stared at her.

She rolled her eyes at him.

'Oh, don't look so shocked, Si. I'm quite a catch, you know.'

Xavier broke into a wide grin.

'Ha! Didn't I say he would try, Véronique?'

'You did, Your Majesty. It is a fair match; a marriage to him would be a good way to seal an alliance between the two Empires. But there is the small matter of logistics...'

Arafel nodded.

'Of course, I won't leave Drachenheim. He is willing to relocate to me. I'm already more senior in rank, more so once I'm Empress, and a ruler in my own right.'

'Well then, you have our congratulations,' Eílís said.

'And ours,' Xavier added.

Silas looked at Rua. Her face reflected the concern he felt for his childhood friend. Arranged marriages were common amongst nobility, but he didn't want her to get hurt.

'Arafel,' Véronique asked, her tone softer than usual. 'How do you feel about it?'

Rua looked startled by this show of kindness, but Silas wasn't.

The Crown Princess gave them a wry smile and picked at her fingernails.

'Well, he's certainly good looking. Educated and well spoken. And he can dance. Let's just say that I wouldn't dismiss him outright.'

Xavier spread his arms wide.

'So where does this leave us? Tianxia are marrying up, so they aren't trying to make enemies. Bashkendir and Sharaafdi seem to be carrying on as normal. Amliga and Ifriqikah are getting friendly with Pontiazza. Tsithia is still annoyed with Iskar, but that isn't new. Hesperia's money problems have mysteriously gone away, and Alekhandros is having its own internal power struggle. All of it seems so... insular, petty almost. Most peculiar is how none of it seems aimed at toppling the Palatinate.'

Arafel looked up from her fingernails, her dark eyes searching for answers.

'So why was someone trying to spy on us?'

***

Silas made a show of admiring the scenery as he tried his best not to maintain eye contact with the others on the carriage. As it was the last day before the coronation, all of the guests had been invited to tour Drachenheim and visit the site of the ceremony to run through the order of service. Arafel had arranged for their alliance to be spread across three groups. The Empress Incumbent would be looking after the dignitaries from Hesperia, Alekhandros, Bashkendir and Tianxia. Her cousin Mayim was with the Eirans, who would be keeping an eye on the visitors from Tsithia, Amliga and Sharaafdi. Which left Serefah with Vertcielle, Pontiazza, Iskar and Ifriqikah.

The twelve-seater carriage was still a tight fit for their eleven passengers. Principe Marco and Jarl Thyge chatted in the back row, their wives staying in Schloss Drachen having booked hairdressers. The Jarl's shieldmaiden Gunnælf stayed silent. In the row facing the Vertciellens was Jarl Rikvald and his sister Sigrid, who were complaining about the Tsithians to Xavier. Next to Sigrid was Queen Aminatu, who made no secret of her delight at being on the same coach as Véronique. The glowering Queen Nakato was on the end, choosing not to say anything.

'Has it changed much?'

Silas looked at the girl sitting beside him. Serefah, like her younger sister Mayim, resembled Arafel in many ways. They all had dark hair and dark eyes that looked haunted by the events from nine years ago. They too, lost their parents in the attack.

'No,' he said, smiling sadly. 'It is just how I remembered it.'

She nodded, looking down at her hands in her lap.

'I know it was hard for you. It was hard for Arafel too. She missed you. When you left. And... I'm sorry if... I wasn't kind to you after it happened.'

Silas shook his head.

'We were just children, back then. So I forgive you for any names you called me when you were eight. I do not know if I can forgive the adults who did the same.'

'Thank you. Arafel said you held no grudge against me, but I had to be sure.'

He tried to lighten her mood.

'I heard from her that you were hoping to come to Fleurys?'

'Ah, yes! Well, if I can pass the Lyceum's entrance exams...'

'Majoring in...?'

'Water. And hopefully specialising in Alchemy.'

'Nice combination. If you need any help, please do not hesitate to ask; if we have some free time after the formalities, perhaps we can Harmonise our Spirit Protocols so you can write to me?'

'Th-thank you so much!'

The stagecoach made its first stop at the Universität, home to the world's leading innovators in technology due to their commitment to blending manufacturing with magic. This was evident from the building's perfectly symmetrical exterior, accented with near-seamless rows of red glass tiles and topped with finely machined spires.

Then they drove down to the water line to admire the Nebel Brücke, the longest bridge in Ciel's Cradle. Connecting Himmelsleiter to the mainland, it was rare to see all the way down its length as the sombre stone structure would disappear into the constant mists of the White Lake.

Turning back uphill, they stopped in the famous Schmuckquartal where the guests were invited into a jewellery workshop with a Fire Master. As he demonstrated some basic techniques with Fire threads, Silas felt a pang of nostalgia. This was what he could have become; one of the paths he was training towards, before his tenth birthday.

Finally, their stagecoach climbed Himmelsleiter to its very peak, stopping at the mouth of a cave that was bustling with activity. They all stepped off the coach and Serefah led them into a cavernous chamber filled with spectacular rock formations; stalactites flowed from the ceiling, some joining together with stalagmites rising like waves from the ground. Jewel-toned reflections bounced around the pools of water amongst the cathedral-like columns of rippling stone, as the torchlight filtered through the massive crystals jutting out from the walls.

Whilst workers filed around them placing chairs and decorations on the stands being constructed, Serafah stopped and turned around to speak to the group.

'Welcome to the Auge – the Eye of the Dragon. As you can see, we are standing above an active volcano; just a few steps away from the crater's edge. Don't worry, we are perfectly safe... for now. Of course, we will all be much safer, once the ceremony is over. As my cousin mentioned last night, the role of Emperor or Empress is unique in Ciel's Cradle as they alone can control the flow of lava in the Auge, which powers much of our industry and commerce.'

She gestured at the black, glassy, table-like rock behind her.

'The Arae Doloris – the Altar of Anguish. This obsidian altar was forged naturally from the rocks during the birth of Himmelsleiter. For the Auge to accept its new ruler, the Empress Incumbent must commit her predecessor to its flames and immediately offer her blood to the altar with the enchanted *Blutdolch*. She must then demonstrate her mastery over the Auge by descending into the active crater and redirecting the lava flow into specially made ceremonial channels that flow up the walls, lined with heat resistant glass. This creates an intricate pattern in molten lava in front of her audience. The result is a once-in-a-generation obsidian sculpture, which will be on display at Schloss Drachen for the rest of her reign. Once this lifetime bond is forged, the Empress cannot be separated from the Auge for long; they will pine for each other and go mad, potentially destroying all of Drachenheim in the process. Hence why all in Ciel's Cradle must understand that when the ruler of the Palatinate dies, we have at most, two weeks, before the Auge consumes us all with its grief.'

***

'Weaver, is it true that you have mastery over all of the five elements?'

Silas quickly swallowed his last spoonful of Gulasch as the grey-haired Empress Dowager of Tianxia regarded him curiously from across the dining table.

'I would not presume to have as much mastery over a single element as a mage who has used it throughout their lifetime, but I can use and cast spells with all five, yes.'

'Oh, Si is just being modest,' Arafel interjected. 'He's younger than me yet he graduated with honours in all elements and has started his PhD.'

'At the Lyceum Arcanus, even?' Premier Yuan said, stroking his beard. 'Impressive.'

Véronique inclined her head at him.

'I will take that as a compliment, Premier.'

'As will I,' said Xavier, with his usual lazy smile.

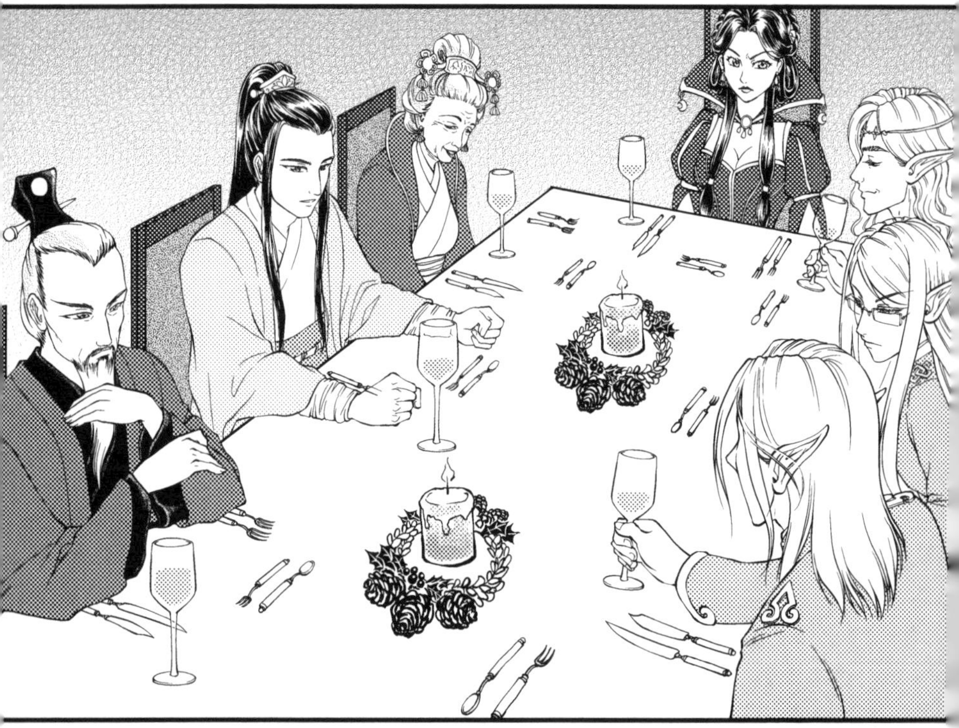

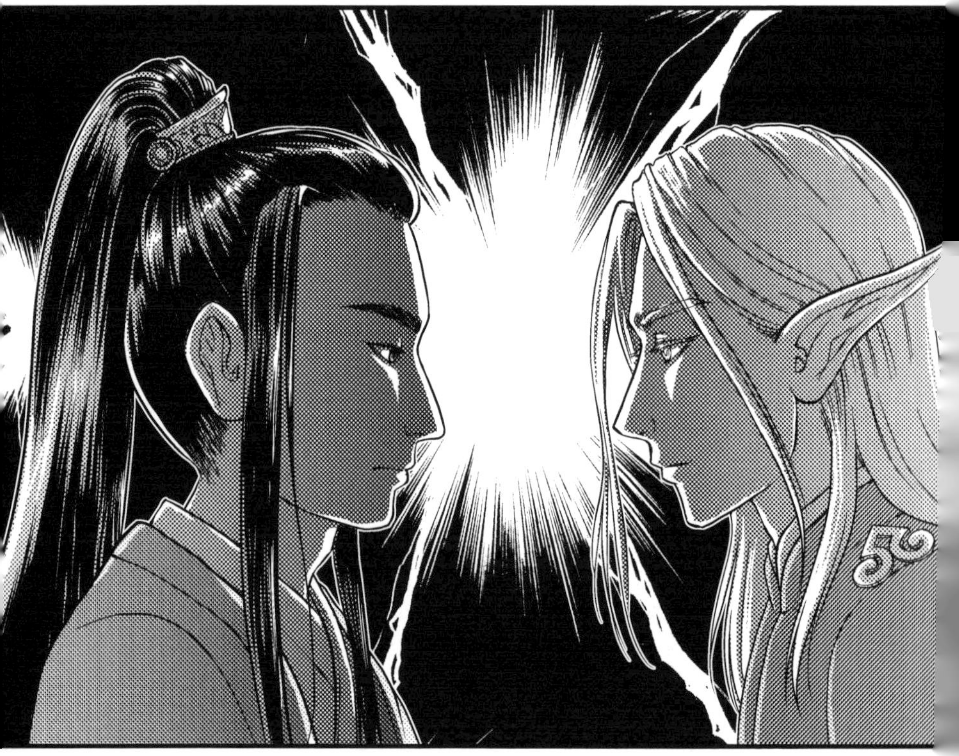

Prince Wei leant back as the soup bowls were taken away and frowned at Arafel.

'You call the Weaver 'Si', Your Highness?'

'It's just a nickname, I've always called him that.'

Silas looked down to adjust the napkin on his lap as he reminisced, smiling.

'From the first day we met. I remember when we used to write to each other as children, I did not correct your spelling when you addressed your letters to 'S-A-I'. And when I told you a year later, you were so embarrassed...'

He glanced up to see Arafel with her face taut as she gave him the smallest shake of her head. He paused for a moment, then noticed that the Tianxian prince was glowering at him intently.

Was Xianrong jealous? He needn't be. In fact, he shouldn't be.

'...That you resolved to never misspell anything again. I am sure I still have some of those letters hidden at the Ambassadade. Actually, there may even be a few in that old library we used to play in—'

'Ah, the fish course is here!' Arafel said, raising her voice over his.

She shot Silas a murderous glare as plates of trout were placed in front of them.

'And we still have three more courses to go,' Xavier chuckled.

***

'Tea? How do you take it?' Eílís asked, as Owyn handed her the teapot.

Flustered that a queen was offering to make it for him whilst his king and his mentor were watching, Silas said the first thing that came into his head.

'Just as it is, thank you.'

She raised an eyebrow at him as she handed him the cup and saucer.

'We've no maids around at this hour, but I can still make a good brew, you know.'

'I-I meant no offence, I did not wish to trouble you!'

'You weren't quite so meek at dinner earlier...'

Xavier laughed and clapped his hands together.

'I had not witnessed such quality entertainment in years! I must thank whoever came up with the seating plan. Putting us with the Shuntien delegation was a stroke of genius. Xianrong was so besotted with the girl, he barely looked at the food on his plate. Of course, every time Silas spoke to her, he clenched his jaw a bit. And you, my boy – you actually played up to it! I'm impressed by your pettiness.'

Silas's ears shook slightly with indignation.

'I never-'

'Really?' Rua said, cutting him off. 'You didn't think all those anecdotes weren't gonna make him just a little bit jealous?'

He sipped his tea.

'Arafel is one of my best friends. If he cannot handle that, he is no gentleman.'

The doorknob to Eílís's chambers clicked and the door swung open. After a second, it swung back and closed. With a swishing sound, Arafel and her cousins appeared.

The white glow of Spirit left the Crown Princess's eyes as she stomped up to Silas and jabbed at his chest with a finger.

'You!' she hissed. 'I have a bone to pick with you, but scan the room first!'

Silas gulped and obeyed, tuning into each spectrum in turn.

'All clear,' he reported.

Véronique's eyes flashed a brighter green as she cast an Air Barrier.

'Done,' she confirmed.

Arafel glared at Silas and took a deep breath.

'You *Dummkopf!* You were winding Xianrong up on purpose, weren't you?! It's all well and good for you, but this engagement isn't yet a done deal and I've not got the biggest pool to choose from! Few men can deal with a wife that comes with as many conditions as I do and *I actually like him*, so Ciel help me, if you wreck this to the point where he bails out or starts rumours about us, I'll set the Auge on you myself!'

Silas cowered under her barrage of words and hung his head.

'I am sorry, Arafel. My conduct was wrong. I suppose I was... testing him. A gentleman should trust his wife to have friends and her own independence. However much I may have irked him, he said nothing of it, so he, most definitely, is.'

She glared at him for a few moments longer before she let out an exasperated sigh.

'Fine! But no more point-scoring! He needs to get used to you first, Ciel help him.'

She shooed Silas along the sofa and sat down heavily.

'So! Any revelations from today?'

Eílís folded her arms.

'Nothing significant to add. Kazimir and Zharykhin seem close. Vadim was very polite to Saif and Ashraqat. Well, he already knows Kaspar; much of their naval trade passes through Bashkendir before going overland to Sharaafdi. Yuma and his warriors didn't really talk much.'

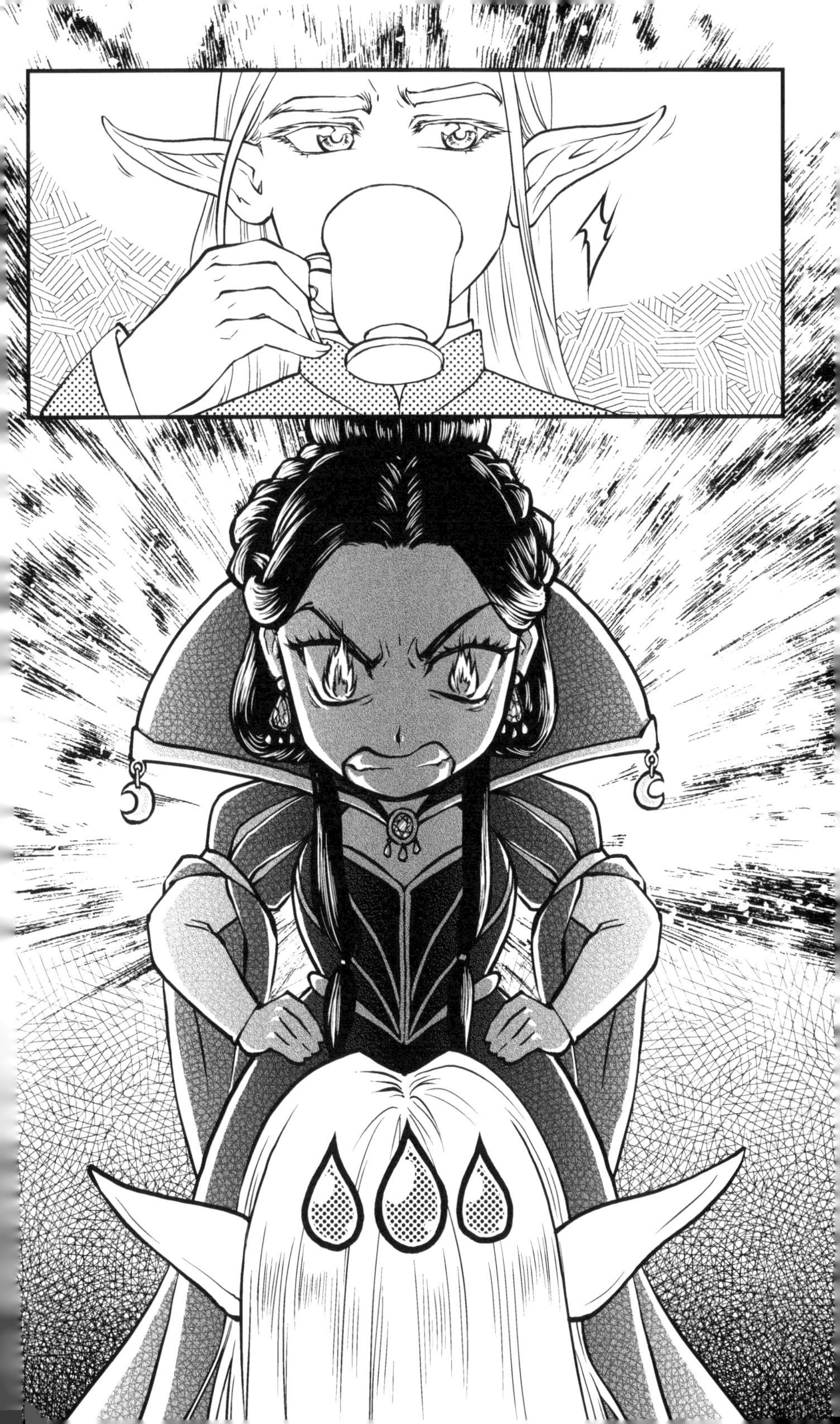

Xavier sighed.

'Our group was the same; just the usual pleasantries and chit-chat. I'll admit much of my ear was taken up by Rikvald and Sigrid complaining about Vadim's fleet. Véronique, did you notice anything?'

The Chancellor adjusted her glasses.

'If the tours were conducted similarly across all three groups, there would have been plenty of opportunities for an assassin to strike. The Schmuckquartal would have been an ideal spot, but other stops on the tour would have sufficed.'

Silas was reminded about her past as a battle mage. Which made him wonder.

'Can we figure out who tried to use the Earth Bore yesterday?'

'Saif is a mage,' Eílís remarked. 'I've heard he shifts the dunes around Sharaafdi if the trade routes get buried under sandstorms. Not sure which element he uses, though.'

'The High Priestess of Alekhandros is always a mage,' Véronique added. 'But most of the rituals require only the basic level of Spirit affinity; she could be a mistress of any element. She did not train at the Lyceum, so I do not have that knowledge to hand.'

'And during dinner, I saw Premier Yuan access a magus inbox to post something for the Empress Dowager,' Arafel recalled. 'But there are over a hundred nobles visiting and not all mages advertise the fact that they are mages.'

Xavier drummed his fingers on his knee.

'We're no closer to finding out who our little spy was. Perhaps it was just that; some opportunistic eavesdropping. And maybe whoever killed the Emperor had a personal vendetta and we're making it all out to be bigger than it is. But we can't risk hoping for the best; we must prepare for the worst.'

Arafel settled her hands in her lap.

'And we're out of time. The ceremony is tomorrow. I cannot delay it without good reason. Even if I did, the Auge itself will not wait much longer.'

Rua closed her eyes and tapped a finger to her lips.

'The ceremony is most definitely the key to all of this. The vital elements are the cremation of the deceased Emperor and the blood-letting of the new Empress. If I wanted to cause havoc, there are three things I'd do. I'd either steal the Emperor's corpse, stop Arafel's blood reaching the altar, or kill Arafel, Serefah and Mayim before any of them could offer their blood.'

'The Emperor's body is being guarded every hour,' Arafel said. 'I, myself, have visited him every night with with Serefah and Mayim. A shared vigil is part of the rituals leading up to the ceremony. I can confirm that it is him.'

'Hmm. So we've got to carry on the ceremony as normal and catch them in the act whilst keeping you all safe. Troublesome. Talk me through the ceremony in more detail.'

'After the visiting dignitaries are seated, the Emperor's coffin will be brought in by the clergy and placed on the altar. The Head Cleric brings in his crown, followed by Drachenheim's nobles. Then the three heirs –myself and my cousins– enter. We position ourselves around the altar and I make a declaration to the Auge. We push the Emperor's coffin into the flames. Then the Head Cleric gives me the *Blutdolch* to cut myself and drip my blood onto the altar. Once enough has been absorbed into the stone, it will glow. Then I must...'

She faltered slightly at this point, but continued, her voice slightly shaking.

'...Descend into the active crater and make my obsidian sculpture. I'm... still a bit nervous about that part. Once it cools, I climb back up and I am crowned. Then I leave with my cousins and the clergy, followed by everyone else.'

Rua's eyes narrowed.

'How soon after cremating the Emperor must you offer your blood to the altar?'

Arafel frowned.

'Once the Emperor's body falls into the lava, the lava will begin to rise up the crater. So... not very long. There are no formal records of exactly how long you can leave it but I have seen my grandfather making it rise and fall. Perhaps... five minutes before it starts getting warmer in the chamber, then another five before it starts getting extremely hot?'

'In that case,' Rua growled. 'I have a plan.'

IX

The Auge's main chamber was rammed full of people in extravagant outfits. Despite being the site of an active volcano, the entrance to the cavern was still wide open to the elements, so everyone had to dress warmly for the wintry morning temperatures.

Those from the Azure Basin were more used to milder winters; the Hesperians shuffled about restlessly in their padded doublets, shivering from the cold with the Pontiazzan delegation and members of the Alekhandrian Order. In stark contrast were the Iskarians and Tsithians, neither of whom looked uncomfortable at all. The former wore full animal pelts down their backs, held in place by their bucklers. The latter embellished their outerwear as much as their indoor clothing; their great coats dripping with jewels and framed with colourful embroidery. From further afield, the Amligans and the Ifriqs were smothered in animal hides and chunky jewellery, their war spears just as richly decorated. The parties from the Desert Corridor and Tianxia looked elegant and serene dressed in their long robes; several layers of silk and brocade wrapped closely around them to stave off the chill.

Silas had been sitting in the Vertciellen section of the audience stands with Xavier and Véronique, but as time went on and the moment of the ceremony approached, he began getting butterflies in his stomach.

'Oh, Silas, do stop fidgeting,' Xavier scolded. 'You're beginning to put me off.'

'It does us no favours if we let any potential assassins know of our wariness,' Véronique whispered. 'Learn to control your feelings more.'

He swallowed, and took a deep breath.

Images of Rua's beaten and bloodied corpse swam before his eyes.

It was so fresh and recent, he had to try very hard not to succumb to panic again.

Logically, she had to do it. Logically, it made sense.

He looked over to the Eirans and counted heads for the tenth time. Everyone was present that should be there. He looked at the small, hooded figure next to Eílís and Owyn. Her fluffy red tail was curled around to rest in her lap.

He prayed that Rua would come out of this better than the last time.

A fanfare played and all of the dignitaries rose to their feet in the stands.

Drums beat a slow and steady rhythm as the coffin of the Emperor was brought in by ten pallbearers, marching in unison to the sound. Gilded dragons glinted on its sides of dark wood as it passed by the chamber's flickering torches. The clerics of Ciel followed closely after, swinging smoking balls of incense from chains. Vocalising without words, they sang a haunting melody which echoed off the rocky walls as they shuffled to the back of the chamber in deeply hooded cloaks.

The elderly Head Cleric of Drachenheim came in, carrying the Imperial crown of the Palatinate. It was both weighty and delicate in appearance; a velvet-cushioned circlet of white ermine topped by glittering diamonds with six stems in silver arching up to a dragon-winged orb.

As the Emperor's coffin was carefully placed on the Arae Doloris by the pallbearers, the Head Cleric walked up to the stone altar. He bowed, then stood to the side, waiting for the aristocrats of Drachenheim to enter the chamber. Wearing rich mantles of brocades and furs, they filed in solemnly and took their places reserved at the front of the stands.

Then the clerics stopped their song and the Imperial Knights lining the walls held their weapons held high in salute.

'All rise for their Imperial Highnesses!'

Three figures in black velvet slowly walked in. Like the clerics, their hoods were long and deep, completely obscuring the faces of the women who wore them. Their cloaks were ornately decorated with twin crescent moons, representing the ancient line of House Aristarchus, keepers of the Auge for thousands of years. Embroidered around the moons were dancing dragons in silver thread; eyes twinkling with inset red rubies. As the women walked, their cloaks billowed about, revealing the hems of their floor-length dresses in rich purple, indigo and violet silk.

They finally stopped in front of the altar and faced the crowd. Their trailing sleeves, also embellished in silver and rubies, glittered as all of three of them raised their cloth-covered hands in unison. Arafel's voice was crystal clear, projecting well in the natural cavern.

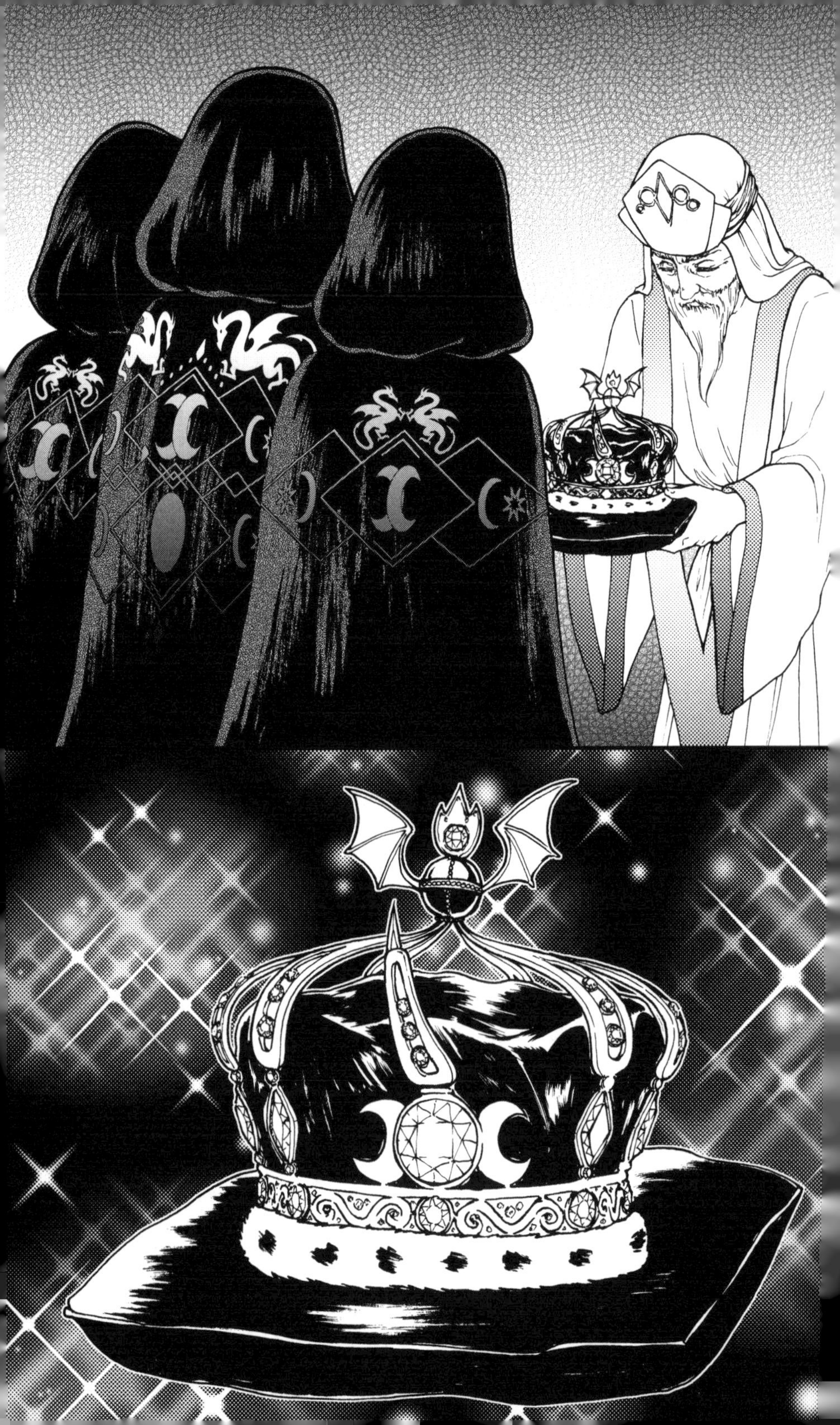

'My most honoured guests. It is with a solemn heart that I welcome you all here today to witness the ancient funeral rites for my grandfather, Emperor Aviur Crescentio Eyzaguirre von und zu Aristarchus. His Imperial Majesty was a great leader, a pioneer of industry and an astute politician. Despite the cruel way in which so many of his line were taken away from him nine years ago, he continued to lead this Empire with wisdom and fortitude. I will be forever grateful for his love and kindness. *Großvater*, I will miss you.'

After an emotional pause to collect herself, she continued.

'I will now begin the ritual.'

The three of them turned around to face the coffin.

'*Audire*, Auge! Hear my cry! The Dragon children of Ciel are here. Your faithful master has passed and longs to return to your embrace. He awaits you on the altar. *Excie! Arae Doloris!*'

As soon as she spoke its name, the altar began to glow, the stone taking on a semi-translucent appearance as a crystalline fire seemed to burn from within. A deep rumble echoed up through the crater, ending with tremors below their feet and a ringing hum as the crystals in the cavern resonated with the vibrations.

'In return for your grant of mastery, your late master finally offers you everything he was, everything he has and everything he will be.'

In unison, the three women pushed the coffin off the altar and into the crater far below. They stepped back, raising their arms.

'Take his body, recognise it. *Accipe!*'

The Auge rumbled again, its crystals humming. The crater glowed brighter and flames leapt up from its centre, the cavern rippling with light from its flash.

'*Audire*, Auge! I hear your cry! You search for a new master, one of the blood of Dragons. I am Arafel, of the blood! And by my blood, you will know me!'

The Head Cleric came forward with the Imperial crown. He stopped, just a few steps shy of them. Then he pressed the enormous diamond centrepiece. With a click, it detached itself from the rest of the crown along with the front silver stem. Jutting out from its end was a short, small blade hidden inside the winged orb. The *Blutdolch* was part of the crown, a reminder of the blood-pact made with the Auge by whoever assumes its office. He held out the crown and its now-detached fleam to the three heirs, his head bowed low.

Before Arafel could take it, there were loud cracks from the ceiling.

Silas gasped as huge chunks of stalactites broke away, just above where the four of them were standing. Before he could react, the women dived forward, pushing the old cleric to the ground and out of the way. The falling rocks crashed into the middle of the cavern, causing clouds of dust to rise.

As the Imperial Knights came rushing to their aid, the Head Cleric got to his feet.

'Your Imperial Majesty! We must continue with the ceremony immediately! Or–'

Then his eyes went wide. He clapped his hand to his neck and dropped like a stone.

Rua's voice called out.

'Stay down!'

Arafel's cloak rippled as its wearer yanked it off, spinning it in a blur so it shielded her. Stretching it out in front of her with her clawed hands, she inspected the cloth, now bristling with small, silver needles. She clicked her tongue in irritation as she tossed the cloak to one side and drew out a pair of daggers from under her skirts, kicking off her high-heeled boots. Her golden eyes fixed on her would-be assassin.

'Okay, the poisoned needles, I understand... but how'd you make the ceiling fall in, Gunnælf?'

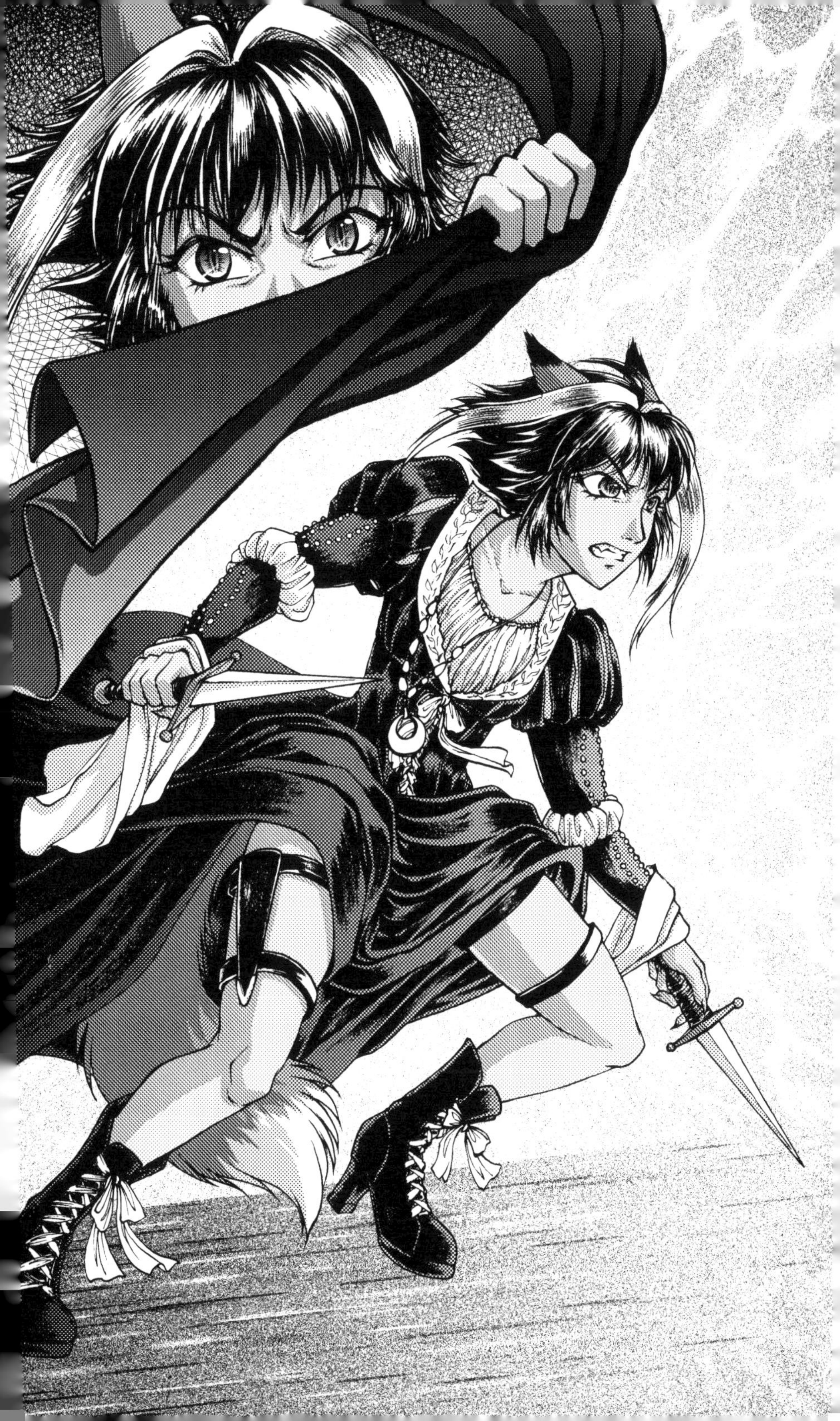

X

Still dressed in Arafel's purple coronation silks, Rua leapt from the floor and onto the first row of the viewing stands, scattering the Drachenheim nobles who were seated there. As she approached the now-disgraced shieldmaiden, Gunnaelf drew her sword and bared her teeth.

'*Bellum Omnium!*' she howled.

Then the entire chamber erupted into chaos.

Screams started as several more of the guests stood up and drew their weapons, turning on their own countrymen.

Silas flinched as he heard the ringing sound of a rapier being drawn from behind him. He turned to see Vertcielle's own Maréchal Lefèvre bearing down on Xavier. Before he could react, the Maréchal was frozen in place by wind chains, struggling to move, eyes bulging from lack of air as it was forcibly withdrawn from his lungs.

Véronique's eyes glowed a glacial green.

'I'm most disappointed, Maréchal. But I will keep you alive for later.'

'Véronique,' Xavier said coolly, drawing his own rapier. 'Wind shields, now, and stay with me. It seems the plot has thickened; there wasn't just one enemy. There were many, all working together from within.'

'What do we do now?' Silas asked in a panic.

'The priority is Arafel. She needs to complete the blood-letting ceremony within the next ten minutes. Or all of us will die. Find her. In the meantime, try to stop as many people as possible from getting killed. That includes yourself. Now go.'

Silas tuned into the Air spectrum and placed a wind shield on himself. His eyes darted around the cavern, searching for her. Rua had been disguised as Arafel, Arafel was in Serefah's robes, and Serefah was disguised as Rua, complete with a false tail. Mayim was the only one who wasn't pretending to be anyone else.

It was vital that Rua was not only in Arafel's place, in case of an assassination attempt, but for Arafel to be one of the three hooded heirs. Her voice had to be authentic and sound as if it was coming from the altar, and she needed to be close enough to offer her actual blood.

Flashes of purple silk caught his attention.

Rua was still incredibly efficient at fighting, even when dressed in a long gown. She deflected every one of Gunnælf's sword strikes whilst simultaneously dispatching anyone else who tried to sneak in a stab to her back. He watched her for a few moments to reassure himself that she would be fine.

He looked towards the Head Cleric's corpse beyond the rubble.

That was where he last saw Arafel and Mayim when Rua caught the poisoned needles, but they weren't there now. Where could they be?

The wind shield rushed in his ears, the air flow speeding up to deflect a blow.

He turned around to see an Ifriq spear heading straight for his forehead.

With no time to incant a spell, he stumbled back and grabbed at the nearest Air thread as he fell to the ground, throwing it at the point of the spear.

The Human holding it was thrown off balance, side-stepping awkwardly.

'Nakato! Not you as well?'

Queen Aminatu now stood over him protectively, her pointed ears trembling with rage as she tipped her spear towards her fellow Ifriq.

'Where is your honour? Have you no shame?!' she bellowed.

The chastised Queen of Umzania hissed in response.

'What of it?! Ifriqikah has no need to curry favour with the Palatinate. Ciel's Cradle can burn in a pool of lava for all I care! We stand for a new world order! We could reign supreme!'

Aminatu had a look of pure disgust on her face.

'What a selfish point of view,' she spat. 'All of Ciel's children are connected. We all have strengths and weaknesses. We compensate and help each other grow, not wipe each other out. Now, fight me, you traitor. At least I can give you an honourable death.'

Silas scrambled out of the way as the queens flew at each other, spears stabbing and spinning in blurs of motion.

'Weaver!' Aminatu called. 'Nakato's guards!'

Umzanian warriors were bearing down on both him and Aminatu.

Instinctively, he switched into the Fire spectrum and grasped multiple red threads.

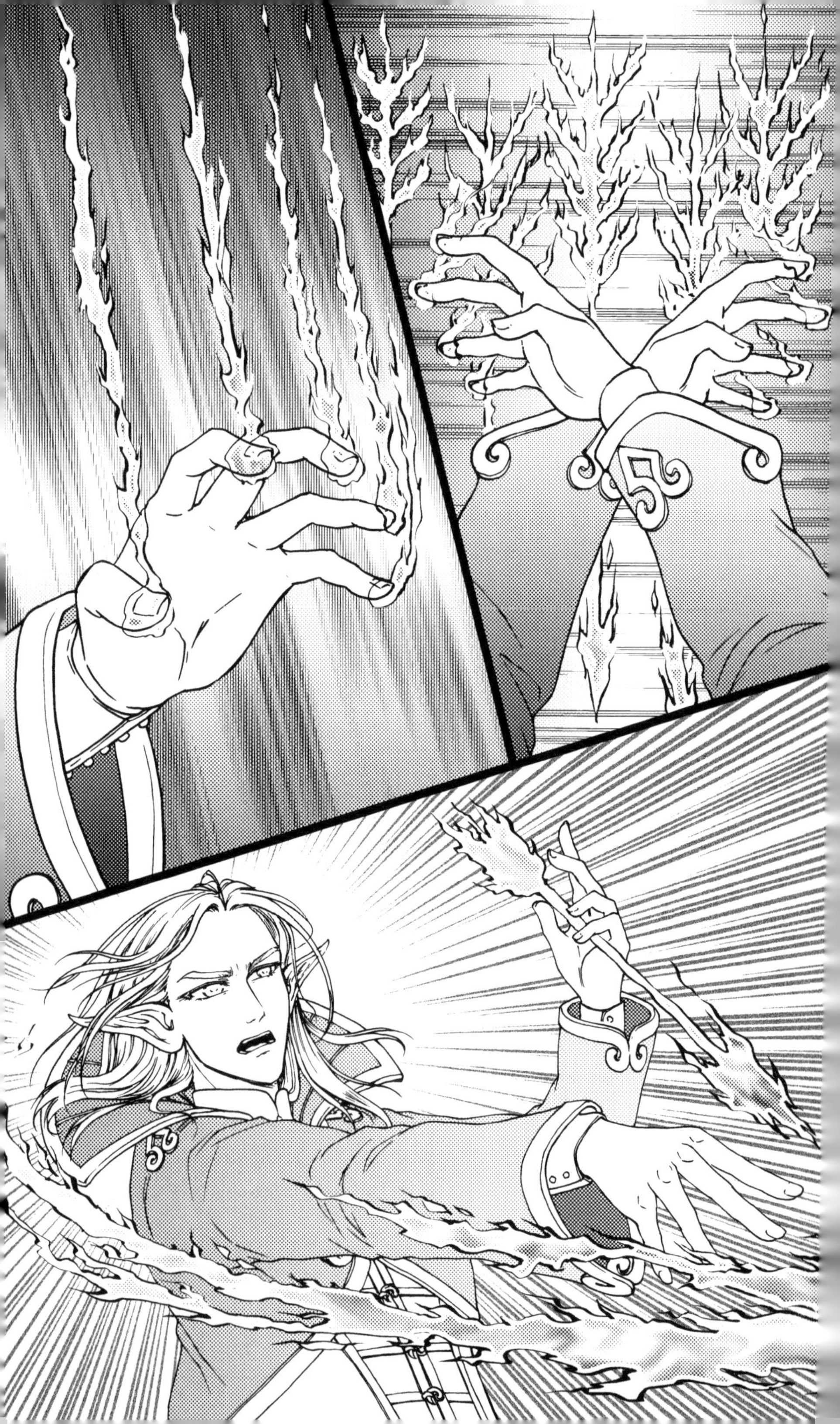

'Ignis, ego præcipio vobis...'

Fire, I command you...

He raked both sets of fingers through the air, drawing multiple fiery lines straight down, then with two sweeps back and forth, added feather-like fletches to the ends. He grabbed them, took aim, and flung them.

'Sagitta ignis!'

Fire arrow!

Darts of flame flew at the guards, setting the wooden shafts of their spears alight and embedding in their chest plates. They dropped their weapons, screaming as they rolled around the cavern floor trying to put the flames out.

Aminatu swept her spear under Nakato's feet, pulling them out from under her. As she fell, the Elf kicked her spear point around with lightning-fast speed, plunging the blade into the Human's throat.

'Foolish girl,' Aminatu said, as Nakato bled out wordlessly.

One of Nakato's remaining warriors threw their flaming spear at her.

'Watch out!' Silas shouted.

Just as she turned and ducked, the spear shuddered and stopped in mid-air, its flames extinguished.

Véronique's hand was outstretched. She made a fist, and the spear snapped in half. Then she flicked her fingers down; the blade planted itself harmlessly into the ground.

'Your Majesty,' she asked the queen, as Xavier followed behind her, his weapons still drawn. 'Are you hurt?'

Aminatu grinned, her teeth a brilliant white against her midnight skin.

'Only my pride. My thanks, Véronique.'

She pulled her spear out of Nakato and walked up close to the Chancellor.

'And how many times must I say it? You can call me Aminatu.'

Véronique quickly dropped her gaze to the floor, her mouth clamped shut.

Xavier flicked back his hair with his main gauche.

'Véronique's a stickler for the rules, Aminatu. Been that way for a hundred years, at least. Can you give us an idea of the conspirators and casualties you've encountered?'

The Nzaidiran Queen huffed.

'Regrettably, we have just dispatched Queen Nakato and her guards. Before I encountered her, I saw Prince Lorencio of Hesperia wound several of the other princes before he was overpowered and executed. Yourselves?'

'Tsar Vadim was stabbed by Baron Zharykhin. He was swiftly avenged by his son. We also lost Jarl Thyge of Sturmgaard to the shieldmaiden Gunnælf, but thankfully not Jarl-kona Liesel. Jarl Rikvald of Orbos and his sister, the shieldmaiden Sigrid have been assisting us with—'

He was interrupted by the booming voice of Owyn.

'BLESTIUM!'

Serefah, still sporting Rua's clothes, came running towards them for safety as the enraged Prince Consort bore down on the Eiran duke, who was locked in combat with Éilís in the far corner.

The battle-hardened queen was holding her own against the duke despite being armed with a mere dagger. He slashed downwards with his sabre only to be caught by the dagger's sturdy hilt. He shook with exertion as he tried to push through, but she held fast.

'You've gone soft, Blestium,' she goaded. 'Shouldn't have turned down so many invitations to my dragon hunts, eh?'

'And you've gone soft in the head, Éilís,' he sputtered. 'Too much peace and our biggest export, our warriors and weaponry, loses its edge.'

Her eyes widened.

'You... you're insane.'

She side-stepped, causing the duke to lurch forwards in a fall. Before he could gather himself, Owyn's dagger hurtled through the air, planting itself between his shoulder blades.

As Silas was about to call to them, a shriek came from behind him.

The High Priestess of Alekhandros was on the floor, clutching at her shoulder.

He could see the Water wall surrounding her waver and shudder.

So she is a Water Mistress.

Her Hierophants were forcing a gap through the wall with their swords; one must have got through.

He held out his hand as Véronique made to step forward.

'I have this.'

He drew a small circle of flames, parallel to the ground, then shaped walls up with his palms like throwing a vase on a pottery wheel.

'*Murus ignis!*'

Fire wall!

He took aim and threw the symbol at the Hierophants. Flames suddenly encircled the High Priestess's Water wall, erupting into a blazing pillar. They staggered back in agony, their arms blackened and charred.

'Your Holiness!' he yelled. 'Drop your wall! This way!'

He grabbed at the trailing tendrils from his Fire wall and pulled them taut towards himself. A gap appeared in the flames and the cylinder stretched into an impenetrable corridor leading back to him.

She picked herself up gingerly, still clutching at her wounded shoulder. The Water wall vanished in clouds of steam and she ran through the corridor to his side.

Silas dismissed the flames and surveyed the chaos.

Aside from the small group they had amassed, several dignitaries and nobles were still running around in panic, trying to escape the assassins. The Imperial Knights had formed a barrier for protection and with the help of the remaining Iskarians, were ushering people out speedily. They found it difficult to do anything more, as every nation appeared to have a sleeper agent in their ranks.

It was also beginning to get uncomfortably warm. How long had it been since the since the rocks fell; five minutes?

But he still couldn't see any sign of Arafel or Mayim.

Then it hit him.

What if they simply couldn't be seen?

XI

Silas shifted his sight into the Spirit spectrum.

There! A bright, white Spirit Fabric, its wispy tendrils bearing her distinct signature. She was hiding in plain sight, back pressed against the altar.

'Maestra,' he said to Véronique. 'I have located Arafel. I must go to her, but it requires a Spirit Fabric.'

The Chancellor nodded.

'Go, I will take care of things here.'

Silas swiftly began drawing the intricate pattern to cast the spell; resembling an Eiran infinity knot of warps and wefts ending in curled edges. He pinched the diagonal corners and pulled them apart, stretching the Fabric then threw it over himself, vanishing from view. He picked his way around the corpses, giving those still fighting a wide berth and made his way to the altar.

'Arafel! What are you doing? You must finish the ceremony–'

'I'm Mayim!'

'Wha... she gave her Spirit Fabric to you?!'

'She couldn't make more than one! She wanted to keep me safe!'

'Where is she?!'

Mayim pointed to the back of the cavern.

'She's out there, trying to get to the *Blutdolch* from Premier Yuan! She saw him grab it from the Head Cleric!'

He tried to suppress his rising panic by talking himself through his new mission.

'Okay... get you to safety, retrieve the *Blutdolch*, find Arafel! You must join up with the others. Here, take my Fabric so Arafel can free herself up for more spells.'

He took a few steps back, then threw his Fabric over Mayim before running to put some distance between them.

'Arafel!' he shouted, hoping she heard him. 'Mayim is safe! Dismiss your Spirit Fa–'

There was a rumbling beneath his feet. Was the Auge getting impatient? No, there was something suspicious about how localised it was...

Silas gasped in sudden realisation and jumped sideways, narrowly missing a stalagmite which burst through the spot where he was standing. His eyes flashed between white and yellow as he tracked the threads of Earth back to its wielder, perched high amongst the crystals jutting out from the walls.

'Premier Yuan.'

The Tianxian diplomat lowered his hands, tucking them into his belt where the diamond hilt of the *Blutdolch* sparkled.

'Do not take this personally, Weaver,' he said. 'This is strictly business.'

'Give me the *Blutdolch*, Premier.'

'...No.'

'*Shenwu! Ni yao zuo shenme?*'

The Empress Dowager and her grandson appeared, flanked by their bodyguards.

The Premier smirked.

'What am I up to? Only trying to advance our great nation. And with that...'

He nodded at one of her guards, who immediately stabbed her in the back.

The other guards recoiled in shock for a moment before grabbing the assassin's arms to prevent him from killing himself or hurting anyone else.

'NO! *Nainai!*'

Xianrong fell to his knees, clutching at his grandmother but it was too late; she was gone. As her blood seeped into his silks, he raised his head, eyes hot with tears.

'Why?!'

The Premier adjusted his flowing sleeves.

'Because I felt petty. I am still rather sore at missing the Crown Princess earlier.'

Xianrong rose and took one of his guard's swords. He spun it with ease, testing its balance. Then he pointed the blade at the Premier.

Yuan smiled.

'Yes, this will be much more fun than burying you under rocks in a 'freak' accident.'

The young prince ran at the Premier, nimbly leaping from rock to rock as he gradually ascended the walls to reach him.

Yuan's eyes began to glow.

'Your Highness!' Silas warned. 'Beware the rocks! Do not keep to the same path!'

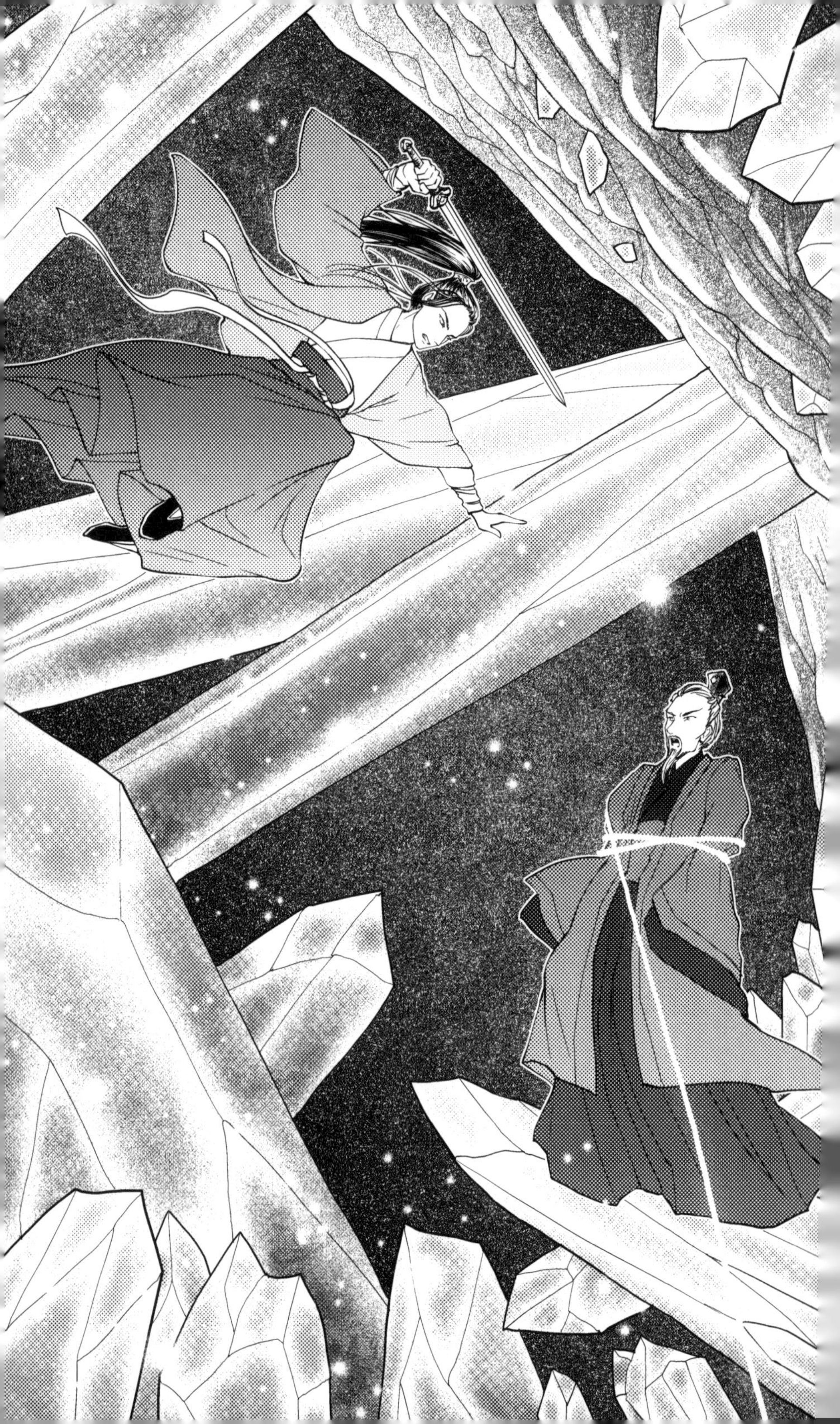

'Guide me, then!' he yelled back.

Silas concentrated hard on reading the flowing Earth threads emanating from the Premier. A spike rippled through the walls like an impossibly fast tidal wave.

'Roll!' he shouted.

The prince dived forward as a crystal spike broke through the wall, stabbing at the air inches above his head.

'Jump!'

He leapt across a chasm that suddenly appeared beneath his feet. He landed heavily on the other side, slightly winded.

'Weaver, if I try to climb that last sheer face, I cannot avoid his attacks!'

The glowing lariat of a Spirit whip cracked around the Premier, lashing his arms to his sides. He struggled to stay upright, his Earth threads dispersing.

'Not if I can help it!' Arafel cried, emerging from the rocks below the Premier. 'Si, get him up there, now!'

Silas promptly obeyed, adding Air to his sight spectra. He threw as many green threads as he could find towards Xianrong.

'Your Highness, jump!'

The gust of wind propelled the prince high into the air. He took aim with his sword. Plummeting down, he rammed his blade straight through Yuan's chest.

'*Buyaolian de dongxi,*' he declared.

'On the contrary...' the Premier replied, as blood bubbled up in his mouth. 'I am only Human. Shame means... nothing to me.'

He slumped back, sliding off the blade as Arafel dismissed her Spirit whip.

'Xianrong!' she called. 'Give me the *Blutdolch* now! Before the Auge takes us all!'

The prince plucked the enchanted dagger from the dead man's belt and dropped it over the edge onto the cave floor.

'Si! Cover me!' she commanded, picking it up and running.

Silas was already drawing the concentric circles out of Air with both hands, incanting to ensure the spell would reach its marks.

'*Aer, fac clypeus ventus pro me et Arafel!*'

Air, form wind shields for me and Arafel!

The air currents whipped around them, deflecting opportunistic arrows as together, they ran as fast as they could.

'I am Arafel, of the blood of Dragons...'

From the corner of his vision, a flash of red fur and purple silks told him that Rua had taken up the rear guard as they advanced on the altar. Barely soon enough; he heard the sound of metal ringing in his ears as blades clashed on his heels.

'By my blood, you will know me!'

The diamond hilt of the *Blutdolch* glowed as she pulled back her sleeve and plunged its point into her inner elbow. The crimson blood that welled around the silver blade was a stark contrast to her pale skin. She fell upon the altar, shaking from shock.

'Expand the shield, Silas,' she muttered. 'My blood must not be stemmed.'

He spun her wind shield out into a wind wall, its perimeter now large enough to surround her as she leant on the altar. No longer kept in place by Air magic, her blood began to flow freely. It pulsed out in a steady stream, barely making a mark on the stone as the altar drank it up equally as fast. Her breathing became hoarse and she grew paler with each passing second.

'*Gottverdammt*, how much more do you need?' she whispered.

Just as Silas was beginning to lose hope, there was a roaring sound in his ears and the Arae Doloris lit up the entire cavern in a blinding flash.

He reeled back, shielding his eyes from the light, then squinted as the room gradually came back into focus.

Arafel looked as though she was glowing from within; her eyes and her veins pulsed with the colour of lava. She was no longer shivering; she was still and serene, her arms spread wide as she completed her address to the altar.

'*Consummatum est.*'

She started to climb onto the altar.

Silas tried to offer a hand to help but flinched from her heat. He couldn't touch her; it was like standing next to a blast furnace.

She stood tall on the glowing stone and threw a burning smile over her shoulder at him. It was both reassuring and unsettling.

'I'll just be a few minutes.'

She took a step and fell, feet first, into the boiling crater below.

He leant over the altar, his heart in his throat.

She was standing on a tiny crust of black, igneous rock, floating like an island in the middle of the lava. She hadn't fallen very far; the molten magma was just a few yards away from reaching the top of the crater. It struck him then, just how close they had come to disaster.

238

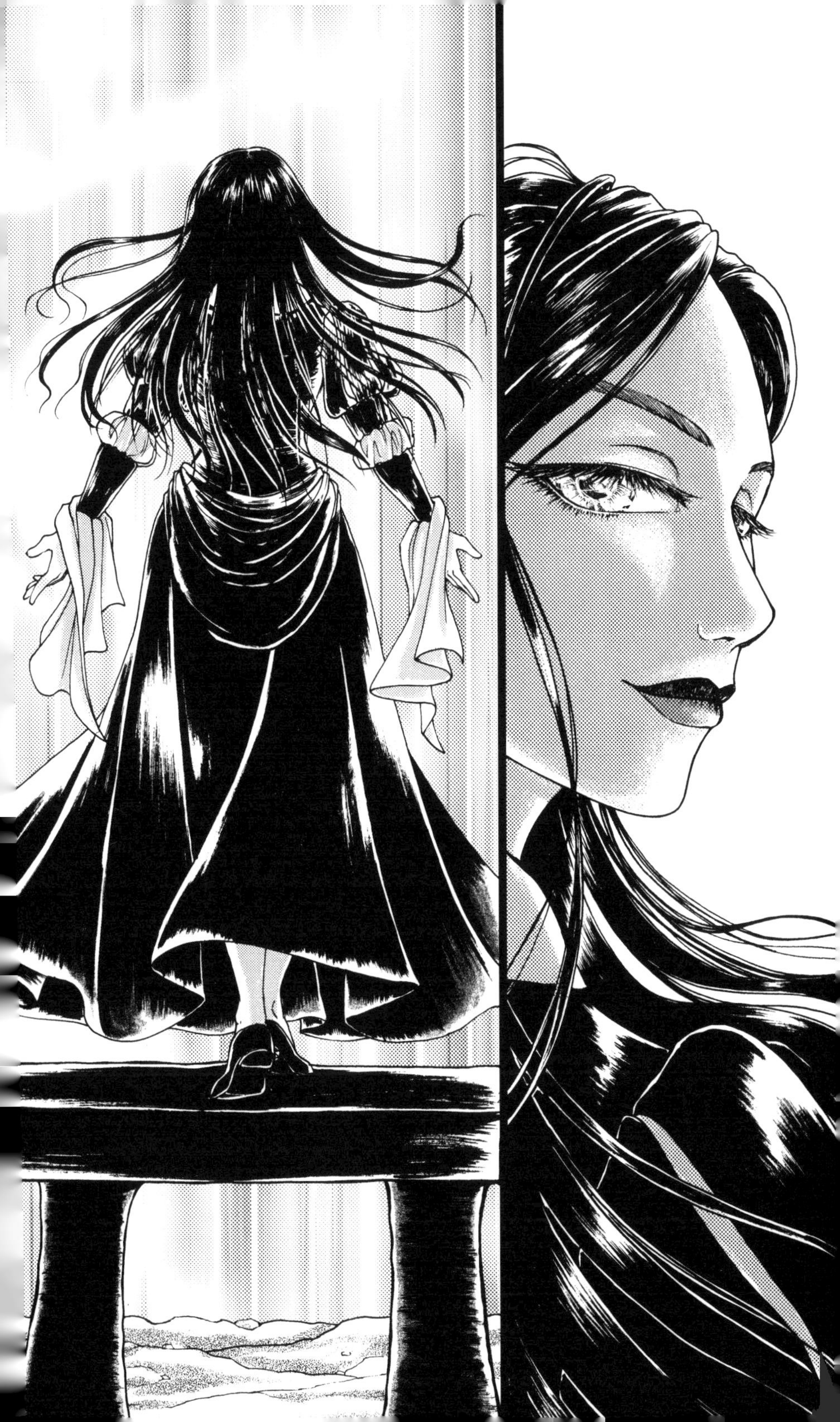

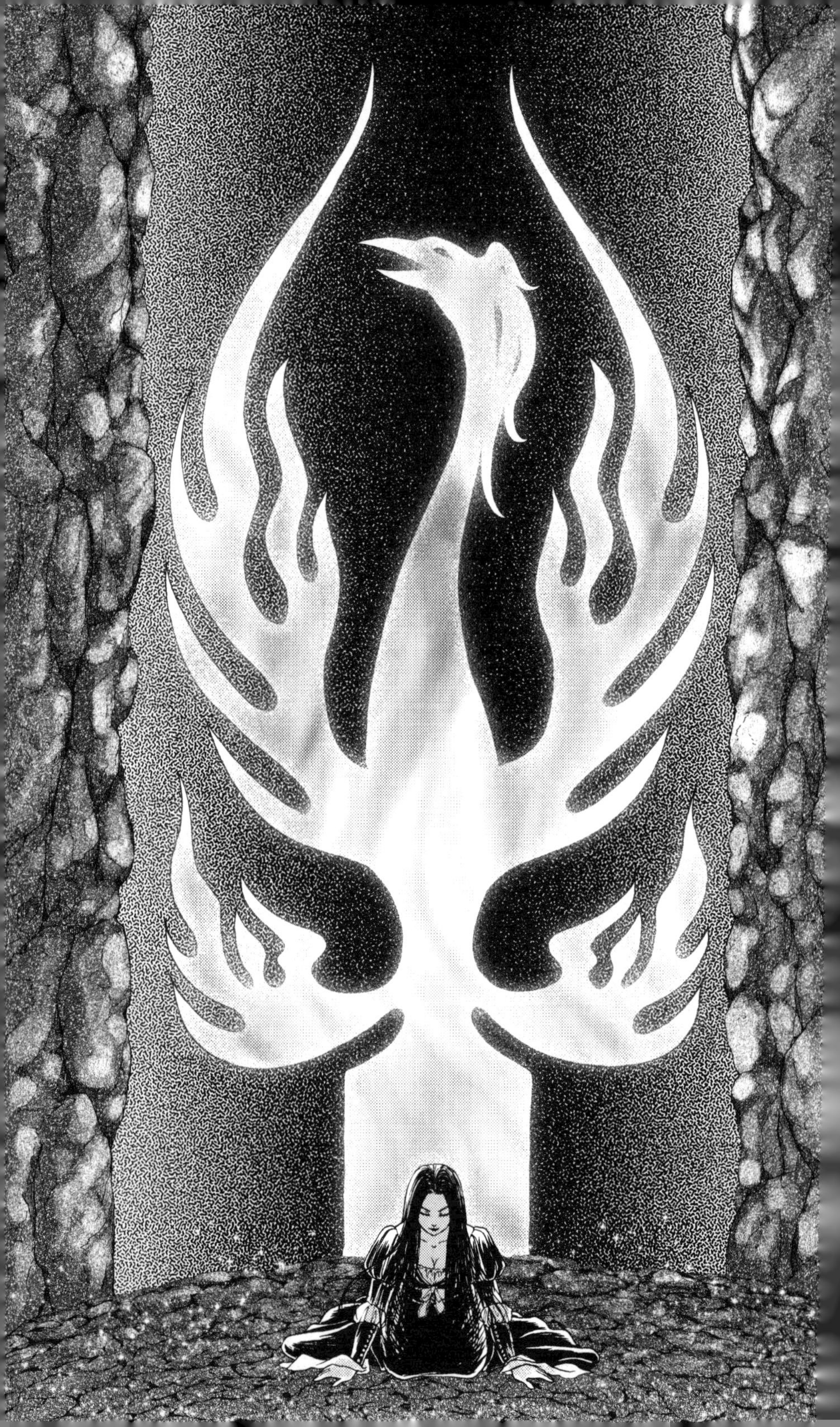

She extended a foot and miraculously, another crust formed as she set it down. She gracefully walked across the lava, leaving a trail of glittering, dark crystals in her wake. She began to laugh as she danced over the surface of the fiery liquid, drawing spirals and flourishes.

When the entire surface looked as if it was coated in black diamonds, she returned to the centre and knelt down. She pressed her palms to the crust. It shuddered and rippled outwards.

The lava began to descend. As the crusted platform lowered, a blazing pattern began to light up the walls of the crater behind her. Slowly, the glass channels filled from the bottom up. Stylised flames in elegant arabesques; feathers sweeping into outstretched wings. She sunk deeper and deeper as her molten sculpture was finally revealed in all of its glory.

A magnificent phoenix, rising from the flames.

It pulsed like a living, breathing thing. After a few moments, she stood up and when her palms left the magma crust, it instantly flashed into a glossy black. She walked over to its base and stroked her hand over the glass, smiling with half-lidded eyes, still glowing with the Auge's fire.

Silas caught his breath. He'd not seen that look on her before.

It was a lover's smile.

XII

It was a rare moment of calm and quiet in the corridors of Schloss Drachen but Silas's thoughts were loud as he strode hand-in-hand with Rua.

No nation was left unscathed from the ceremony. Every country had sleeper agents, activated by Gunnælf's cry. Bellum Omnium. It was the name of their secret society and their ethos: all-out war. From the few agents they were able to capture alive, the Imperial Knights determined that the group's aim was to destabilise Ciel's Cradle and seed discontent in order to plunge its nations into warring with each other.

Upon hearing this, it took several hours for Rua to release her rage on the practise dummies in the knights' training grounds. Éilís offered to replace all ten of them within a fortnight and Arafel called for an emergency meeting with all of the remaining heads of state. By the end of that day, everyone agreed that it was essential to form a coalition of peace that would work together to prevent further wars.

The last major conflict in Ciel's Cradle began when Vertcielle invaded Eira four hundred years ago, drawing in neighbouring countries who were keen to support their allies or exploit the situation. When Eira shook free of her invaders ninety years later, the conflict spilt over into the rest of the continent, carrying on for another hundred years. Although this was in their history books, what truly hammered the point home was the presence of Rua. The visiting dignitaries were shocked to discover how much the Dagger of Ciel was involved in key moments of the Great Wars as she recounted her experiences, confirmed facts and corrected hearsay. It was a sudden and sobering realisation that the Dagger was more than a fancy title. The living legend was sat in front of them. The relative peace and prosperity of the past two centuries wasn't mere chance; much of it was due to just one person and it took her a very long time to achieve it. Whilst she now had the Weaver as her partner, she could do with more support from everyone, especially as the enemy had become more organised.

The past few days had been a flurry of meetings; from immediate concerns such as tracking down the agents who had escaped during the ceremony and identifying the extent of Bellum Omnium's influence in each nation's courts, to more long term goals like fostering more international exchange programmes, establishing direct lines of communication with additional security protocols and scheduling the sharing of intelligence on a regular basis. Even though Ciel's Cradle was the initial target of Bellum Omnium, the representatives from Amliga, Ifriqikah and Tianxia were keen to participate as they felt responsible for the sleeper agents in their ranks.

Despite all of this, Éilís and Xavier both agreed that the current threat of assassination had passed, so Silas and Rua could stay with each other in the evenings. It was a welcome relief to finally hold her in his arms again, to kiss her unreservedly and feel her comforting warmth beside him at night. The constant, gnawing panic in his belly that started when he arrived in Drachenheim and grew in the lead up to the ceremony fell away as soon as he was with her, where he was meant to be.

The wounds of his soul were healing and with her help, he would take this last step.

These particular marble hallways were so familiar to Silas; they haunted his childhood memories and recurring nightmares but it felt strangely dissociative seeing them again, now that he was much taller. He wouldn't have dared to return to this part of the palace without Rua by his side. The warmth of her hand nestled in his was keeping him grounded. For a few minutes they walked, the click-clack of his heels on the stone breaking the silence before he spoke.

'Arafel did me a great service. Ensuring that all of my engagements thus far were not held in this wing.'

'This was where it all happened, huh?'

'Yes.'

They kept walking, Rua's wrapped feet padding quietly, his court shoes less so when they rounded a corner and Silas hesitated as he recognised the latched gate leading to the cliff side courtyard.

'You don't need to do this if you aren't ready, love,' Rua said.

He took a deep breath and squeezed her hand, looking down at her worried face.

'I think I am,' he said, managing a weak smile. 'I want to.'

He bent down to kiss her, lingering on her lips for a few seconds before he stepped away from her and unlatched the gate.

'Besides, she is expecting me. Can you... wait for me here?'

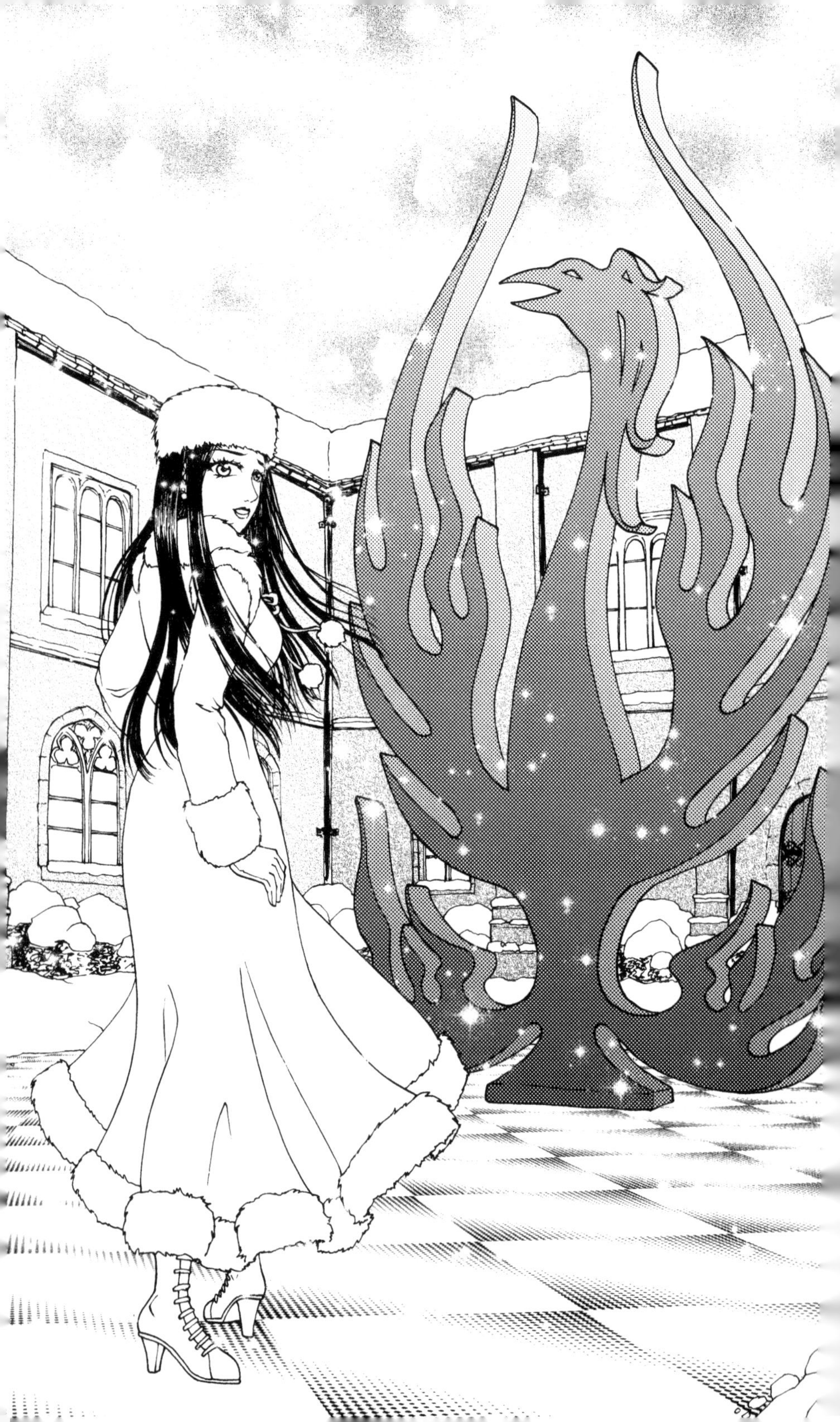

'Of course, love. Take as long as you need. I'll be nearby, just shout and I'll come.'

'Thank you.'

He took another deep breath to steel himself, then pushed open the gate.

The crisp, icy air of the wintry morning stung his cheeks as he stepped outside and closed the gate behind him. He stood and stared, his breath forming clouds.

When he was last in this courtyard, it was lit by glowing purple sigils of dark summoning magic. This time, the overcast sky was a hazy white, the familiar hedges and boulders under a thin blanket of snow. Towering over the centre of the courtyard was the newly-installed obsidian phoenix sculpture, its glossy, black stone making it look even more incongruous in its snowy surroundings.

In front of the sculpture was Arafel, dressed in a long, white fur coat and hat. Her jet-black hair hung loose, fluttering around her waist as she turned to face him.

'...Si. You came.'

'How could I refuse? I hope I did not keep you waiting too long.'

'No. Even if you hadn't come at all, I'd understand. That's why I dressed warmly.'

She pointed at an iron garden bench.

'Do you think you could warm this up?'

Silas nodded and engaged the Fire spectrum, directing a thread through the bench. He removed a glove to test the iron's temperature before they both sat down.

For a minute, they sat in the snowy stillness, gazing at the statue.

'I'd always planned to put my sculpture here,' Arafel stated. 'As my way of taking this courtyard back. For all that the Dark Goddess took away from me, I wasn't going to let her sully this part of Schloss Drachen. This was where some of my dearest memories were made. This was where we used to play hide-and-seek together. Do you remember that time when I was so sure you wouldn't be able to find me, but my hair was peeking out from behind that rock?'

Silas smiled.

'You were convinced that I had cheated. Your mother had to step in and tell you that your hair was showing. Then you insisted on a trim that evening.'

'And you also had your hair trimmed in solidarity!'

His smile waned as he continued to look at the rock in question.

'That rock was also how I managed to climb through the window to find you in the library when... when it happened. When I had to become the Weaver.'

He shut his eyes tight.

'To save you from a monster, I became a monster to everyone else.'

He felt her hands close tightly over his and he opened his eyes to her fierce gaze.

'No,' she declared. 'Not to me. Never to me. And never to anyone else who mattered. We can't undo the past. Yes, this was where our lives changed. But this was also where we survived. We lived. And whilst we live, we hope. So this place, this courtyard, this statue... represents hope. After that day, I was revered as a symbol of hope and new beginnings. But you and your powers also represent hope. They didn't know it back then, but they sure as hell know it now. Deep down, you know that who you are and what you do is right. So it's time to own it.'

Silas's tears were hot, spilling over his cheeks as they were squeezed out by the painful grip around his heart from years of internalising his childhood banishment.

Arafel lowered his head to her shoulder and he allowed the pain to engulf him, forcing his tears out until the tightness in his chest went away.

The cutting looks and cruel words in his memories would never disappear entirely, but he could choose to lessen their blows by accepting that he, the Weaver, was created by Ciel as a force for good. He had been ostracised not because of his powers, but because they were afraid.

When his breathing calmed, he straightened up and gave her a grateful smile.

'Thank you.'

She squeezed his shoulder companionably.

'You're welcome.'

The clouds overhead began to clear and the sun shone brighter through the disappearing veil of white, making the snow glimmer and the phoenix sculpture glisten.

'Would you mind if I called for Rua to come out here?' Silas asked Arafel. 'She has been waiting for us inside and I do not wish for her to worry any longer than necessary.'

'Oh, I hadn't realised! Please do.'

He cleared his throat and raised his voice in the direction of the gate.

'Rua! Please can you join us?'

It only took a few seconds before the gate opened and she came bounding into the garden, her face flooding with relief when she saw that he was smiling.

'Hey!' said Rua. 'Budge up, you two.'

They scooted along the bench as she sat down. Her ears pricked up suddenly.

'Whoa! This bench is warm! Did you do that, love? I could get used to this...'

'I-I can only warm up metal benches—' Silas warned her.

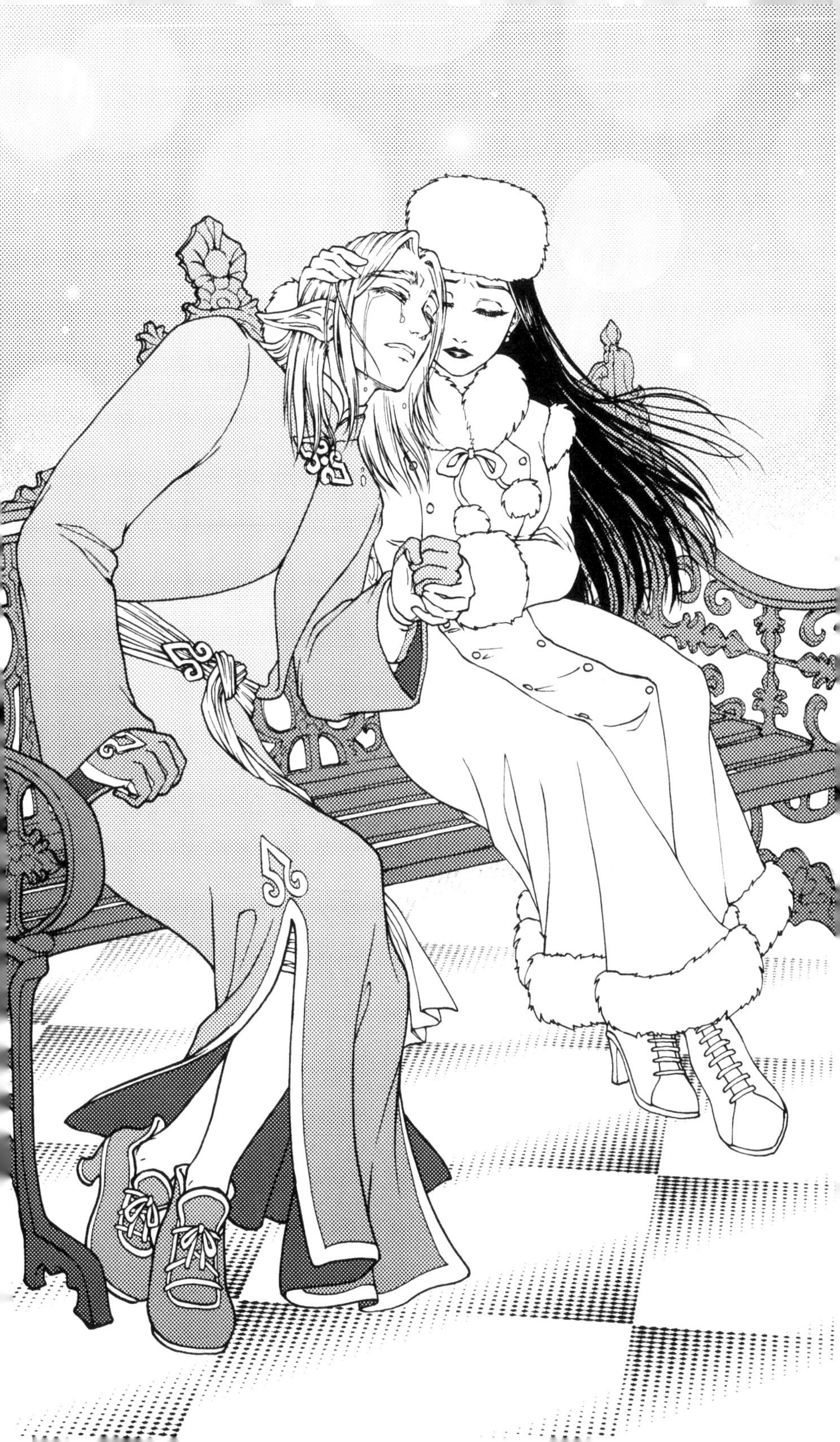

'...By Ciel, that statue really is something!' she rambled on. 'I didn't think it was that big when it was still in the walls of the Auge, but placed here, it's huge! Look at all that obsidian... hey, I wonder how many knives you could make out of a piece that big? I love obsidian blades, they're so nice to use!'

Arafel giggled.

'I'll be more than happy to make you an obsidian blade, after all that you've done for us. Actually, I can make as many as you want, now that I control the lava.'

Silas recalled that moment in the Auge when she touched the glass.

'We have not had much chance to speak in private since the ceremony,' he said. 'When you made the sculpture, you looked... different. How do you feel?'

Arafel's big, brown eyes widened. Then she looked away, her brow furrowed.

'Different? Yes, definitely. I mean... on some level, I feel as I always have. I'm still me. But I feel... like I'm both fully formed... and augmented somehow. Like there was a part of me that wasn't there before and now I am whole and complete and... more. Much more. Like I am enveloped and connected yet spread about and dispersed, and I feel so deep and far down, yet high, all at once? Urgh! It's hard to explain.'

'N-no, I... somewhat understand.'

Rua stood up and went to Arafel's side, patting her shoulder.

'I understand very well. When I was touched by Ciel, it felt like I was emptied out, then filled up again with... sunshine. I know that I contain much more than me now.'

Arafel nodded emphatically, then held Silas's gaze, her expression fearful.

'But what they all said about needing to stay close to the Auge... I already know. It loves me. It wants me. I can feel its fire, burning in my veins. Comforting me and wanting to be comforted. I cannot lose this fire now that it is part of me, it would be like... ripping all of my bones out of my body. I would rather die than be without it. And that's... scary.'

Now it was Silas's turn to reassure her as he held her hands.

'You are one of the strongest people I know and that is no small statement considering the circles we keep. Ciel herself spoke to you, knowing that you were capable of handling all of this power. You are intelligent, compassionate, kind and brave. We love you. We trust you. And we will support you.'

Her eyes were bright as he welcomed her into his arms, giving her a tight squeeze.

'And you'll be alright with visiting me here, now?' she asked, her voice wavering.

'Of course. No more excuses.'

Arafel leant back and blinked away the tears that were welling up in her eyes, fanning at them with her hands. She laughed.

'Urgh, look at the state of us! And I've got to– Oh! Actually, would you both like to join us? I'm supposed to be meeting Xianrong for lunch now. I had planned for it to be a casual thing, so it could just be us four.'

'We'd love to!' Rua said eagerly. 'I'm starving!'

'Already?' asked Silas incredulously.

Arafel laughed again.

'Wonderful! Walk with me, then.'

Silas rose, offering both women an arm each.

Together, the three of them began making their way back to the garden gate.

'How're things going with your fiancé?' Rua asked.

'Ciel bless his soul,' Arafel lamented. 'Losing his grandmother like that was very tough, but avenging her has eased his pain somewhat. When he isn't keeping himself busy with work and the coalition meetings, I've been spending a lot of private time with him. He's coming through it. I'd like to think my company soothes him.'

Then she stopped in her tracks, holding them all back by the snow-covered rose bushes in the border planting. She released a melancholy sigh.

'A pity it's winter. Xianrong loves roses and was keen to see the differences between Tianxian varieties and ours. But how can you make a rose bloom in the snow?'

Rua nudged Silas with her elbow, giving him an expectant look.

He beamed, his eyes now flickering between yellow and blue.

'I have just the thing.'

In the next volume...

Breaking The Ice

In the aftermath of Bellum Omnium's attempt to assassinate the leaders of Ciel's Cradle at Arafel's coronation, the trail of the main instigator goes cold... literally. Rua and Silas head north to the icy shores of Iskar, where they discover a lot more than their quarry have gone missing. Joining forces with their Dwarven friend Morten and his caravan-load of jewels, they decide to try the ever-fruitful tactic of following the money.

A Line In The Sand

The grim truth behind the promised wealth and riches in the Iskarian mines is revealed with Rua and Silas determined to rescue all of those already ensnared in the illusion. The sands of time revolve once more as Rua is forced to revisit the Desert Corridor to shut down a smuggling ring with the added horrors of trafficking. Much is already at stake but when Silas goes missing in action, will her fury get in the way of the mission?

ACKNOWLEDGEMENTS

I can't believe we have finally made it! I know it's been a long time coming despite me mostly writing 80% of it in November 2015 during NaNoWriMo (National Novel Writing Month). Honestly, I really wanted to get it out in 2017, but a new baby (an actual one, not a book baby) then postnatal depression then big contracts in 2019 (because money) then PANDEMIC... But it's here and I really, REALLY hope you loved it.

Okay, time for the fun things about Rua and Silas's world! I'd always intended for it to be a lot like ours between 1600-1800 as it is both advanced and hindered by magic / longer-lived races, so I base much of the culture and most obviously, language, on real life equivalents. Many place names are explained in the story but in case you were wondering, I used a lot of Irish Gaelic, Scottish Gaelic, French and German. For example, Dúnragnhildt means Castle of Battle Counsel, Bàrrathair means Father's Mount and is a pun on Ballater, a village in the Scottish Cairngorms I frequently visit on holiday. People's names were also fun to create: Tianxian is based on Mandarin Chinese, so Wei Xianrong is 'Magnificent Virtuous Honour', Empress Dowager Wei Xianwen is 'Wise/Civil' and Premier Yuan Shenwu is 'Ambition Unyielding Sorcery'. Of course, I had Rua sing some Irish folk songs again. This time I featured 'Eibhlín a Rún' and 'Mo Ghile Mear' - both are absolutely gorgeous tunes, I suggest looking them up.

Now I must finish on my thank yous... Fans of the first book! You were and still are incredible at cheering me on; seeing your obvious love for my characters brings me so much joy. This includes my eldest son Kris who was fascinated by the first book which I read at bedtimes (paraphrased at times and I will definitely need to do that when we read this book together, haha). NEO Magazine! Thank you for the features and kind reviews. The Old Buttery nursery for looking after my youngest child so I could focus on writing! Walk The Moon, Secret Garden, Thomas Bergersen/Two Steps From Hell, Blue Stahli - thank you for inspiring and motivating me with your music! Morag Lewis for reading the awful first draft and giving suggestions. En Gingerboom for the friendly and expert eye on my graphics and design work (especially when I was tired and made terrible choices which needed fixing!). Finally, as always, my beautiful husband Matthew, who has gone through so much because of me and still sticks around despite it. To me, you are as close to perfect as is humanly possible. I will love you forever.

Ciao for now,

Sonia

GRAPHIC NOVELS FROM SWEATDROP STUDIOS

Dragon Heir
REBORN
EMMA VIECELI

Dragon Heir

EMMA VIECELI

In this world, the Spirits govern all. You live by your spirit sign, you serve the Spirit World.

Protus, one of four Dragon Heirs, sets out on a journey to gather the heirs and take them to the location chosen for Spiratu's Ritual of Transcendence. This act will leave the four young men free of the dangerous dragon spirits they have harboured since they were born; free to begin their mortal lives with Spiratu's blessing.

However, in a world where fate has spawned not one but two sets of Dragon Heirs, what guarantee is there that a prophecy so ancient can be fulfilled at all? And just what could failure mean for the Dragon's human hosts?

ISBN: 9781905038299 *Action, Fantasy*

MORAG LEWIS
NOBODY'S LIBRARY
VOLUME ONE

NOBODY'S LIBRARY

MORAG LEWIS

The Great Library has been derelict for years, its precious books scattered across the worlds, its mages, scholars and librarians long gone - until now. One mage has returned, and to him falls the task of restoring what has been lost. But he will find himself collecting more than just books...

Available volumes:
Volume 1 - ISBN: 9781905038558
Volume 2 - ISBN: 9781905038619 Fantasy

£4.00
sweatdrop

Rebel

EN GINGERBOOM

A-Level student Elisabeth Graves starts to wonder if her girlfriend might be a vampire, or if she's just been watching too much anime. A full-colour short romance story!

Romance, Supernatural

The
Witch-Hare
Irina Richards

The Witch-Hare

IRINA RICHARDS

Three women.
Three different time periods.
One extraordinary gift...

For centuries, people have heard stories of witch-hares - magical beings who could shapeshift between human and animal forms. Could these stories be true?

Inspired by Welsh legends, this book will take you on a fascinating journey through the folklore and landscape of Wales.

ISBN: 9781905038619

Fantasy, Historical

ANTHOLOGIES & MAGAZINES

Blue is for Boys	Various Authors
Cold Sweat and Tears	Various Authors
Drop Dead Monstrous	Various Authors
Pink is for Girls	Various Authors
Shimmering Drop	Various Authors
Sparkling Drop	Various Authors
Stardust	Various Authors
Sugardrops	Various Authors
Telling Tales	Various Authors
The Drop	Various Authors

GRAPHIC NOVELS & BOOKS

A Pocketful of Clouds	Morag Lewis
Ambient Rhythm	Morag Lewis
Aya Takeo	Sonia Leong
Chemical Blue	Irina Richards
Dragon Heir: Reborn	Emma Vieceli
Fantasma	Selina Dean
Jarred	Ruth Keattch
Looking for the Sun	Morag Lewis
Love Stuffing	Sonia Leong
Nobody's Library	Morag Lewis
Once Upon a Time...	Sonia Leong
Patchwork Sky	Morag Lewis
Pearls and Twine	Selina Dean
Sun Fish Moon Fish	Morag Lewis
Sushi and the Beginning of the World	Selina Dean
The Chronicles of Ciel	Sonia Leong
The Witch-Hare	Irina Richards
Trade Winds	Morag Lewis
White Violet	Shazleen Khan

COMICS & SINGLE ISSUES

Allsorts	Morag Lewis, Emma Vieceli and En Gingerboom
All That Matters	Morag Lewis
Artifaxis	Morag Lewis
Bell Ringers	Selina Dean
Chocoberry	Joanna Zhou
Defenders of the Sunset City	Morag Lewis
FujoFujo	Sonia Leong
Harajuku Zoo	Joanna Zhou
Jigsaw Pieces	Morag Lewis
Koneko	Selina Dean
Letters to England	Rebecca Burgess
Mini Murder Mysteries	Morag Lewis
Rel El	En Gingerboom
Sunny's Field	Selina Dean
Sushi and the End of the World	Selina Dean
The Triad	Rowan Clair
Twenty Thirty Three	En Gingerboom
Views From Another Place	Sergei and Morag Lewis

sweatdrop studios
INDEPENDENT ART & COMICS COLLABORATIVE